SURVIVORS OF STALINGRAD

SURVIVORS OF STALINGRAD

Eyewitness Accounts from the Sixth Army, 1942–1943

Edited by REINHOLD BUSCH

Translated by GEOFFREY BROOKS

Foreword by ROGER MOORHOUSE

Frontline Books, London

Originally published in German in 2012 as Der Untergang der 6. Armee

The English edition first published in 2014 and reprinted in 2016 by
FRONTLINE BOOKS
An imprint of
Pen & Sword Books Ltd
47 Church Street, Barnsley
South Yorkshire
S70 2AS

ISBN 978 1 84832 766 5

A CIP catalogue record for this book is
available from the British Library

Printed and bound in England
By CPI Group (UK) Ltd, Croydon, CR0 4YY

Pen & Sword Books Ltd incorporates the Imprints of Pen & Sword Aviation,
Pen & Sword Family History, Pen & Sword Maritime, Pen & Sword Military,
Pen & Sword Discovery, Pen & Sword Politics, Pen & Sword Atlas,
Pen & Sword Archaeology, Wharncliffe Local History, Leo Cooper,
Wharncliffe True Crime, Wharncliffe Transport, Pen & Sword Select,
Pen & Sword Military Classics, The Praetorian Press, Claymore Press,
Remember When, Seaforth Publishing and Frontline Publishing

For a complete list of Pen & Sword titles please contact
PEN & SWORD BOOKS LIMITED
47 Church Street, Barnsley, South Yorkshire, S70 2AS, England
E-mail: enquiries@pen-and-sword.co.uk
Website: www.pen-and-sword.co.uk

CONTENTS

ILLUSTRATIONS

FOREWORD

by Roger Moorhouse

The battle for Stalingrad still carries enormous resonance. Like 'Kursk' or 'Anzio', the name alone conveys its meaning. One of the bloodiest battles in history, consuming over a million lives at a conservative estimate, it was also one of the most important, signalling a genuine watershed in the conflict: what Churchill called a 'climacteric'.

Unusually, Stalingrad's significance was clearly evident even at the time. For the Soviets its defence was as much symbolic as strategic. As well as controlling the approaches to the oil-rich Caucasus and sitting on the western bank of the mighty Volga river, one of Russia's most formidable natural obstacles, it was the city that bore Stalin's name. For propaganda reasons alone, therefore, its surrender was unthinkable.

Militarily, too, the battle for Stalingrad was profoundly significant. Where the Red Army had struggled to come to terms with the German doctrine of Blitzkrieg over the previous two summers, at Stalingrad it launched an audacious Blitzkrieg of its own, sending armoured columns deep into the Axis rear, hitting at the more lightly defended flanks of the salient – where the Italians, Hungarians and Romanians held the line – and cutting off the German Sixth Army in a shrinking pocket to the west of the city, effectively besieging the besiegers. It was an astonishing reversal, finally and conclusively demonstrating the truth of Stalin's optimistic assertion from July 1941 that no army was invincible. After this success, the Wehrmacht's spell was broken and the Red Army's generals hardly looked back. To paraphrase one of Churchill's neatest aphorisms: before Stalingrad the Red Army scarcely had a victory, after Stalingrad it scarcely had a defeat.

The Germans, too, were well aware of Stalingrad's importance. The city lay on the high-water mark of Axis expansion and its loss heralded an ebb-tide that would sweep Soviet forces, with few interruptions, all the way to Berlin. The associated loss of the Caucasus was also a grievous blow, denying Hitler access to the vital Soviet oil-fields of Baku, Maikop and Grozny, without which, he had earlier confessed, he would be unable to continue his war.[1] Stalingrad, therefore, was highly significant both as a strategic and a military turning point in the wider history of the Second World War.

Far from being concealed from the German people, as is so often assumed, or wished away with a propagandist's flourish, the defeat at Stalingrad was acknowledged for the catastrophe to Hitler's ambitions that it was. The news was announced on German radio to the accompaniment of the sombre *adagio* to Bruckner's Seventh Symphony, and three days of official mourning followed. Two weeks later, Propaganda Minister Joseph Goebbels would give his response to the crisis. In his famed 'Total War' speech in Berlin, he cited the defeat at Stalingrad as a wake-up call to the German people; opening their eyes to the 'true nature' of the war against the Bolsheviks, and to their 'historic duty' to defend Western civilization. It was a duty whose importance would brook no half-measures, no compromises; instead, he declared, 'total war' was the demand of the hour.[2] In the aftermath, Nazi Germany would belatedly adopt a war economy, sacrificing most of the remaining civilian comforts for a strict prioritisation of the war effort. Too little, it would prove, too late.

Yet, aside from the propaganda and the posturing, Stalingrad's profoundest consequences were human. The true death toll of the battle – military and civilian, Soviet and German – will never be known for sure; such was the slaughter that the proper retrieval, identification and burial of the dead was simply impossible. In total, it has been suggested that as many as two million people died in the battle. In addition, for the 90,000 or so Axis soldiers taken captive by the Soviets, their torments were not yet at an end. Condemned to punitive hard labour in the infamous camps of the Gulag, few would survive. Barely 6 per cent of them would ever see their homelands again.

All sides suffered, of course, but this book concentrates our attention specifically on the experiences of German soldiers. Its editor, Reinhold Busch, has spent many years collecting, collating and evaluating first-hand accounts of the battle, primarily with an interest in the history of the medical units involved. The accounts assembled here are a by-product of that process, the myriad eyewitness testimonies of German soldiers of all ranks, all faiths and all political affiliations – a cross-section of German fighting men. More than any other volume, perhaps, this book gives a voice

---

1. Quoted in Ian Kershaw, *Hitler 1936–1945: Nemesis* (London, 2000), p. 514.
2. Quoted in Roger Moorhouse, *Berlin at War: Life and Death in Hitler's Capital, 1939–1945* (London, 2010), p. 338.

to the German soldiers of Stalingrad: it tells their grim story of the battle, in their own words.

There is much here to satisfy the enthusiast for the tactics or technology of the Second World War. At times, indeed, it is rather like eavesdropping on a convention of Stalingrad veterans as they swap stories, reminisce and remember their comrades that did not make it home. It is certainly not a book for the faint-hearted or the squeamish, therefore. It can be breathless stuff, recreating the confused frenzy of military action by dropping the reader into a narrative often with little by way of context or introduction. Some of the accounts hold little back, relating searing, terrifying episodes of combat; the urban 'Rattenkrieg' or 'Rat War', which some veterans described as being 'worse than hell'. It is all here; from the hideous cacophony of the Katyusha rockets – the infamous 'Stalin Organ' – to the visceral horror of facing an onrushing T-34 without anti-tank weapons; from the unseen death at a sniper's hand to the brutal reality of hand-to-hand fighting.

In the lull between battles, there were other tribulations. The extreme cold took a heavy toll that winter. In temperatures as low as -30°C and lacking adequate winter clothing, German soldiers were at the very least prey to frostbite. Many simply froze to death, often prone ready for action, or curled up, showing the burrowing impulse that is distinctive of hypothermia. For many of them, just falling asleep constituted a death sentence. The bodies would be stacked en masse for burial, as not even a makeshift grave could be hewn from the frozen earth.

The shortage of food was another constant, as the already measly ration allocation dwindled to nothing by the final days of the siege. Once the stores and iron rations had been exhausted, the spoiled remnants had been consumed, and the horses that had carried the army eastwards had been slaughtered and eaten, all that was left was gnawing hunger, made all the more insistent by the Soviet tactic of shouting across the frontlines offering hot soup and bread as a seductive inducement to defect.

As if all that were not enough, all of the men, it seems, suffered infestations of lice, many also had scabies, diphtheria, jaundice, dysentery, or the mysterious Volhynia fever. Wounded men, too, were ubiquitous, from those silently awaiting death to those still fighting on the frontline – all of them suffering from the inadequate medical care that was available. Even among those that survived Stalingrad, few emerged without a scratch. One soldier, who was one of the last to escape the siege, came home with over forty wounds; his family were told to prepare for the worst.

This is a truly remarkable book. Informative and enlightening, it can be by turns horrifying and uplifting, showcasing not only man's inhumanity to his fellow man, but also the indomitability of the human spirit. There are vignettes here that will stay with you for a long time. The young infantryman, for instance, eager for combat, who pushed his way to the front of the queue to be transported to Stalingrad, only to rue his keenness when he realized that he had hastened into a murderous trap. Or the NCO rescued unconscious from a pile of the dead and dying because his comrades spotted his familiar regimental collar tabs. Or the gravely injured soldier who is given a blood transfusion, and to his astonishment sees that the donor is his Russian doctor.

This book does not sentimentalize or over-dramatize events, rather it gives readers a genuine sense of the horrors, the sights and the smells of the battle for Stalingrad; the stacked piles of the dead, the distant rattle of the T-34 and the stench of putrefaction. It can be harrowing, certainly, but that should in no way be construed as a criticism; it is more accurately a tribute to the skills of the editor in bringing together such a compelling selection of quite excellent first-hand accounts of one of the Second World War's most climactic military confrontations.

This is a truly valuable addition to the available English-language literature on the Battle for Stalingrad. And, as such, it is a book that deserves to be read by anyone with an interest in the war on the Eastern Front, or indeed in the Second World War in general – albeit with the tiny caveat that it might induce the occasional bad dream.

Roger Moorhouse, 2014

EDITOR'S INTRODUCTION

Seventy years after the German Sixth Army surrendered at Stalingrad, this highly dramatic event has lost none of its allure. The fascination which the battle for the city has exercised for decades, and continues to exercise, on people of all continents – be they historians, military men, politicians or philosophers – is astounding. To take one example, one needs only to read the lively internet discussions in various forums, in which even young people talk about details of the battle and look for the biographies of those involved. Tens of thousands of German soldiers are still missing: their families have no closure. New graves are found daily in the tortured ground of the former encirclement. Since the fall of the Soviet Union, German veterans of Stalingrad or their relatives regularly make the journey to Volgograd, as the city is now called, to visit the new military cemetery at Rossoshka or to meet Russian veterans. The list of books on the subject is longer with every passing year.

Since 2003 I have been working on a series of books with the title *History of Medicine – The Surgeons of Stalingrad* of which, to date, seven volumes have appeared in German and the series is continuing. It has been my purpose to publish the memoirs of former members of the Sixth Army medical units and to reconstruct the story of the field hospitals and main dressing stations at Stalingrad. This subject has been almost totally neglected in history even though by the end of January 1943 the majority of the men within the encirclement were unfit through frostbite, wounds or illness, and froze or starved to death, or vegetated with other units, in cellars, emergency hospitals and dressing stations.

In my research for previously unpublished material there has come into my hands almost as a by-product well over a hundred interviews, manuscripts, diaries and privately published books together with articles published in magazines or Stalingrad veterans' circulars which were only available to a limited readership and which I evaluated for my history of the medical units. Because I considered the greater part of it suitable for a book, I spoke to Ares

Verlag of Graz, Austria and I am grateful to its publishing director, Herr Dvorak-Stocker, for agreeing to publish my collection of eyewitness reports. I based these reports on the following criteria: preference was given to personal experiences, neither too long nor too short, and which in particular did not dwell on the military situation. No accounts by German medical corps personnel are included, since these are the foundation for my book *The Surgeons of Stalingrad.* I was also anxious to include as wide a range of ranks as possible, from the private soldier to general, and to look for accounts which reflect the drama of Stalingrad in a particularly impressive manner. Where they occur, the italicized potted biographies which provide the lead-in and epilogue to each report, and in most cases the title, were provided by myself as editor.

The book embraces essays by soldiers who were either captured at the surrender and returned home after the war, or did not experience the end of the battle by reason of having been transported out previously sick or wounded, and the pilots or aircrew who flew into the encirclement. For those readers who are not familiar with the events at Stalingrad I have prepared a short preface omitting any assessment of motivation and especially moral judgement. Many of the authors in this book have adopted this or that stance, from which the reader himself can draw his own picture.

PREFACE

After the setback at the gates of Moscow in the winter of 1941, Hitler decided against a major offensive in the area of Army Group Centre and turned his military planning to operations in the southern sector. Here the Soviets had suffered a serious defeat at Kharkov in May 1942, and this strengthened the prospects for more military victories.

Against the advice of his generals, Hitler wanted to achieve two objectives at the same time: to close down river traffic at Stalingrad on the Volga and with it the transport of strategic war materials from central Asia and the Caucasus; and to capture the Caucasian oilfields. To extend the frontline to Stalingrad meant having a flank 700 kilometres long. Fifty divisions would be required to protect it, not to mention the difficulties of keeping them supplied. The entire operation could only succeed if the Soviet fronts were all to be collapsed completely, that is to say, if the Red Army was prepared to risk everything on preventing it. Instead, their units fell back into the hinterland. When the spearhead of XIV Panzer Corps approached the city and reached the Volga between 19 August and 2 September 1942, Soviet troops were holding out in the ruins along a stretch of the river from where they could not be expelled. In the months which followed, the German units sent to eject them bled out in the waves of attacks made to clear the ruins of houses and factories of Soviet forces. During this time the city was reduced to rubble and ashes.

On 19 November the Soviets began a major offensive from north and south against the weak flanks, which were protected by inadequately-equipped Romanian, Italian and Hungarian forces. Within only four days the spearheads of the two Soviet armies met at Kalatch east of the Don and thus encircled the Sixth Army. This also threatened to cut off Fourth Panzer Army, well forward in the Caucasus. Strategically, now was the time to swiftly withdraw the twenty-two German and two Romanian divisions while it was still possible, or to order the break-out from the Stalingrad Pocket in order to shorten the front. The Commander-in-Chief, Sixth Army, General Friedrich

Paulus,[1] therefore telexed Hitler with a request for freedom of manoeuvre. All Hitler's military advisers were convinced that it would be impossible to supply the 280,000 men in the encirclement from the air. Thus it was understood at Sixth Army that preparations should be made accordingly when, on the morning of 24 November – against the advice of his experts – Göring boasted that the Luftwaffe could do it. This fell in with what Hitler wanted, to hold the city at all costs, leaving Paulus appalled and his commanders resigned. Only General Walther von Seydlitz-Kurzbach[2] rebelled and in a memorandum of 25 November called for an immediate withdrawal. Paulus did not have the courage to oppose a Führer-order, and, in his eyes, such an act of disobedience threatened to destroy all authority. Seydlitz-Kurzbach gave in.

Nevertheless on 12 December 1942 Operation 'Wintergewitter' ('Winter Thunderstorm') began. This was an attempt to break out of the encirclement with insufficient forces. Seven days later the relief divisions were only 50 kilometres from the south-western edge of the Pocket when the operation came to a halt in the face of increasing Soviet counter-attacks. Thus another round of preparations to break out was brought to a standstill. By then, however, their chances of success had become doubtful: the first men had starved to death. At this late stage it was at last clear that there would be no relief and the fate of those in the Stalingrad Pocket was sealed, especially since the main German frontline was falling ever farther back from Stalingrad and not even 10 per cent of the supplies required by Sixth Army were arriving.

---

1. Friedrich Paulus (b. Breitenau-Gershagen, 23 September 1890, d. Dresden. 1 February 1957). Joined Army as ensign 1910: 1911 Lieutenant, 1918 Captain. End of 1920s Staff, 5th Division, Stuttgart, and Staff Training Leader. 1938 Chief of General Staff XVI Army Corps, 1939 Chief of General Staff, Army Group 4, Leipzig (later renamed Sixth Army). 1940 Lieutenant-General General-QM I and Deputy Chief of the Army General Staff: worked on the concept of Operation 'Barbarossa'. 5 January 1942 General, C-in-C Sixth Army: 31 January 1943 Field-Marshal. After the attempt on Hitler's life entered BdO (Bund deutscher Offiziere), witness at Nuremberg. 17 November 1953 released from Soviet captivity, lived out his retirement in Dresden.
2. Walther von Seydlitz-Kurzbach (b. 22 August 1888 Hamburg, d. 28 April 1976 Bremen). 1908 entered Army, WWI 1917 Captain, 1930 Major, 1936 Colonel, 1941 Lieutenant-General. 1 June 1942 General of Artillery, 4 May 1942 Commanding-General LI Army Corps. 11 September 1943–3 November 1945 in Soviet captivity president of BdO: 8 July 1950 sentenced to death for alleged war crimes, commuted to 25 years' imprisonment, 6 October 1955 released from Soviet captivity.

From this point on the objective was to organize the defence within the Pocket and tie down as many Soviet forces at Stalingrad as possible. At the beginning of December 1942, the Soviets launched massive attacks at the western perimeter of the Pocket and the so-called Northern Boundary: the Germans held both positions but with heavy casualties. An ultimatum to capitulate was declined by the recently promoted General Paulus: this was followed on 10 January 1943 by a major Soviet offensive against the Pocket, now being slowly squeezed from west to east. With grim determination the last defensive forces mobilized into 'fortress battalions' formed from dispersed units and the men from the rearward services.

The loss of the last airfield, Stalingradski, in the western suburbs of the city on 23 January signalled that the last hope of salvation was gone. The remnants of Sixth Army made a more or less hasty retreat into the ruins of the city. On 26 January Paulus and his Staff occupied a cellar of the Univermag department store on Red Square. The remnants of the 297th Infantry Division were the first to lay down their weapons and accept captivity. Despite the desperate situation, diminishing ammunition and provisions, and no prospect of relief, Hitler ordered those in the encirclement at Stalingrad to fight to the last round. Seydlitz-Kurzbach ordered his corps to fire off what was left of their ammunition and cease fighting, at which he was relieved of command and consideration given to placing him under arrest. On 27 January the Pocket was divided into two halves, north and south, which continued the struggle independent of each other.

On 31 January, Paulus, newly promoted the previous day to the rank of field-marshal, led his Staff and headquarters escort 'personally' into captivity without signing a formal instrument of capitulation. He informed the Soviets that he would not order the northern Pocket to surrender, and so the latter fought on until 2 February. About 90,000 mostly wounded, sick and half-starved soldiers, many with frostbite, went into captivity: around 140,000 had fallen, and approximately 35,000 were flown out. Most of the prisoners died on forced marches across Russia or in the death camps around Stalingrad: only about 6,000 lived to see their Homeland again.

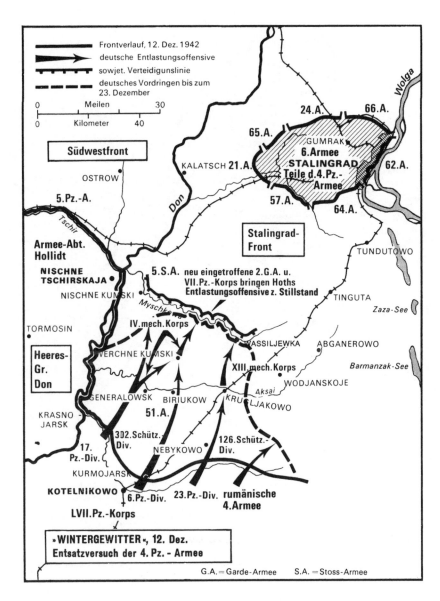

Map 1: 'Operation *Wintergewitter*, 12 December, Relief Attempt by 4.Pz.Armee'.
The relief attempt by Army Group Hoth gave hope of rescue briefly, but was
condemned to failure by the numerical superiority of the Soviets. (*See Chapter 3*).
Key, top left: Front line, 12 December 1942; German relief offensive; Soviet defensive
line; German advance up to 23 December.

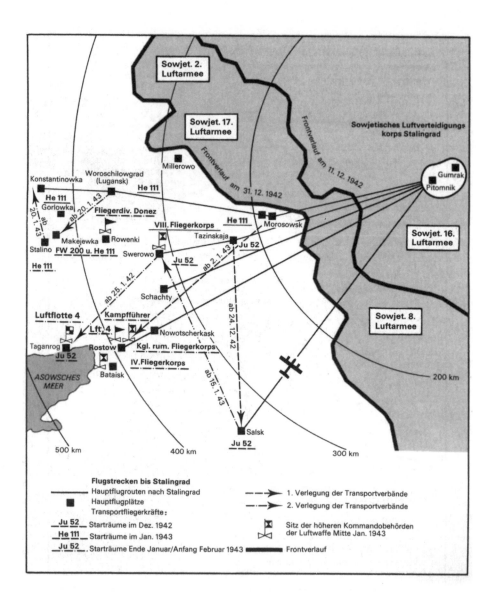

Map 2: Flight paths to Stalingrad. Key, bottom left: Main flight routes to Stalingrad/Main airfields/Transport aircraft; Ju 52 take-off areas in December 1942; He 111 take-off areas in January 1943; Ju 52 take-off areas end of January/beginning February 1943. Bottom right: arrows showing transfer of transport groups; base of the Luftwaffe Higher Command authorities, mid-January 1943; route of main front line.

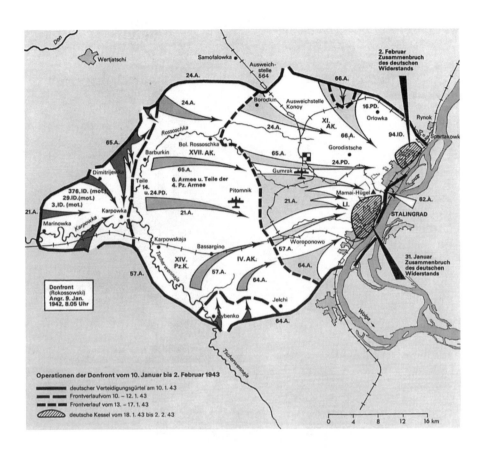

Map 3: The situation in the Stalingrad Pocket between 10 January 1943 and the final capitulation on 2 February 1943.

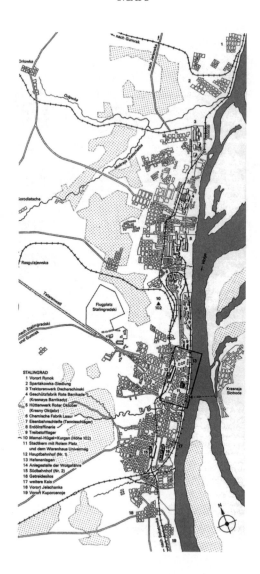

Map 4: Map of the Stalingrad inner city marked with principal combat locations. Key: 1. Rynok suburb. 2. Spartakovka settlement. 3. Dshershinski tractor works. 4. Red Barricade ordnance factory. 5. Red October metal works. 6. Lasur chemical factory. 7. Railway loop ('Tennis Racquet'). 8. Oil refinery. 9. Fuel dump. 10. Hill 102. 11. City centre with Red Square and Univermag department store. 12. Main railway station (No.1). 13. Port installations. 14. Mooring quay for Volga ferries. 15. South railway station (No.2). 16. Grain silos. 17. Other quays. 18. Yelshanka suburb. 19. Kuporosnoye suburb.

1. GOTTFRIED VON BISMARCK:

I Flew into the Pocket[1]

Gottfried von Bismarck was born on 8 January 1921. After obtaining his school-leaving certificate in 1939 he performed his compulsory RAD labour service, and during the Polish campaign was a soldier training in civil engineering. From October 1939 he did his basic military training with the 9th Infantry Regiment at Potsdam before being drafted to the 176th Regiment in the 76th Infantry Division. After the French campaign he attended the War Academy and obtained his commission in January 1941. Afterwards he served with a training unit in Romania, and the Russian Front.

. . . That meant for us infantrymen a march on foot of about 950 kilometres through dust, or after the slightest rainfall, deep mud, weighed down with all our battle gear: 70 kilometres daily!

Many of us were able to sleep while marching, taking a position in the middle of the column and being pushed in the right direction on the bends. I could even sleep running. Because as platoon commander I had to lead from the front I used to hold the tail of the company commander's horse to remain on course.

The Russians offered heavy resistance only at the river crossings. Thus we reached the Donets basin rapidly – too rapidly – and were surprised there by the early onset of winter, stifling our advance. In that Russian winter of 1941 bitter defensive fighting alternated with periods of relative quiet. Both were hard to endure, for unlike the Russians we had no winter clothing, and temperatures could fall to -30°C. Casualties due to frostbite were substantial, and so those who survived this winter were awarded a medal which we called 'The Order of the Frozen Meat'.[2]

---

1. Privately printed in connection with the presentation of documentation by the Military-Historical Institute entitled *Stalingrad. Ereignis – Wirkung – Symbol.* With the kind permission of Frau Ehrengard von Bismarck, Aachen.
2. This was the 'Ostmedaille' awarded for the 'Winter Battle in the East, 1941/42'.

In the spring of 1942 we left our winter positions and after great long marches and some bitter fighting to break out of encircling movements we reached the Don. On 21 August our 178th Regiment broke through the northern bridgehead over the Don at Wertyatshi, and then our panzers – despite the stiffest Russian resistance – got through to the Volga north of Stalingrad in a few days.

In September, my 76th Division had settled in the so-called Northern Boundary between the Don and Volga in steppe country with deep gorges, and dug in laboriously. A double-trench system enabled us to reach all command positions from the bunkers. In front of our lines we laid six rows of minefields and barbed wire, and dug in behind them immobilized Russian T-34s with working turrets for defence against tanks. We had the feeling: here we are safe, here the Russians cannot touch us.

In Stalingrad itself the fighting began man to man and house to house for every square metre – a struggle on the western banks of the Volga, where the Russians had dug in and were clinging to a slope 300 metres wide which fell steeply down to the river. Because the area being fought for was so narrow there was no question of using heavy weapons here. In the end we never took this strip because we never managed to prevent the Russians keeping it supplied – and it was a struggle which often involved grotesque situations. Thus once I visited a company commander I had befriended in whose sector there was a house where the Germans were in the cellar and first floor and the Russians on the ground floor. Fearing the approach of winter nobody wanted to demolish the house, but nobody wanted to give up the positions held. During the day there would be bitter fighting, but with humane features. Thus at night there was tacit agreement that a kind of truce would exist so that the wounded could be brought out and the fighting men supplied with rations.

A serious problem for us as a horse-drawn unit was how to accommodate the horses out of the cold and provide their fodder. In the bald, barren steppe – no trees, no bushes – this was not possible, even the wood to construct our underground bunkers had to be procured from hundreds of kilometres away on the other side of the Don. Our horses had to be sent back over the river, except for the small number needed for the supply carts. The catastrophic outcome of this measure was that later when we were building up the Pocket and had to pull in the flanks we lost nearly all our heavy guns because we could not move them without the horses.

In November 1942 in our sector on the Stalingrad flank it was relatively

2

quiet, and the Army lifted the ban on furloughs. So now there was leave! We drew lots and I got Christmas, but then an elderly reserve officer came and asked me to change with him. He had almost immediate leave, but had just received news that his daughter was getting married at Christmas. I was quite prepared to change, as a practical soldier I said to myself, 'You have what you have. Who knows if this leave-taking will last until Christmas or whether you will be still alive to see it? Therefore – OK, and off home!' Two days later, on 15 November I sat in the leave train at Kalatch, last station on the Stalingrad line: the railway bridge over the Don was still down. On 19 November, only four days later, the Russians launched their major offensive, and on 22nd they bottled up the Sixth Army. I had a wonderful, peaceful four weeks of leave on our estate. It was the last time that I knew my Pomeranian home.

Because the press and radio were silent on the situation in Stalingrad, neither I nor the lower military command centres, and certainly not the German people, had any hint of the catastrophe that was building there. Had my reserve Battalion at Potsdam, which I visited before I left for the front, even heard it rumoured about the true situation, they would definitely have tried to hold me back, but they had no reason to do so because of the lack of information. Therefore when my leave ended on 14 December I took the eastbound train from Berlin.

When the train stopped at Kharkov, the order came: 'Officers and men of the Sixth Army alight! Officers to the Führer-reserve!' We had no hint of what that meant, but word gradually got around that 'something was not right' at Stalingrad. We accepted it with the stoic calm of the veteran soldier: that the Sixth Army could be encircled was unimaginable! After a few days at Kharkov we moved to the Führer-reserve at Rostov on the Don, where rumours of a Pocket at Stalingrad were rife. I was given orders to act as liaison officer with the Romanian Army. Together with about forty other officers with orders to report to the most far-flung command centres, we were sent off by train from Rostov to the east; I had to find the Romanian Army. I was unable to find out exactly where their Army Staff was located. As I discovered later, at this point in time it no longer existed, not to mention Romanian forces! All Romanians – except for those trapped in the Pocket – had fled west in panic leaving all their weapons and equipment behind.

At Tshir, about 280 kilometres from Stalingrad, we received orders that the men aboard this present train were to form a battlegroup to defend the town. The ratio of men to officers in this battlegroup was about 6:1; the officers – all made platoon commanders irrespective of their rank – carried the heaviest

3

weapons we had, namely our pistols. The NCOs and men had only their sidearms. The men were mainly members of the Sixth Army supply units: bakers, ostlers, drivers; therefore soldiers without any combat experience, which made the whole exercise senseless. That was on 23 December.

Next day also we camped in the, thanks be to God, heated train at the station platform because nothing else was available and from there we defended Tshir. No enemy showed up. We had no inkling of the overall military situation, but it was clear to us that not even here, 280 kilometres this side of Stalingrad, was there a functional defensive front. We got confirmation of this from an ambulance train heading westwards on the neighbouring track. It was 24 December – Christmas Eve – and none of us had thought of it! These were the last wounded flown out of the Pocket to Morosovskaya and loaded in goods wagons there, just a few hours before the Russians captured the airfield.

When I saw the haggard and wounded, fed only the barest essentials, on the straw in the goods wagons I suddenly remembered my Christmas tree, which my mother had given me to celebrate Christmas on the steppe and which I had brought along with me in a large sack, contrary to all common sense. It was cold with a biting frost but no wind, and so we quickly set up the Christmas tree on the station platform and lit candles on it. Soldiers and the walking wounded gathered around it at first hesitantly, others opened the doors of the goods wagons. Some began to softly hum 'Silent Night, Holy Night', others joined in. It was a rough-hewn, very moving choir. Afterwards it fell quiet, very quiet. We were all alone with our thoughts, far, far from here. Then someone started up with another well-known German carol and all joined in almost fervently. Despite everything, hope gleamed eternal. Seldom before had a Christmas evening and the Christian message moved me so deeply and filled me with so much confidence as on that night.

Over the next few days we played at soldiers, so to speak, simply to sort out who was who. I recall two reconnaissance patrols, four officers in an Opel P4 in an ice-bound street. Armament: four pistols. The other was in a locomotive with a Russian driver, Russian fireman and three officers scouting the railway line ahead to the east. This was also totally ridiculous and not a little dangerous because the Russians used to fly over by night in their 'sewing machine', a slow fighter-bomber. We always had two tanker wagons full of fuel on these runs.

On 30 December I got new orders: I was to return to Army Group Don at Novotsherkassk and report to the registry which had received a request from

4

my division in the Pocket, where practically all officers of the original permanent company were casualties. After the turbulent to-and-fro of recent days I was happy to return to my own unit even if it was encircled for the moment. The idea that the situation could become critical or even hopeless did not occur to me because I assumed that officers were continually being flown in.

My flight was scheduled for the next day. Looking through the composition of the Staff I noticed that a cousin of my sister-in-law, Alexander Stahlberg,[3] whom I knew well, was personal adjutant to Manstein. I rang him and he said, 'Come at once, the Field-Marshal is having his midday nap.' We had just started our happy family chat when suddenly – unexpectedly early – Manstein appeared. I reported myself: he asked who I was and where I was bound. To my reply, 'From the so-called defensive front on the way to Stalingrad' he cut in: 'What do you mean by "so-called" defensive front?' To my rather forward response, 'Do you wish to know exactly, Herr Field-Marshal?' he ordered me to take supper with him and his Staff to make my report. It was the only time that a mere second lieutenant had been invited to dine within this noble circle. Manstein mentions this evening in his book *Verlorene Siege* as does Stahlberg in *Die verdammte Pflicht*. Stahlberg wrote that it was my 'Prussian devotion to duty' which motivated me to return to the Pocket. That sounds good, but is untrue. I was a soldier, had my orders and had to carry them out.

Next morning I was taken to the airfield and shown an He 111 bomber. The bomb-bays were crammed with bread and ammunition and the wings full of fuel for the vehicles in the Pocket. The airfield was a simple meadow without a runway. Because of the unevenness of the terrain and the gross overloading the undercarriage collapsed shortly before take-off and the aircraft slid hundreds of metres on its belly. By some miracle it did not burst into flames: the three-man crew and I were unhurt. So, back to the flight office for the next attempt. There I met a Luftwaffe officer I knew. He said: 'You're crazy, flying into the Pocket! I've got a courier flight to Berlin. Come with me, tonight we'll have a coffee at Kranzler's.' This was the first time my

---

3. Alexander Stahlberg (b. Stettin, 12 September 1912, died Schloss Bloemersheim, 9 January 1995) was the adjutant to Reich Chancellor Franz von Papen in 1933. In 1938 he was commissioned as a Lieutenant in the Wehrmacht and became Manstein's adjutant. He was a cousin of Colonel Henning von Treskow, a member of the military resistance. His final rank was Captain. After the war he became a businessman.

'Prussian devotion to duty' had been put to the test. I declined and arrived punctually for the second take-off attempt.

It was a flight of three machines without fighter escort. None of our fighters was available. We were attacked by Russian fighters and the other two machines were apparently hit. They did not attempt to land, but discarded their cargoes. Our aircraft put down. As soon as one of our machines arrived, the Russian artillery would bombard the airfield. There was therefore no time to lose. Quickly out, unload, wounded aboard, and then take off again. It was very dangerous to be anywhere near the airfield, many men had been hit by cargo jettisoned from the air – even bread is pretty hard when frozen solid. I hastened to get away from the place. I think I was one of the last officers to be flown in. A few days later the Russians captured this airfield.

I was taken to my Division, reported to the commanding officer and passed him Manstein's message as I had been instructed, namely that the situation was 'a miserable one, but not hopeless'. He gave me strict orders not to make this judgement by the commanding general known. I replied that I could not keep it quiet. I considered it unreasonable and psychologically wrong to pretend to the fighting troops that the situation was other than what we knew it was.

That night I was taken to my regiment at the front where, 30 kilometres west of Stalingrad in the steppe, they had set up a provisional defensive line. The regiment still consisted of only two battalions each with two battlegroups. Apart from the regimental adjutant I never met an officer of the original core staff. There were just the six of us when our strength should have been forty-five. I took command of a battlegroup with about thirty men; my predecessor had been seriously wounded the day before. I met nobody from my old pioneer platoon, they had all fallen. It was difficult to lead a squad whose members I did not know and with whom I only had contact at night because they were located in dribs and drabs in trenches on the flat, snow-covered steppe. One could only move about when the moon was not visible or under thick overcast. Food – when there was any – was brought up by night to the battlegroup command post, a hole covered over by aircraft parts, illuminated by diverting a telephone cable. Our well-constructed positions were now occupied by the Russians while we on the other hand were on the open steppe, where we had had to scrape out holes in the frozen ground from under a metre of snow and in temperatures of -15 to -20°C.

What was the situation in the Pocket, what had changed in Stalingrad during my absence over the last six weeks? The army was now starving, there were no reserves of provisions. Nowhere near enough could be supplied from the air. Gradually the rations got less and less until finally one had to scavenge for food. The increasingly desperate situation worsened the plight of the wounded and sick. Even the most basic medical materials were lacking: bandages, medication, narcotics, not to mention warm bunkers. The wounded and sick in the Pocket had almost no chance of survival. Therefore every wounded man who could crawl tried to seize a place in an aircraft, if necessary by brute force. This led to ghastly scenes at the airfield. The fuel the aircraft brought in was not even enough for the couple of still-operational panzers to get back into action. There was no fuel for the ambulances. As far as possible, the wounded had to be retrieved and transported by sledge. The last of the horses were useless as carriers and insufficient in numbers as a reserve for food.

Yet the worst of all was the lack of practically any ammunition, either for light or heavy weapons. Such artillery as there was required the approval of the divisional commander for every round fired. The chances of beating off a Russian attack in these circumstances, something with which we had to reckon daily, were very slim.

That, then, was Stalingrad on 4 January 1943: no possibility of getting a bit of warmth, no chance of survival for the wounded, no ammunition, no weapons to fight off Russian tanks, no prospect of relief from outside the Pocket. It was and remains a marvel that the men were still willing to fight on under these circumstances!

On 8 January I was twenty-two years of age, and on 10 January the end began. The enemy launched a massive attack from the north. We succeeded in holding our trenches for a whole day, then the Russians near us broke through and in order not to be cut off we had to pull back in the face of a strong enemy force. Night by night a little bit further east, closer to Stalingrad. By day one half of my squad slept: the other half had to try to keep the advancing Russians at bay. On the marches to the rear each night, every vehicle found immobile was ransacked for anything edible. If we were lucky, and something was found, it would be shared around. The trouble was, whenever something to eat was found, my battlegroup would suddenly grow in size to over 100 men. In the darkness it was difficult to pick out my own. We towed the wounded on makeshift sledges through the deep snow. Otherwise we could do nothing, our own strength did not extend to anything else.

Each night we discussed if and how one might make his way through to the west. I knew how far away the nearest German troops were and therefore condemned every idea – alone or in groups – as totally hopeless. Hundreds of kilometres of snow-covered steppe, hardly any chance of hiding oneself, no chance of finding anything to eat, and because of the months of hunger no reserves of strength to endure a forced march of that length. We gave up the idea. Some tried it all the same, but none made it. Meanwhile it was clear to us all that every man of us who survived had to reckon with being made a prisoner of the Russians, but it was never spoken of openly. We could all remember the dreadful sight of the endless columns of half-starved, apathetic, resigned Russian prisoners of war, and none of us could or would imagine the tables being turned on us like that. Meanwhile the Pocket had been divided up into three parts. We had no airfields any longer and accordingly no line of supply. By night aircraft dropped containers of food. Whoever found one kept it. A large number of these containers fell into the hands of the Russians.

On 31 January the southern Pocket under Paulus surrendered. The day before he had been made a field-marshal and had called upon us to 'fight to the last round'. We in the northern Pocket held out. It was a macabre thing to sit in the cellar of a wrecked house in the ruins of Stalingrad listening to our obituary. This was Göring's famous eulogy in which he compared us with the Spartans who had knowingly sacrificed their lives defending a strategically decisive isthmus against a superior Persian force in order to halt them. When Göring in concluding his speech quoted the last message of the fallen Thermopylae warriors: 'Wanderer, come to Sparta and tell them you have seen us lying dead as the law required', then we knew that we had finally been written off. A whole army – sacrificed for nothing! We could not credit it! The embitterment was boundless . . .

On 2 February it was all over. The shooting stopped. Prisoners were taken quietly without any excesses by the conquering troops. Tacit understanding for the defeated enemy? Both sides were sick to death of it and happy that it was finally, finally, over.

At the end of December 1949 in a mock trial on trumped-up charges, Gottfried von Bismarck was sentenced to twenty-five years' labour camp. The basis of the arraignment was the fact that Soviet prisoners of war had been required to work on his family estate in Pomerania. He spent the next five years' in hard, forced labour underground. In 1955 after almost thirteen years of captivity he was freed as a result of the efforts of Federal Chancellor Konrad Adenauer. In vain, together with others, he attempted to have the West German Federal Republic recognize those condemned to forced labour to be 'victims of Stalinism' and compensated financially: 'It hurts that this should fall on apparently deaf ears amongst our politicians!' He studied at the Essen School of Mining, worked as a blaster with Thyssens, sinking shafts, and finally set up his own business exporting to the East. He died on 8 January 2001.

2. MICHAEL DEIML:

Last Flight into the Pocket[1]

Michael Deiml (b. Auerbach/Oberpfalz, 28 March 1918, d. Pegnitz, 9 February 2009) was trained as bomber crew and took part in the operations to supply the encircled Sixth Army. After the war and until his retirement he was in the police service.

After my training as gunner/flight mechanic from December 1939 to March 1940 at Bomber Crew School 4, Thorn/West Prussia, and then at Reserve Bomber Group 3 at Cracow, from 1 April 1940 until 30 September 1940 I served with KG 55, the 'Griffin Squadron'. With my first crew I flew twenty missions against France and nine against England. This crew (pilot Lieutenant Müller) was shot down over the English Channel by RAF fighters in the spring of 1941. All were lost. At the time I was interned in the Luftwaffe Field Hospital at Munich-Oberföhring with a middle ear infection, my place being taken by Sergeant Simon, who therefore died for me.

After my recovery at the bomber crews' convalescent company, Quedlinburg, on 1 October 1941 I returned to KG 55 in Russia, and was attached to 7th Squadron in No. 3 Group. With my new crew, on 7 October 1941 I took off from Kirovograd for my thirtieth mission. Because of my many excursions to the front – 387 flights over enemy territory – it is not possible to comment on these individually, but I would like to write something about my participation as an airman in the Battle of Stalingrad.

After the Caucasus and other operations around the Black Sea, my missions over the Stalingrad area began with my 139th flight. On 21 August 1942 we flew two attacks against Russian troops, taking off at 0630 and 1340 hrs from Kramatorskaya airfield west of Stalingrad. After several attacks each

---

1. This report was written in 1999 and placed at the Editor's disposal. Along with the typescript the author supplied his flight log which confirms all the related missions and landings in the Stalingrad Pocket.

day on 23 August 1942 we transferred to the Morosovskaya airfield, and next day we began concentrated bombing attacks on Stalingrad. We took off at 0630, 1130 and 1515 hrs and made high level attacks on the city, particularly the railway station, usually under very heavy anti-aircraft fire. Thus with my crew under Sergeant-Major Dietrich we flew nearly every day until 3 October 1942 from the airfields at Kramatorskaya, Morosovskaya and Tazinskaya for Stalingrad and the inner city. In this period of six weeks since beginning afresh, I flew fifty-eight missions, on each of which we would be two to four-and-a-half hours in the air. Our orders were: drop your bombs on the target area. In the Kalmuck steppe there were many gorges: one especially large one – we called it Gratshi-Valley (north-west of Stalingrad) – we had to attack time and time again in the effort to wipe out the Russian troops there, their positions and supply base. In Gratshi Valley there were an awfully large number of Russians. To support our ground forces we were very often called upon to attack these Russian troops, usually in daylight raids. We used to attack other targets in the city area such as railway stations, industrial plants and airfields, including east of the Volga, both day and night. We were frequently engaged by AA guns and fighters, and our aircraft was often hit, but luckily all crew members escaped harm.

I recall especially the last mission with my second crew under Dietrich, my 196th. We took off from Kramatorskaya in our Heinkel 111 G1+BD at 2045 hrs on 2 October 1942. Towards 2300 hrs we arrived east of Stalingrad on the other side of the Volga to attack some airfields. We were illuminated by searchlights and the Russian AA guns fired at us but failed to inflict damage. Our radio receiver was down so we could not ascertain our position. Our base could hear us because the two transmitters were still working. As we discovered later, we flew close to our target and then continued disoriented into the night. Finally we decided we should fly south to reach the Sea of Azov because even at night one could distinguish between land and water, enabling us to orient ourselves by the coastline. As we had no idea of our position, we were worried about overflying Russian-occupied territory. The observer Lieutenant Winkler shouted to pilot Dietrich, 'Willi, fly west, or we will reach Ivan!' To fall into Russian hands was commonly feared then. After some consideration of the pros and cons we held to our course south because we were running short of fuel. Towards 0430 hrs we reached the Sea of Azov. When we sorted out where we were at a very murky first light, we found that there was not enough fuel to reach the nearest friendly airfields at Nikolayev and Mariupol and so had to make an emergency wheels-up landing in a meadow 15 kilometres north of Berdyansk. We lowered the undercarriage, but then retracted it. If we had tried a conventional landing, we would have touched down at 150kms/hr on a highway low on the contour line and which we could not see from the air. The slightest overshoot on landing and the consequences would have been our deaths. We spent the next few days walking back to our airfield in stages.

In October 1942 our pilot, Sergeant-Major Dietrich, was transferred to No. 4 Group as an instructor and the crew was disbanded to make good losses in other machines. At first I was in reserve, and after December furlough I rejoined my unit at Novotsherkassk airfield. On 18 January 1943 I flew a low level mission with Corporal Püschel against enemy troops on the southern Don east of Novotsherkassk. After this I joined my third crew under Corporal Adrian. I was the flight mechanic: gunner was Corporal Werner Deiters, radioman Leading Private Werner Schubert, observer Leading Private Willi König. As our troops had been bottled up since 22 November 1942, we now flew only supply operations. We dropped containers of provisions and sacks of bread, landing to pick up wounded men, occasionally a war correspondent and a shot-down aircrew.

The first mission with my third crew, my 198th war flight, was on 12 January 1943. Aboard He 111 G1+DS we took off from Novotsherkassk at 0745 hrs and landed at 0955 hrs at Pitomnik airfield. Here there were masses of wounded German soldiers, also OT[2] people, nearly all of them middle-aged. They wore a light olive-green uniform. When asked how they came to be trapped in the Pocket, they said they had been repairing the road between Kalatch and Stalingrad. After setting down an Army leading private, who had brought some spare parts for his unit from Germany, we began unloading the food containers with the help of the OT men.

After that we took out about twenty sacks of large loaves and distributed them there. Eight wounded and a war correspondent were brought aboard then we rolled out to the airstrip. Although the aircraft had been seriously damaged by heavy AA fire on the way in – the tail unit and rear fuselage had been holed by fifty AA shells – it could still fly! The machine was not a transport but a bomber, with bomb-bays, supplementary tanks etc, in the

---

2. OT = Organization Todt, which grew during the war into an enormous public works organization employing many foreign workers and concerns in the execution of construction plans important for the war effort both in the Reich and the occupied territories. Named after Dr Fritz Todt (1891–1942), engineer, 1933 General Inspector of Roadbuilding and 1940–2 Reich Minister for Armaments and Munitions.

interior, and we could only take eight passengers. We left Pitomnik at 1050 hrs and landed at Novotsherkassk at 1210 hrs.

Once the Russians captured Pitomnik on 15 October 1942, we still had Gumrak airfield, but this was in a very dangerous condition with shell craters, wreckage of machines and equipment strewn everywhere, and so only a few landings were made at Gumrak, and under great difficulty. The squadrons involved in these supply operations now received from the Führer's Plenipotentiary, Field-Marshal Milch[3] the order, 'Landings must be made!' Through running losses, our Group, 3/KG 55 had meanwhile been reduced from twenty-seven to twelve crews. For the operation on 18 January for the mission 'Landing at Gumrak' only three of the crews were operational: the rest had damaged aircraft, men off sick and so on. We three crews – piloted by Corporal Peter Adrian, Lieutenant Georg Leipold and Leading Private Heinz Danz – were driven in a small lorry from quarters to Novotsherkassk airfield. It was bitterly cold, more than -20°C, at altitude more than -40°C. On the way there, Sergeant-Major Lochner from Bad Berneck said to us he had a bad feeling about this mission. At the airfield the ground personnel had warmed up the aircraft motors, and after the first mechanic had turned off the warming machine and reported the machine clear for take-off we got in and rolled to the airstrip.

In He 111 G1+AR we took off at 2040 hrs and reached Gumrak around 2200 hrs. We could not land but had to go round again because of obstacles on the landing strip: at the third lamp was a presumably damaged aircraft which never moved. We repeated this procedure eight to ten times, each time lowering the undercarriage and then retracting it. Despite our orders we could not land in those circumstances or we would have hit this aircraft. So we dropped our provisions containers, opened the entry flap in the lower fuselage and, standing over it in an icy draught, tossed out the twenty bags of bread we had brought with us. Some Russian fighters were in the vicinity but did not attack. Danz' crew copied us, indicating that they did not intend to land. Leipold's crew failed to return from this mission and remain missing. Whether the Russian fighters got them is unknown.

Similar obstacles were encountered there on our next mission on 20 January 1943, also flown at night. We set off in He 111 G1+ZR at 0130 hrs

---

3. Erhard Milch (b. Wilhelmshaven, 30 March 1892, d. Wuppertal, 25 January 1972): 1939–45 General-Inspector of the Luftwaffe, 1941–4 General in charge of Luftwaffe planning. 1947 sentenced to life imprisonment by a US military tribunal, released 1954.

from Novotsherkassk and circled Gumrak airfield for ninety minutes without being able to land. We dropped out the provisions and landed back after four and a half hours flying time at 0555 hrs at Novotsherkassk. Because we had failed to land at Gumrak contrary to our orders, we had to submit a written report to which we received no answer. Over Gumrak by day we would have been able to get a clear picture as to the overall situation at the airfield and would definitely have been able to put down – but day flights had now been ruled out.

After the loss of Pitomnik, between 17 and 21 August 1943 we flew ten missions both night and day dropping containers of provisions and attacking Russian troops, weapons and artillery emplacements, primarily near our airfield at Novotsherkassk and east of Rostov-on-Don. After we lost Gumrak, our last airfield, about 10 kilometres west of Stalingrad on 21 January, all we had left within the Pocket was the emergency field at Stalingradski which had been set up closer to the city centre. This possibility was only open on 22 and 23 January, and then fell to the Russians. On 22 January 1943 at 0905 hrs we left Novotsherkassk with our He 111 G1+CR, and landed at 1045 hrs at this emergency airfield which we called Stalingradskaya. There a very sad sight met our eyes. In the icy temperatures, -30°C and lower, we met our soldiers, lightly clad in uniforms of thin material, starving, frozen together and almost motionless. Unloading the provisions containers and bread sacks a still able anti-aircraft artillery captain said that he wanted to give his will, which he had in his overcoat pocket, to the last machine to land. Next day on our last landing he was nowhere to be seen. During this stop we had to leave the propellers turning since there was no machine available to warm the motors up. In addition to the provisions we took fuel from our tanks for the vehicles at the airfield which had run dry. Of the many wounded present we could only fly a few out with us, since we had to take five men of an aircraft shot down in the Pocket. We left at 1125 hrs and landed at Novotsherkassk ninety minutes later.

After landing we then took the aircraft to Stalino to be loaded with infantry munition packed in bomb casings. Then we left Stalino for the Pocket and dropped these supplies to our troops. We got back to Novotsherkassk at 1950 hrs. With the same machine we took off at 0725 hrs on the morning of 23 January 1943 and landed at Stalingradski at 0920 hrs. While unloading the bread sacks suddenly we came under fire from Russian fighters. I jumped out of the aircraft at once and replied with an MG 15. Luckily neither our aircraft nor its crew, nor any of the wounded lying around us were hit. Whilst we were there the Russians did not try again. In great haste we finished unloading the bread sacks, and suddenly heard a dull thump. Looking towards the direction from where the noise had come we saw a headless soldier falling nearing the rotating propeller of the port motor. There was blood on the undercarriage left side but no other remains visible. Two field-gendarmes collected and identified the body. Despite the emotion we all felt we had to unload the rest of the cargo as quickly as possible, for we had to reckon on renewed air attacks by the Russians.

We rolled out to the airstrip with eight wounded aboard. Very many of them, including those we had seen the day before, we had to leave behind in the Pocket. There was one wounded man with his arm in plaster whom I had noticed the previous day and again he was not chosen to come. Before we took off, Adrian said I should get out and bend one of the elevators at the rear to stop it jamming. It had been damaged on landing by hitting frozen snow standing 30–40 centimetres high. After opening the entry flap on the lower fuselage I got down, went to the rear end of the aircraft and bent the elevator back into shape. While I was doing this a wounded man stole into the aircraft through the open flap. When I followed him inside he looked at me in agitation, as if fighting for his life, his eyes begging me to let him leave with us. I can never forget that look. Although we were already loaded to the limit I let him into the interior and said nothing to Corporal Adrian, the pilot and commander of the crew, about the additional wounded man. As a result of all these events and activities we had been at the airfield for 90 minutes and left on the return flight at 1045 hrs. During this short stay at Stalingradski we saw no other German aircraft. If any landed after us, or how many, I do not know. Stalingradski fell to the Russians that same day and the last German aircraft had left Stalingrad.

From 24 to 29 January 1943 we flew another seven missions with provisions containers which we dropped into the Pocket, the last being on the night of 28 January. In He 111 G1+FR we took off and landed each time at Novotsherkassk: out at 2055 hrs, back at 2335 hrs, dropping over the Pocket at 2230 hrs; on 29 January out at 0045 hrs, back at 0315 hrs, dropping over the southern Pocket, the larger one, at about 0200 hrs. The centre of Stalingrad was already in Russian hands and the smaller Pocket was to the north. We had to fly at an altitude of 300 metres to ensure that the provisions really did reach our troops. Then at low level eastwards, over the Volga and Kalmuck steppe before rising to 3,500 metres for the remaining leg to Novotsherkassk. The final drop was confirmed from inside the Pocket by radio.

14

I took part in eighty-one missions in the Battle of Stalingrad. Fifty-nine of these were air attacks and raids and twenty-two were operations to deliver provisions and to fly out wounded from the Pocket. All data mentioned is recorded in my flight logs, still in my possession. Flight personnel had to keep them and enter all flights and missions. These entries were then confirmed by the command centres of the time.

In many of my missions I had several life-threatening experiences. My third crew under Corporal Peter Adrian was shot down by Russian fighters over the village of Marefa near Kharkov on 5 March 1943. The aircraft burst into flames upon hitting the ground and all aboard were killed. I was absent from this flight through illness. Sergeant-Major Ramsberger had taken my place and so died for me. The third of the three remaining crews I mentioned earlier commanded by Leading Private Heinz Danz crashed killing all aboard on 10 August 1943. With my fourth and last crew under Captain Schmidt that same month the wireless operator beside me was killed and the observer wounded in an attack by Russian fighters. Despite my numerous flights in an operational career lasting nearly four years between 1940 and 1944 I returned home intact after the war.

Fifty-six years later, on 12 May 1999, I flew to Stalingrad, today called Volgograd, for the eighty-second time, but with the Condor airline for the dedication of the Rossoschka military cemetery on 13 May arranged by the German War Graves Commission (VDK).

3. WILHELM EISING:
Despatch Rider at Divisional HQ[1]

Wilhelm Eising served as a motorcycle despatch rider with the HQ of 16th Panzer Division at Stalingrad. After home leave in November 1942 he did not return to the Pocket.

We broke camp in the early morning of 24 August. We were hoping to reach the Volga in two to three hours. Even before we got to the railway line and the Tatar Wall we came across a unit of 3rd Infantry Division in action. We went no farther: during the night Russians on the flank had attacked the supply line to Stalingrad and blocked it completely.

With the support of two Ju 88s the 3rd Division unit opened the way. We passed the Rollbahn which had been cleared of the enemy. The Ju 88 fighter-bomber attack had had a fearsome effect, but no less ghastly was the following scene: a large supply convoy had been attacked from the flank during the night by Russians and destroyed. The lorry drivers had been shot where they sat: the assistant drivers who had attempted to flee lay stabbed or clubbed to death near the vehicles. We found neither wounded nor survivors: the vehicles had been plundered and the dead relieved of their effects. The body strippers had been!

Continuing on the way to our unit we came across some Russian tanks near the railway line. We availed ourselves of the favourable terrain to make a timely disappearance. Later we had to avoid enemy groups twice more. Two Stukas returning at low level from Stalingrad fired on us with their MGs: we fired off smoke flares in time to warn the Stukas which followed. Our whole route went across enemy territory. Shortly before nightfall we reached the safety of the Balka,[2] our future home. Lieutenant Heise made his report. Only

---

1. This report appeared in *Unsere 16*, edition 162, 41st year, Oct 1993: in edition 164, April 1994, and edition 165, 42nd year, July 1994.
2. Balka: a deeply-incised narrow gulley or gully in the steppe, in which habitable caves can be dug into the walls.

afterwards did we understand how much luck had been on our side on the way through the supposed corridor.

The Division lay encircled on the Volga: all supply routes were cut off. In the east the front stretched along the Volga from Akatova in the north past Vinnovka and Latashinka in the south. There it turned off from the river bank inland towards Rynok and Spartakovka (tractor works). The South Front, which extended to north-west of the steppe village of Orlovka, began at this dangerous so-called corner angle. The West Front west of the command post both sides of the dairy farm was occupied by reserves like a strongpoint. The dominating heights in the north down to the Volga, the so-called Northern Boundary, were captured on this day and fortified. Thus the Division had a hedgehog defence with three fronts at the Volga. The divisional command post was located at the heart of the hedgehog in a Balka about a kilometre north of Orlovka. At the narrowest part the South Front and North Front were separated by only two or three kilometres. In the Balka, work had been carried out feverishly above ground to create protection. Angular one-man holes, dug into the sidewalls of the Balka, offered secure protection. Even the General[3] contented himself with such a hole.

At the end of August the Russians brought reinforcements from the city and attacked the south-east corner – the corner angle – with superior forces from Rynok and Sparovka. Also south-west of Orlovka, at the join with the 3rd Motorised Infantry Division, which had arrived meanwhile, the most bitter fighting developed. While serving at the orders-bus one heard only the most worrying reports: proven officers had fallen, company strengths were shrinking. The whole hedgehog embraced just one valley and two heights around it! Every minor retreat could have dire consequences for the entire Division. Because the supply routes were interrupted, we were short of fuel and ammunition: transport aircraft dropped bomb casings full of provisions. It was not possible to bring the wounded back from the collection point at the main dressing station and so they remained under enemy fire. Even convoys with panzer protection could not force a way through to the west.

---

3. Lieutenant-General Hans Valentin Hube (b. Naumburg, 29 October 1890, d. aircraft crash, 21 April 1944), commanding officer 16th Panzer Division from June 1940: Knight's Cross 1941, Oak Leaves and Swords 1942, Diamonds 20 April 1944, final rank General. His successor at 16th Panzer Division on 15 September 1942 was Major-General Günther Angern (b. Kolberg, 5 March 1893, d. Stalingrad, 2 February 1943): 1940 Knight's Cross and German Cross in gold: 21 January 1943 final rank Lieutenant-General.

Although Rynok was captured by our forces on 27 August, it was yielded the following day. A convoy of vehicles with panzer protection reached our hedgehog position, however. The attempt to bring back the seriously wounded failed. In the ratio of respective strengths one German company equalled one Russian regiment. Franz Beerlage my neighbour saw the situation as hopeless and painted everything in the darkest colours.

Our aircraft attacked the northern area of the city without pause: harbour installations and factories burned. There was so much smoke that it darkened the sun. On the banks of the Volga the Russian AA barked, sprinkling the skies with little black clouds from the exploding shells. The Russian attacks came not only from north and south, they even brought gunboats up in support. Here our pioneers had a strong position and inflicted heavy losses on the Russians. During a trip there I visited my friend Horstkötter[4] from Ochtrup of No. 2 Pioneer Company. Sadly I learned of his death a few days later.

On 1 September we despatch riders lay in our angular holes in the earth, covered with tarpaulin against rain. Bunker building was announced: prisoners brought for interrogation helped us with it. They were all eager and willing for the reward of bread and cigarettes. When they came under accurate rifle fire while removing railways sleepers from the nearby embankment they were not prepared to assist, however; they did not like the idea of falling to friendly fire in captivity! Only after it got dark could they be reasoned with. There were amongst them also a worker from the Stalingrad factories who had been armed a few days previously. The Ic Staff officer sent him back into the city with a mission.

At the beginning of September the fighting on the South Front between Spartakovka and Orlovka abated. It looked as though the Russians were withdrawing troops from here because west of us a strong German Army Group had got to within 10 kilometres of the corridor and the city. On a map in the orders-bus, in which the frontline was marked out daily with pins, we followed the advance of these German forces. At night one could see by the traces of light visible for kilometres how the front was changing to the south of the city, from where the sounds of battle emanated.

On 2 September the supply road to the Don was clear again, but remained threatened on the flanks. While the men began to be optimistic at the

---

4. Driver Heinrich Horstkötter (b. Brake, 23 June 1912) fell on 22 September 1942 according to the German War Graves Commission.

approach of Hoth's[5] Army Group, on the basis of the most recent reports we despatch riders were not confident that it bode well for the near future. The Russians were sending up strong forces from the Voronesh area. Our commanders reckoned on heavy fighting along the Northern Boundary, which the Russians attacked during the month in overwhelming numbers and using every weapon they could lay their hands on. Beyond the dominating heights to the north the horizon was a single curtain of black smoke. The impression made by the Stalin Organs was tremendous: clouds of dense dust rose up to a great height and enveloped the terrain in black night, from within which the impact flashed. The Russian infantry was supported by massed tanks. Our Companies shrank into small groups, and the Russians penetrated here and there. Therefore sections of infantry regiments were moved from the South Front to shore up the Northern Boundary.

Lieutenant Heise was given the job of assembling everyone available at Divisional HQ and sending them to the exposed corner angle at Rynok and Spartakovka: I accompanied him as his messenger. We were shown to a well-constructed Company command post by a sergeant of the 64th. We could only occupy the line sparsely, the next man often not even being in sight, the brushwood preventing it. A Russian attack in this situation would have been disastrous! We found two dead in the position, removed by the baggage-train during the night. When it was quiet, we could hear lively movement from the direction of the city suburbs. The constant rattle of tank tracks did not bode well: each day the Russians maintained a nuisance with mortars.

The terrain immediately before us was overgrown with scrub and allowed only a limited field of vision, but from the command post one had a good view with field glasses. Before us were the housing blocks of Spartakovka: there was a collective farm in the gully not visible to us. In mid-September tall columns of smoke stood above the city. Air attacks and the troops attacking from the south and west were continuing their work of destruction.

In mid-September Lieutenant Heise was recalled to the divisional command post in the Balka, and I went back to my old trench there. The sounds of German units advancing from the south were louder. At night the

---

5. General Hermann Hoth (b. Neuruppin, 12 April 1885, d. Goslar, 25 January 1979) took command of Fourth Panzer Army on 1 June 1942, attacking Stalingrad from the south. In December he attempted unsuccessfully to prise open the Stalingrad Pocket from the south. In the OKW trials in 1946 Hoth was sentenced to 15 years' imprisonment, but was released after serving eight.

frontline could be picked out by the glow. General Hube left us to become Corps-General. Meanwhile I now knew every battalion command post between Rynok and Orlovka. I delivered mail to the companies. One evening I was on the road to Captain Goldmann's command post. At twilight after passing an observation post I knew, I saw some figures silhouetted on the horizon. I rode nearer, dismounted and approached the group. As I felt that I had strayed off the right road, I asked them where the Captain's command post was. Suddenly I saw they were Russians! They did not seem to grasp the situation: I crept into the undergrowth and stayed there a while before finally escaping. Probably the people in the observation post had seen my mistake, but could not warn me in time.

Another night I rode to a company command post which had been set up beneath the wreck of a Russian tank and spent hours priming hand grenades. As I had not been able to get away from there before it got light, I had to take part in an attack by the 64th Regiment in the early hours. The same thing happened at Orlovka a few days later.

Even with the Captain's Group I was not spared an attack. The collective farm in the gully was the objective. The unit sustained heavy losses: a number of NCOs of the field-gendarme troop well known to me fell. Only three weeks before, with men of the baggage train, they had come into the frontline for the first time.

At the end of the month Orlovka was the centrepoint of events. This steppe village, only a few hundred metres behind the railway line to the south of us, had several gulches running through it and was therefore a natural fortification. One fine autumn morning Stukas dived-bombed it and then artillery and mortars softened it up in preparation for the attack. The village held out that day. On 30 September the performance was repeated. We watched from our command post as Orlovka was captured during the late afternoon. That day is embossed on my memory: on a postcard I received from home that day I noted: 'Stukas over Orlovka, 30.9.42.'

Towards the evening, Captain von Alvensleben,[6] camp-follower and friend of the General, sent me into the ruined village to search for icons. I drove there thinking the place would be abandoned and free of the enemy. Most of the wooden housing either side of the main road had been destroyed. I saw neither civilians nor German infantry. I parked my motorcycle in the garden of a fine-looking house. I crept from one house to the next: everywhere there

---

6. Udo von Alvensleben was Staff officer Ib of 16th Panzer Division.

was a deathly hush. As I was about to cross the road I heard the report of a rifle aimed at me: the bullet whistled past close. I took cover behind a house. As the light was failing I waited for night to fall before returning. My journey into the gulley had not been unobserved: the officers were annoyed about it. Over the next few days Orlovka was cleansed and certified free of the enemy.

At the beginning of October some panzer grenadiers came to join us. Near Major Wota's[7] command post I was hit by a splinter which went through my trousers and tore open a few centimetres of my abdomen below the navel. Initially it was an insignificant wound, but after a few days it became inflamed and began to seep pus. A Sergeant-Major, a pharmacist, who was serving in the gully only fifty metres from the senior field surgeon,[8] attended to me. During this period I spent carefree days in my hole in the earth. Only the morning visit of some Russian tanks, which appeared not far from the gully, caused me any discomfort.

As there had been no relief for six weeks the men had gone to seed: they were unshaven, unwashed and lousy. This was something rarely seen previously at Division! The new MG 42 arrived. We familiarized ourselves with it and the effect of this 'Hitler-saw' was demonstrated on a stake in the gully. We were all suitably impressed, but the expenditure of ammunition was enormous.

During the first days of October the new divisional commander, General Angern, came to the gully. We hardly got to know him for every day he drove off to the command posts in a VW- Kübelwagen. One day Fritz Giltjes had the luck to drive him. Fritz did not know every command post, however, and so the pair of them landed up at the frontline, immediately before the Russians! Everything turned out well, however, and the General showed he had a sense of humour. We often laughed about it, only Fritz was cross.

On 10 October General Paulus showed up at the command post. We thought that was a bad sign! Franz Beerlage predicted it correctly, for on 14 October there was renewed activity north of Stalingrad and next day the

7. Major Kurt Wota (b. Stolp, 19 May 1903, d. in Jelabuga officers' camp 1943) was commanding officer, 1st Battalion, 79th Panzer Grenadier Regiment, 16th Panzer Division. Decorations: German Cross in gold, 29 August 1942.
8. Senior Field Surgeon Dr Werner Gerlach (b. Zwickau, 14 August 1903, d. Ottobrunn, 17 February 1982). Divisional surgeon, 16th Panzer Division. Soviet captivity 1943–53, from his homecoming until 1971 was established as a surgeon in Nuremberg. His book *Das dunkle Tal* was edited by myself and re-released in 2006.

fighting flared up around Rynok and Spartakovka. After a two-day struggle the west end of Spartakovka was taken but with heavy losses. The Russians pulled back to Rynock, the last remaining bridgehead. Here on the edge of the village all our attacks were beaten off. The Division suffered heavy casualties for little achieved. Over the next few days it rained: the Balka became a quagmire. It was wet and cold, and we shuddered to think about the winter. In this second half of October, Lieutenant Heise gathered men up into a troop, not for Rynok and Spartakovka, but to the Don where winter quarters had to be erected. We drove via Orlovka, Gorodishtche and along the Tatar Wall to Stalingrad-Centre.

The curious were banned from entering the city centre. Since we were in a motorized group we risked it and entered. As in the suburbs, most of the housing here was of wood. This mass of housing ran down from the heights to the Volga: the various city neighbourhoods were separated off by gorges or gullies. In the centre was the old Zarizyn, in the outskirts to the south and north along the Volga industrial and port installations. The city centre with the main railway station and 'Red Square' was a heap of rubble, the multi-storied buildings shell-damaged and gutted. Here and there half a chimney stack stood surrounded by the ashes of wooden dwellings. The population had either fled or taken shelter in the suburbs in ruins, cellars and caves.

We drove over the Zariza into the southern part of the city: along the Volga more gutted tall buildings. Farther on we saw in the distance the grain silo towering over everything and round about a landscape of rubble. The wrecks of tanks and vehicles lined the road. In the many gullies, holes had been dug into the slopes, huts and tiny wooden houses made of wreckage shafted into the walls of the Balka. The caves were given privacy by means of doors and curtains over the entrances. Old people, women and children, clothed in rags and tatters, sat warming themselves before open fires. An undefinable stench of burnt material, sewage and putrefaction overlay the scene. On the roads leading out of the city people had gathered to head westwards in small treks.

At Karpovka we drove to a major supply depot where we received more instructions on building winter quarters on the Don. At Marinovka we reached our destination, a village on a minor tributary of the Don. Here it was peaceful. The population had been told to excavate holes in the ground the size of bunkers: the work had proceeded without enthusiasm. After a few days Fritz Giltjes and I drove back to Stalingrad in the VW-Kübel to fetch provisions. We passed the night in the Balka.

The fighting in the Division's sector had meanwhile died down, but no bright moonlit night was allowed to pass in which the Russian bombers did not make their presence felt; then the 'Owls of the Rollbahn' or 'sewing machines' as these Ilyushin fighter-bombers were known would come screaming over in rolling attacks – no minute passed without the roar of their motors, without the whistle and crash of their bombs. We often marvelled that the casualties were not greater.

After one such night, similar to which we experienced countless times, Fritz and I left the Balka, our home in a hole for eight weeks. We drove back to the Don in the hope that the fighting would die down in the winter and we could peacefully inhabit our winter quarters. Before we neared Orlovka, we passed once more the cemetery near the railway line which had grown appallingly over recent days. Daily we watched the people from the baggage-train unloading and burying their dead colleagues. A worn path led to the main dressing station, originated by the medical orderlies who were obliged to constantly follow this route with hand-barrows and tarpaulins.

Past Orlovka we came to Gorodishtche. Heading eastwards and to our left we left behind us the suburbs of Spartakovka, the northern sector of the city with the still fought-over tractor works, the 'Red Barricade' ordnance factory and the 'Red October' smelting works and drove along the periphery of the city to the turn off for Kalatch. There was an enormous amount of traffic on this road and miserable columns of refugees such as we had never seen before. Just outside Kalatch we turned off to the south and in the afternoon, full of happy expectation, were reunited with our small group under Lieutenant Heise.

With the usual rations we had brought along a few litres of red wine. Lacking a suitable keg I had poured it into a water canister I had found lying in the Balka. That evening Fritz Giltjes was given the job of preparing mulled claret. We had become a happy circle as Fritz brought the last of it to the boil. After using our fingers to remove floating mould and wiping off specks of dirt, Fritz, by nature oversensitive, declined to have any more. Although we considered this to be a bad sign we all drank up except Lieutenant Heise. He ordered Fritz: 'You old low-brow, drink up!' Fritz, who had now suspected something, drank and retched. When we examined the canister more closely we found some dehydrated mice stuck to the bottom. In the last few weeks the Balka had experienced an indescribable plague of mice. We had only been able to put some of the provisions in zinc ammunition boxes, and in one night the mice made short work of the bread we had left lying around outside them.

When not setting up the winter quarters we stole time to angle in the tributary waters of the Don. Somebody came up with the idea that it would be better done with a hand grenade. It worked, but the dead fish lay on the bottom. Although it was not very deep, the fish could only be retrieved by diving down for them. Nobody wanted to go in, because it was already below freezing at night and the water was very cold. We drew lots, and I lost. The fish were very slippery and difficult to grasp with bare hands, and I had to use my bound-up shirt for the purpose. We were guaranteed a good meal for the next few days!

At the beginning of November the road took me to the Staff quarters which I had not seen since Makeyevka. Our CSM, Sergeant-Major Kohl, ruled the roost here. I could hardly believe my ears when I was told that I was in line for leave and could take it. Lieutenant Heise's squad would be informed. Short and sweet, and I was dismissed. Next morning I was on the road to Tchir station and arrived home after a journey lasting six days. Lieutenant Gustav Heise and Corporal Franz Beerlage remain listed as missing at Stalingrad.

4. ANDREAS ENGEL:

An Impressive Experience[1]

Andreas Engel, born on 24 June 1915 at Bebra, was a type-setter and from 1936 a professional soldier. He served in Poland and France with the 15th Regiment: at Stalingrad he was a sergeant with the Staff of 1st Battalion 15th Panzer Grenadier Regiment in the 29th Motorized Infantry Division.

On 18 or 19 November 1942, 1st Battalion 15th Panzer Grenadier Regiment was resting in balkas, deep gullies in the steppe, about 60 kilometres from Stalingrad. After the fierce fighting for the city it was up to strength in personnel and equipment and fully refreshed. It was rumoured that the division was to be transferred to the Caucasus for the conquest of Astrakhan. Morale was good; we had procured wood, doors and other building materials from Stalingrad and had made ourselves cosy.

Our comfort did not last for long. A surprise operational order interrupted our well-deserved rest. At once the fighting arm set off for an unknown destination; for the time being the baggage-train and services remained behind. Major Müller von Berneck had assumed command of the battalion a few days before, and from him I received instructions next day to take a lorry loaded with mortar bombs and MG ammunition and follow the Battalion. From the east one could hear heavy artillery fire which was increasing in volume.

The following day at noon Staff Corporal Michels and I set out for an unknown destination. After leaving the balka we discovered to our astonishment that our 29th Artillery Company had taken up positions there and was firing towards the direction in which our orders required us to travel. As we saw no German soldiers after that, we proceeded with the greatest watchfulness.

---

1. This report appeared in *Falkenblatt*, 29th Infantry Division bulletin, 1982, p.10

Suddenly two fighter aircraft approached at low level. I thought they were German by the black crosses. We were therefore flabbergasted when they opened fire on us. I was hit in the upper left thigh: instinctively I left myself drop free of the vehicle. My colleague Michels had been hit in the heel and he also lay on the Rollbahn. The terrain was sloping and fortunately our vehicle came to a stop about 100 metres away. As we observed with relief, the ammunition was undamaged.

From ahead a disorderly mob of soldiers in earth-brown uniforms was approaching. Our assumption that these were Russians was happily disproved: they were Romanians, deserting. They applied emergency dressings and drove our vehicle back to us. Only the radiator and tyres had been shot up. At our request they lifted us back into the motor and we set off back, stopping every 50 metres, and so reached our baggage-train.

My colleague Wetzlar, lorry-section leader, drove me to the nearest dressing station. After two hours this was hastily abandoned: we were to be transported out from Kalatch. We never got there, for the Russians had taken it and cut off our way to the west. The ambulance driver turned about and delivered us in the middle of the night to the Army Casualty Collection Centre. Scarcely had I been bedded down on straw than I heard MG fire. Whoever could still walk fled this inhospitable place. There were only a few of us who seemed to have been left to an uncertain fate. We had a sergeant, who had taken over the protection of the collection centre with a platoon, to thank that we got out of there. He stopped some fleeing vehicles at gunpoint, had them load us aboard and head back eastwards.

I was delivered to the dressing station of 100th Jäger Division and here I lay until Christmas in a primitive, cold shack. I was not doing well: the wound had not been treated properly and a phlegmone (a suppurating infection of the soft areas) had set in. Every day the rations were reduced: a slice of bread and now and again some horsemeat broth. Morale was at rock-bottom.

After Christmas I crept out in the hope of convincing a passing vehicle of our Division to take me out of this desolate place. If I was going to die, then better amongst the colleagues of my unit! When a vehicle appeared I dragged myself on to the roadway, forcing it to stop: it was an anti-aircraft signals truck. The squad leader, a sergeant, brought me to the nearest airfield. The crowd here was unimaginable! My hopes sank to zero. Next morning an aircraft came: at gunpoint the crew stopped the machine from being stormed. As a wounded man unable to walk I had the great fortune to secure a place and be flown out.

A little later our machine landed on a military air strip. We heaved a sigh of relief, for we were beyond Russian AA guns and fighters. The Stalingrad Pocket lay like a chaotic nightmare behind us. The crew left the aircraft: medical personnel appeared and freed us from the paper sacks in which we had been wrapped. A nearby stone barracks took us in. An officer made us undertake to say nothing about our experiences and the situation in the Pocket – this was a Führer-order! I did not like it, but it did not interest me particularly, for the great fortune to be out of it outweighed everything.

Eat, sleep and not freeze any more – that is what we wanted! We did not have to wait long for food. I weighed only 89 pounds and had no time to lose. My stomach was unable to retain the 'chicken and rice' which I gobbled up and the doctor quickly sent for 'had a very loud conversation' with the orderly who had apparently served it to me against medical instructions.

A few hours later we made a journey to a Luftwaffe field hospital. The luxury was inconceivable for an infantryman – I thought I must be in heaven! Deloused, a snow-white bed and rations which got better with every passing day. I could have stayed here for months but the front was getting closer and we were moved to Stalino.[2] Here a doctor decided I was not fit to be transported. This made me unhappy, for to be on the safe side I wanted to 'gain territory'. With the help of a nurse, who had the fullest understanding of my situation, I arranged to be put aboard a provisional hospital train two days later. This was composed of goods-wagons converted for the purpose. Plank-beds had been installed, in the centre was a round iron stove into which coal lying around had to be shovelled. One could not stay on the plank-beds long, the warmth from the stove did not extend that far. Whoever was able, therefore, laid his bed on the heap of coals. Soon we were all as black as the ace of spades-but who cared? How long it took us to get to Kiev I cannot say. Many a good comrade was unloaded on the way: his earthly journey ended.

Sergeant Andreas Engel stayed only a short while at Field Hospital 505, Kiev, then was put aboard a hospital train via Cracow to Oberschreiberhau in the Riesengebirge of Silesia and cared for in the hospital section 'Lehrerheim' by Catholic nurses. In June 1943 he went to the Convalescent Company at Kassel, and rejoined his unit, 1st Battalion 15th Panzer Grenadier Regiment, some weeks later in Italy. He was wounded again in December 1944 and treated at the Cortina d'Ampezzo hospital. After the war he worked with the Kassel city administration. He died on 30 July 2002.

---

2. Stalino, today Donetsk, is in south-east Ukraine. It had numerous military field hospitals.

5. EITEL-HEINZ FENSKE:

Sardine Tins in my Trousers[1]

Eitel-Heinz Fenske (b. Neuendorf/Danzig, 8 August 1924) attended technical college at Marienwerder, 1 April 1941 joined the civil service: 1 October 1941 Government Inspectorate: 5 December 1941 conscripted, trained as radio operator/telephonist at Allenstein. 13 May 1944 drafted to 44th Infantry Division and on 18 May 1944 at Balakleya/Don joined the Staff of 3rd Battalion 131st Infantry Regiment as a signaller.

It was before midnight on 17 November 1942. It was getting colder and colder; the moon lit the night. At ten o'clock I was on duty at the switchboard of the field telephone exchange at Battalion and was due to be relieved at 0200 hrs. There were no special problems with the connections to the command posts and other units.

Some of the companies were reporting hearing very loud engine noises. I left my post for a moment to listen for myself and then made a report to the adjutant. Then of a sudden towards 0200 hrs there was this infernal racket to the left of us amongst the Romanian 3rd Infantry Division. A bombardment by artillery and Stalin Organs – I had never heard the like of it! Under the full moon we could follow it with the naked eye. The companies all wanted to make a report at the same time. All the little flaps at my switchboard fell: I could give them a 'collective reply'.

Our commanding officer appeared at my side; we watched the inferno from our low hill. We saw the rolls of fire slowly shift from the communication trenches to the command posts and how the Romanian troops came scurrying out like black ants – this comparison impressed itself upon us because of their dark greatcoats and black sheepskin headgear. The Russian spearhead was coming up from the Kletskaya and Serafimowich area, immediately after the bombardment an endless convoy of tracked vehicles carrying infantry, but

---

1 This report appeared in the 44th bulletin of the 'Former Reichsgrenadier Division *Hoch und Deutschmeister* Comradeship' issue 173, December 2003.

also horse-drawn carts with mortars and ammunition. The Russian advance reached to the Don bridgehead.

On 19 November I received a telephoned report from 44th Infantry Division which I had to pass immediately to the Battalion commander: '...the German Sixth Army units have been encircled, the Stalingrad Pocket is a fact! The II/131 is leaving for the south-east and is abandoning its positions!' We dismantled our telephone exchange, loaded it on our horse-drawn wagon and took along everything we thought valuable. As a telephonist I had been issued white-green-grey winter clothing because I was often alone and had to repair severed telephone wires outside. Thus I had a special advantage over my colleagues: a reversible anorak filled with cotton-wool flock which would be worn with the grey-green or white side outwards depending on the weather conditions and over the uniform. This camouflage suit was to have an important function for my survival and not only on account of temperatures which could sink to -40°C without a roof over my head.

On our retreat we came to a giant clothing and equipment depot, and almost every infantryman disappeared inside to find what he could. 'Why weren't we supplied from here with some of this weeks ago?' was our question. Sentries wanted to force us back at gunpoint. A couple of brave souls informed these guardians that they would be simply gunned down should they not care to stand aside! The sentries disappeared, our way within was open. The smokers availed themselves of cartons of cigarettes: French cognac was also an objective. What a pitiful error to make when one reflects on what the coming weeks held! As a non-smoker I ignored the 'delicacies' and filled the legs of my protective winter clothing with tins of Portuguese sardines with a key attached to the underside to open them. That was to prove a godsend. Two bottles of cognac went into my haversack: I was thinking, if it stays as cold as it is now, then a drop of cognac in melted snow might be a real lifesaver. Thus I had made good provision for the weeks ahead, for on our retreat towards Stalingrad we received only small amounts of bread. A can of sardines in oil per day was a diet rich in fat, all the better to resist the cold.

On 21 November a Russian cavalry regiment supported by infantry attacked our new defensive line at Verchnaya-Businovka. If we had not had the 177th SP Battalion with us, our prospects of survival would have been poor. They did tremendously well! On 23 November the new main frontline was set up in the Golobayatal at Ludsiyenskoye, fortifying the Don bridgehead. My commanding officer ordered me to reconnoitre the situation and send running reports by radio to Battalion HQ. I headed west to the Don at Akimaski where

I saw almost nobody but Romanian troops, some without weapons, setting off for the west on their own. I crossed the Don bridge built by German pioneers; on the other side were a few detached houses. Night was falling. Because I would only be able to recognize the new battalion command post in daylight, I had to look for somewhere to spend the night. I settled in the upper floor of a house, cuddled my loaded carbine and rested my head on my walkie-talkie. Because I did not know if I could trust the Romanians, dozens of whom had also sought refuge in this house, it was an uneasy night. Before falling asleep I was thinking: will they steal my rifle, my clothing and my radio set or even kill me? When I awoke I found that I still had all my belongings.

Now I thought about the west. If I had had the courage, I could have posed as a straggler and joined the German troops outside the Pocket who were arriving from the west. Nevertheless I decided to return to my unit and carry out my mission, re-crossed the Don bridge eastwards and at midday reached the battalion command post and reported my findings. Our commanding officer wanted to know if our division could shift west over the Don. All only in theory! A group of officers appeared, amongst them some generals. Suddenly I received the order to present myself and state my observations. Before me stood Generals von Seydlitz and Paulus. 'Gefreiter Fenske, report what you have seen!' Thereupon I set out my experiences and the situation at the massive wooden bridge. Later I learned that at that time it was being planned to break through to the west over this bridge.

On 28 November the bridgehead was abandoned, and our pioneers blew up the wooden bridge. All the same, the Russians used the wreckage to get up the east bank. A new frontline was set up at Baburkin. Left of us was the 134th Regiment, then the remnants of the 132nd Infantry Regiment. The 177th SP Battalion which had been attached to us kept the Russian tanks at bay: with the infantry we were ready for whatever happened. The major Russian tank offensive of 4 December was beaten off with their help. In four weeks they destroyed almost one hundred T-34s! We began a counter-attack towards Hill 124.5 near Baburkin: the SPs went ahead and came under heavy fire from Russian anti-tank guns (which we called 'Ratch-boom'). I was hit by a splinter in the left wrist, and suddenly had a swelling the size of an egg with blood beneath it. As a trained ambulance man I treated it correctly and made a small cut with my jack-knife so that the blood could drain out. I held the wound against the ice-cold armour plates to cool it. Fortunately the splinter was a ricochet, otherwise I might have lost my hand.

On the late afternoon of 12 December we made a counter-attack after the

Russians had breached our lines. Around 1700 hrs a shell fell 100 metres left of us, another 50 metres right of us and the third exploded amidst our seven-man squad. The night was quiet: all I had seen was a bright, lilac-coloured light and heard a loud retort. As I grew aware of my situation, I found that I could not move my right side. 'I cannot stand, the temperature is forty below, I shall freeze to death', these were my thoughts. It had fallen deathly quiet: of our group there was only one other survivor, and he could not speak. Was this the end of my life? I was only eighteen years old! The 15cm shell had had full effect.

Suddenly I heard the snorting of a horse, and soft commands. A sledge passed close by me. When I realized that it was a German-speaking ostler, I made myself known. The comrade stopped and asked how many survivors there were. I replied that apart from me there was one more, he was gurgling. Our comrade brought us to an airfield and unloaded us in rooms used by the ground staff.

I was treated the same evening. Forty-eight shell splinters had entered the right side of my body. A few days later my upper thigh swelled up out of the dressing – gangrene, blood poisoning and sepsis in my right leg. There were only two alternatives: amputation or drainage under narcotics. Junior surgeon Dr Hubert Haidinger[2] had the courage to choose the second way. So I kept my leg but had paralysis. What would have happened to me, a seriously wounded soldier, if they had decided to break out of the Pocket?

At Christmas 1942 the Russians had a kind of ceasefire. The medics put cotton wool swabs on thistle bushes and called them Christmas trees. We received a bottle of champagne and half a tablet of Belgian chocolate – and Hitler's speech. 'Stop work, give it a rest!' came over the loudspeakers to all parts of the straw-bedded hall. Our divisional chaplain Czygan[3] wrote a letter for me to my sister and parents which actually arrived in March.

---

2. Dr Hubert Haidinger (b. Gunskirchen, 27 January 1913, d. Gunskirchen, 8 May 2003) served at the main dressing station, No. 2 Medical Company, 60th Infantry Division. Taken prisoner by the Soviets at Stalingrad, after the war he became senior health officer in his home town. An honorary citizen of his homeland, for decades he was Federal Chairman of the Stalingrad League of Austria.

3. Richard Czygan (b. 23 November 1892, Cronau) was the evangelical divisional chaplain of 60th Infantry Division. He has not been heard of since 30 January 1943 at Dmitriyevka, where according to eyewitnesses he was murdered at a military hospital together with the wounded by Soviet forces.

December 28th was the day of my transfer-out. We were wrapped in so-called air-transport sacks, three-layered paper sacks about two metres long, so that we did not freeze to death in temperatures of -50°C whilst in the air. So, as one lay, one was put into the sack. A medic drove several times from our 'steppe-pony's hut' to the airstrip: first the married men with children, then those without, and if there was still any room in the aircraft, the others took their chances. It lasted many hours: our little house was almost deserted, just a few wounded in their packages on the straw. We kept thinking, they've forgotten us. Then suddenly the sound of engines – was it the Russians or the long-awaited medic? It was the latter!

It was already dark when our three-engined Ju 52 landed at Salsk after a thirty-minute flight. Medics brought the sixteen wounded into a large hall, yawning with emptiness. This had certainly been a place where they stored the provisions and other supplies to be flown into the Pocket. Field bunks of several tiers were ready – good for us, for we were in the truest sense of the term 'in a compartment under a roof'! For the first time in weeks we received a warm, light stew, tea and bread. The medical care was excellent and satisfying. My dressings, several days old, were changed, the drainage tube in my upper thigh cleaned so that my body could regenerate itself. Thanks to Marevenil-Prontosil my temperature was down: every day I was given ten to twenty large pills, very difficult to swallow. Suddenly it fell quiet, whispers and murmurs, there was an air of unease, they said: 'The Russians are advancing westwards, the Salsk airfield is threatened and will be evacuated in the next few days!'

Early one morning we were loaded into a provisional hospital train and taken to a school in Rostov which had been converted into a field hospital. Here there were beds with white sheets and coverings and hot food again! Many of my fellow-wounded could not keep it down and gave it away. Our treatment by medics in grey – not soldiers but middle-aged men under obligation to serve and wearing an armband with the letters 'DRK' – German Red Cross – and military surgeons was very good. There were also some Russian female doctors who served in that role or as nurses.

When I noticed that my temperature was rising, the good-looking female Russian doctor looking after me arrived with medication to reduce my fever. She examined me and found that I had blood poisoning, which was spreading. Because I was getting increasingly weaker, the doctors decided on a blood transfusion. 'But where do we get the blood from, when we have none in storage?' they asked, standing around my bed. After my condition had grown considerably worse, a trolley was wheeled up beside my bed. I was astonished to see the Russian doctor lay herself down on it so that the Wehrmacht doctors could set up a transfusion line between 'the saviour of my life' and myself. When it was quiet, she said to me in good German, 'You poor little boy, you must be suffering so much. I shall help you!' My condition improved rapidly: my 'white-clad wife' often came to my bedside and comforted me with the words, 'You getting better and soon go home.' Even today I cannot get over what she did for me. I have one or two litres of the blood of a beautiful Russian girl circulating in my veins!

In preparation for a long journey, each wounded man received a loaf of bread and a tin of lard. We were to be taken to the port at Rostov, where hospital ships picked up all the wounded from the southern front and carried them through the Black Sea and Mediterranean to Italy or France. Suddenly it was all stopped, the bread and tins of meat collected up again. The reason we discovered a few days later: Russian submarines had torpedoed two German hospital ships full of wounded. Hundreds of German, Italian and Romanian soldiers drowned. It was a terrible thing – and I had almost been there!

Then came a report which gave us some relief: the population of Vienna and environs had donated an 'Auxiliary Hospital Train Vienna', consisting of fifty goods wagons in which three-tiered bunks of wooden posts and webbing had been installed, filled with food, clothing and medication, and sent to the east pulled by two locomotives: the remnants of Sixth Army were to be brought home. The Viennese had taken Regiment No. 134 *Hoch und Deutschmeister* to their hearts. Unloading the consignments and loading the wounded lasted a whole day – I was aboard! For seven to ten days we clanked past Kharkov and Lemberg to Krzeszowice near Cracow, which the Germans in the Reich Gouvernement called 'Reichshof'.

Daily around midday the train would stop: it was still very cold. They served us hot tea and a slice of bread. Nobody looked at our wounds, there was no medical treatment or care. Men who died on the way were unloaded at the next station and left on the platform. It was scarcely imaginable: the non-walking wounded had no chance of visiting a toilet: one did it down the wall. Happy were those who had the uppermost bunks. Despite the cold outside of -20°C to -25°C, one can imagine the stench. At Krzeszowice we were lodged in a large former school. In the gymnasium, especially the shower room, we were all stripped naked, i.e. our dressings were cut away with large scissors, thrown into a large container and burnt, unfortunately also with my haversack containing exposed film and other souvenirs. The stinking uniforms and whatever else remained, including the enormous infestation of lice, went into the boiler-room. After that we were laid out on large trestle such as is used in slaughterhouses to depilate the bodies of boiled pigs, smeared with yellow soft soap and then scrubbed head to toe. Finally we were given anti-lice preparations for the hairy areas of the body, the wounds attended to medically and dressings applied. Then we were given white night-shirts and a hospital bed. 'Is this not the first stage before heaven?' I was not the only one to ask. Shortly afterwards a pretty Polish girl brought some white loaves, cut them into large slices, covered them with butter and handed them round. Thirteen men ate and ate until there was none left. It was hard to put into words what I discovered next: in the recess above my breastbone the lice had eaten into the flesh because I could only move my left arm but not extend it far enough upwards to get at them! Near me lay Karl-Schmidt Walter, later in Germany a well-known opera singer who not only befriended me but would also burst into glorious aria and operatic songs several times a day. He had been shot in one lung, and so it demanded a lot of him, but he wanted to give pleasure to the 'Stalingraders'.

At last March came and with it the longed-for return of warmer weather and spring sunshine. Because I could now walk with crutches I was allowed out into the schoolyard and garden. After good treatment I was soon fit to make the trip home. I did not hear so well in my right ear, I had a middle-ear inflammation caused by the blast on 12 December 1942 which ruptured my eardrum.

It was explained we would have to go home (to Austria) by way of Germany if we did not want to be 'living skeletons' and 'a sight for sore eyes'. How much one had to eat to increase one's weight from a 'skeleton' of 35 kilos to around 70 kilos! In the emergency hospital things were pretty lively. The Stalingrad survivors were spoon-fed and coddled and finally went 'home to the Reich' in a Super-Hospital Train.

Until 1945 Fenske, promoted to Leading Private, underwent numerous operations and never returned to frontline duty. In hospital he was taken prisoner by the Americans. After the war he continued his career in public administration, until reaching pensionable age in 1979 he was administrative director of the hospitals in the Calw region. Today he lives in retirement at Hengersberg.

6. JOACHIM FEURICH:

For Me the War Was Soon Over[1]

Joachim Feurich (b. Chemnitz, 2 June 1923) obtained his school-leaving certificate and was called up on 23 March 1942 to the 185th Grenadier Regiment at Zwickau. Following basic training he attended a course for active officers of the reserve. As a private soldier he joined the 94th Infantry Division heading for Stalingrad.

On 23 October we finally arrived at our destination and de-trained at Tchir on the Don. This was where the railway line to Stalingrad ended, the final section having been destroyed at Tchir. Here I saw my first shell craters, which made me think. We also had to watch out, they said, the Russians might suddenly fire on us with long-range artillery. I could not imagine what that would be like; in the event nothing like it occurred.

We took our packs and marched to the 94th Infantry Division's training camp, the unit with the Saxon-swords symbol you can see on Meissen porcelain. Here they provided further training for the fresh young arrivals from the Reich before sending them off to individual units. We found ourselves instructors again, though we ROB (Reserve-Officer Aspirants) were still privates. All at once we were giving orders. A foretaste of the unpleasantness in Russia was the dysentery which suddenly assailed me and which forced me to spend much time on the toilet despite the low temperatures. That was bad enough, but the toilet was simply a beam laid across a pit in the open air to one side of the camp: anything but suitable for long stays. My battle against cold and dysentery was finally won with coal and medication – things were looking up.

Contrary to my expectations Stalingrad was not yet fully in German hands: the fighting was accompanied by very high casualties. Orders came for me to move up to the front where I would gain the necessary experience which we

---

1. This previously unpublished essay was given to me by the author as a typescript for publication.

as officer-applicants had to show if we wanted to be promoted. Together with the other ROBs we picked up our combat gear and rifles and then set off. With a zest for action we reached Kalatch, got into a waiting ammunition train – and headed for Stalingrad. Pioneers had restored the railway line from here: it was single-track. We were still far from the real events at Stalingrad, but near enough to hear the rumbling and thundering from the horizon. When I had got comfortable as best I could in the open wagon, I looked at the big shells surrounded by duckboarding and read on a plaque: *Only to be fired on orders of the Führer!* These were therefore the notorious 'Stukas on Foot', as the infantry called them, shells so made that when they exploded there were hardly any splinters but created instead a kind of low or negative pressure which tore the lungs of all living beings over a huge area. It was said that Stalin had threatened to use gas if these shells were used at the front, therefore they were kept in reserve.

It was a strange feeling to be going to the front on a munitions train, yet I did not consider the danger to be as great as it actually was. We even smoked and stared up at the grey November sky. Then we heard it and later spotted it too: a lone aircraft humming around, its motor noise betraying it as Russian. The train picked up speed, went faster and faster, and suddenly as if at a command nearly all leapt out, tumbled over and ran to the right into the countryside.

One companion had remained aboard with me: even today I can give no plausible reason for it. The attacker was following the railway line heading direct for our train. The aircraft was an old type nicknamed a 'sewing machine' because its motor sounded like the typical 'put-put-put' of one. Its *modus operandi* was to cut the motor suddenly and then come at its target rather like a glider. The aircraft had no bomb racks, the bombs were tossed out from the cabin by hand. Before the bomb hit, the motor would be re-started and the aircraft would then make itself scarce. We were gambling with our lives by remaining on that ammunition train, for the bomb-aimer was unlikely to miss such a large target. At any rate it was clear to me that we would see the bomb falling. What then? The train was racing along and there was no more time for reflection. The machine flew over us and away without dropping anything; probably he had no bombs left. Then he machine-gunned our comrades in the fields, whom we could still see. He had ignored the train, not even fired a single round at us. We came out of it as heroes: we had stared death in the face.

Towards evening we reached Gumrak, the last station before Stalingrad: here the railway line ended, for the town was not yet in our hands. There was still bitter fighting. We collected up all the abandoned packs, put them into the station building and waited for our comrades to turn up on foot. Tired and dispirited, but without having suffered casualties, they arrived at midnight to receive sympathetic smiles from the pair of us.

Towards noon the day after we had orders to pick up our packs and march. First we went a bit to the north, then headed east again. Now we could hear the thunder of the guns really well and it fell quiet amongst us, each man immersed in his own thoughts. Across trenches and flat country, through gorges and over shell craters we went on and on in single file. We reached the Orlovka gorge and shortly afterwards the command post of the 267th Regiment, to which I had been attached.

The frontline on the Northern Boundary where I now found myself was strangely quiet. It was 19 November, and when I managed finally to report to the company commander it was already late in the evening. I had seen nothing of Stalingrad itself. It was not possible to do so for our forces had come up from the west and set up a sort of northern frontline with the Volga on the right hand. Stalingrad was on the river to the south. We were on the reverse slope of a gorge diagonal to the Volga, the Russians were about 200 metres away on a similar slope on another gorge.

The Russians had launched an offensive that day and broke through the positions at the border between a Romanian and an Italian division before advancing some distance to the westward and then wheeling south. This had created the Stalingrad Pocket in which a whole army was encircled. We were practically prisoners in a giant sack. At the time I knew nothing of this and only learned about it much later.

Our company commander was a second lieutenant whose name I do not remember. I think his surname might have been Hirsch. He was delighted to have me as a reinforcement to his company which had shrunk to ten men. He sat down in the cave and gave me a short situation report. I understood it had been strangely quiet since yesterday, hardly a shot being fired. Because he was suspicious of this, at first light I was to take two men and put up a barbed wire fence in front of our position.

My two companions wore steel helmets as we climbed cautiously out of the trench, carrying a roll of barbed wire, wooden stakes and hammers. I took my cap off but felt anything but heroic as I replaced it with a steel helmet. When nothing happened we stood up and began to hammer the posts into the hard ground. I would indicate the next spot, one of the men held the post and the other hammered it home. We were sure that the Russians would not notice any of this. Suddenly something took my legs away and I fell to the ground. I had not heard a shot, but felt something like a whiplash at my right thigh. Like lightning my companions had taken cover in the trench, but I was lying out in the open practically in no man's land, luckily in a small depression, for now the shooting really began. It was a damned awkward situation to be in, for I could not move my leg, and therefore could not crawl away. Then I heard my name being called softly and I replied I had been wounded in the leg. My colleagues threw me a rope and dragged me back into the trench.

The shooting went on merrily, leaving me with the great fear of being hit again. Everything went off well, however, and I finally landed up back in the company commander's cave. There they cut open my trouser leg to expose a large and bloody wound on my outer right thigh. There was material and metal splinters in the wound – 'a Blighty one' as the British would say, and as my colleagues informed me enviously.

Thus the war was over for me before it had barely begun. Nothing would come of the heroism I foresaw for myself: I would not even be part of our conquest of Stalingrad. I had acted like a dope, revealed myself as the soldier in charge to the Russian marksman, and I was his priority. I had made an excellent target, and it was only due to the inaccuracy of the Russian carbine that the round had hit my leg. I had believed on that 20 November that luck would smile on me because my dance partner Anneliese at the Café Wenig in Chemnitz was celebrating her eighteenth birthday. When I reflect on it today, knowing what I know, then it really was a lucky day, although then I saw things quite differently.

When it got dark, two medical orderlies came with a stretcher, loaded me on it and carried me to the most advanced rearward post. They went ducked down in the trenches: because the stretcher was too long, they simply lifted it and myself above their heads. Thus I swayed at ground height, but above the trench at the rear end, and I guessed that all the incoming rifle fire was aimed at me. However none of it hit.

On the way we had to pause for a Russian artillery barrage, the stretcher-bearers in the trench, myself outside. Finally we reached a collection centre for the wounded. I was loaded beside other wounded on a cart spread with straw and drawn by a steppe-pony. A Russian working for the Germans brought the vehicle at a fast trot to the main dressing station. Here some wounded were lying around: I joined them. My only wish was to get a tetanus jab as quickly as possible. When I finally got it I was there with my comrade Seurig from Chemnitz, who had attended the ROB course with me at Zwickau. He had his right arm in a sling. I heard him say confidently that he would soon be back with his unit, the wound was not so bad. That was the last time I saw him, he is listed as Missing in Russia.

After a while they put me in an ambulance and we headed westwards. After a while the vehicle stopped suddenly and I heard the driver murmur 'Russians'. Then we turned about and raced back the way we had come. We had run into Russian troops: in the darkness they had failed to recognize the German ambulance. That was a stroke of luck!

The ambulance finally reached Gumrak. The surgery for operations had been set up in the railway station building, and this is where I was treated. Having no anaesthetic my wound was treated in the following manner: using bandage scissors the surgeon cut away the ribbons of flesh surrounding the big hole in my leg and extracted the pieces of material and splinters. I only witnessed the first part, then I passed out from the pain. When I came to, my leg was bound to a metal splint and I was being carried to an auxiliary hospital train. This consisted of cattle trucks in which three tiers of plank beds had been installed, each with a mattress of sacking filled with straw. There were already twenty or so wounded there. I lay in the topmost bed, right below the ceiling. Whenever I tried to sit up I banged my head. A medical orderly had charge of each individual wagon and sat at a table and chair near the sliding door. I was wearing my uniform jacket and shirt, and had a long sock on the left leg. I had a woollen blanket for protection against the cold, but that was all. The train could not go west, for the Russians had closed the Pocket. The only chance of getting home was to be flown out. Only a few were lucky enough to have the 'right type' of wound to justify it.

From now on I had time to indulge my thoughts at leisure. The daily rations and having the dressing changed in the station building every five days was the only break. Now and again at night I heard the 'sewing machine' put-putting nearer, the motor would cut out, a bomb would explode, sometimes near, at other times far off, then it would leave. It grew slowly more desolate, for the food became more sparse: soon we were down to a cup of broth with small bits of pork and a slice of frozen bread per day. We no longer had a cigarette ration: I had to have a smoke. I offered the medical orderly my nail clippers for three cigarettes. These only helped for a short while.

When I was next taken to the station building, a young doctor attended me. He noticed my Saxon accent and upon learning that I came from Chemnitz promised to put my name on the list to be flown out of the Pocket. This list bore only the names of the most serious cases, men who would never again be fit for the front. This doctor, who also came from Chemnitz, wanted me to speak to his wife after my arrival to keep her up to date about where I had last seen him. He told me that my wound had been caused by an explosive bullet. It had happened to strike my pocket-knife and explode. This kind of rifle bullet was like a grenade which upon striking a solid mass – bone for example – exploded and tore open a giant wound. For me it was a minor miracle, for otherwise the entire leg would have been torn off. They found a corkscrew in the wound too. I had kept it for some time in my trousers and then lost track of it.

When finally I was brought out on the evening of 5 December, my fellow-sufferers in the wagon were rightly envious. I was loaded on a stretcher in an ambulance with other wounded, and then we left for the airstrip. 'Best of luck, comrade, and a happy homecoming!' they wished me in parting. What irony was concealed in the word 'homecoming'! On the way our ambulance ran into a snowdrift and landed on its side. We all tumbled amongst each other, then it fell quiet for some time. When finally the door was torn open and we were freed from our precarious situation, much time had passed. Another ambulance had drawn up, loaded us in, and the journey continued. Upon arriving at last at the destination, the word 'homecoming' came true, for we were back at Gumrak and my empty bed under the ceiling in the same wagon awaited me. My world collapsed: I was bitterly disappointed and howled into my stinking blanket. All hope was gone, and I saw no way out any more.

In this forlorn situation I turned to prayer for the first time in my life. What would the Russians do about wounded Germans who arrived in their hands? It was clear to me that we would either starve or freeze to death or be shot out of hand. Next day I tried to pass a note to the doctor in the station building, but was unsuccessful. Hope sprang up that he could put me down for another flight out of the Pocket. I had to wait another five days before they brought me in to change the dressings. Here finally I met him again, and he promised to try to get me on the list again.

I had to wait two whole weeks. I always asked the person attending me if that particular doctor was around. Probably he was taking a rest when my dressings were being changed in the station building. My hopes sank ever deeper: I was in a pitiful state. Haggard and my skin scabby – we all had scabies – unwashed for ages, the leg bound tightly to a metal splint and full of lice: depression seized me as I looked at the inevitable grim end to my life. The dressings were of crepe paper: there was no medication, and neither the doctors nor nurses ever spoke an encouraging word. The lice were the worst, nesting under the dressing and moving about in hordes. They could not be got at under the dressing. White grubs lived in the wound, eating the pus.

On 19 December an ambulance came, loaded me aboard and drove me to the airfield at Pitomnik west of Gumrak. We were accompanied by cold, snow and icy storms. Whoever had to live out in the open stood no chance of surviving. I was taken to a marquee near the Rollbahn. Squashed together like sardines in a tin were wounded men, some bedded on straw, the others on the bare earth. I sat up a little and saw by the flickering flames of a stove in the middle of the marquee eight long rows of men laid out. At the far end of these the transporting out had begun. I was therefore amongst the last who should or might be flown out today if enough aircraft landed. A medical orderly wrapped me in a paper sack, similar to a cement bag. It gave some protection against the cold: I had left my blanket back in the wagon. I did not hear any aircraft arrive, but when they took off I thought I could hear the loud howling of their motors.

On that night of 20 December a total of seventeen aircraft brought munitions and provisions into the Pocket, and took wounded out when they left. It was a long while before the rows in front of me were fetched out, but finally the hour came. I was borne on a stretcher to a place in the marquee where hours before a Russian shell had hit and shredded the canvas. The wounded who had been in that spot had previously been removed to an aircraft, and so nobody had been killed.

The pilot stood in the open door of the cabin and made a negative sign when I was carried up, but then he pointed to a free spot and I was the last man to be loaded into the machine. Almost at once the motors howled, the aircraft gathered speed and then we lifted off away from Pitomnik. It was an He 111, as I learned later, as safe an aircraft as the Ju 52. In the last machine but one that night I was flown out of the Stalingrad encirclement, and the cold was much worse than on the ground, for I was lying on bare metal. Suddenly we were hit by Russian AA fire: the machine wobbled a bit, then carried on. The motors hummed softly and in harmony. I pressed down on my left thumb the whole time; it was a talisman for luck. I did it for years afterwards.

Outside the Pocket we landed at Tazinskaya and were taken from there to a railway station building. It was well lit and beautifully warm. Mattresses had been laid out on the floor: one of them was assigned to me. The first thing we received was the so-called 'Führerpaket' for Stalingrad soldiers, a small pack of cigarettes, Schoka-Kola, biscuits and sweets. I thought it quite wonderful that our Führer should remember us like that. We were served drinks and food. If necessary the dressings were changed. I fell asleep exhausted, and when I awoke many hours later I was told that Aircraft 15 and 17 had been shot down by the Russians. I would have shared the same fate had I not by a hair's breadth been found room on Aircraft 16! My feet had frostbite, but not so severe as to require amputation.

Towards evening there was great unrest amongst the doctors and medics. Orders were given, an unparalleled hectic state prevailed. We were told that Russian tanks were close to Tazinskaya and that the wounded and care personnel were to be transported out at once. Great haste was the watchword. An empty goods train stood on the tracks and took us all. I was set down in a corner of a wagon, on the bare floor packed closely together with other comrades. The journey began before the arrival of the Russians. The train stopped once and the doors were torn open for other walking-wounded soldiers to climb in. They had to squeeze in between us, for there was no more space available on the floor.

We were told that a military hospital nearby was being evacuated as quickly as possible so as not to fall into Russian hands. Then the train set off again. We had no shortage of provisions. Thus the hours passed, and I lost track of whether it was night or day. In the wagon it was always dark. All one could hear was the rattling of the wheels and the whimpering of those in pain who felt it worse when the buffers of the wagon clashed with the next ahead or behind. That was how we spent Christmas Eve. I cannot describe the morale. All I know is that one of our comrades began to sing Christmas carols. It was in strange contrast to the rattling of the wheels, the clatter of the sliding doors, the cursing and sobbing with pain, the loud prayers of the believers, the groaning and whimpering. Although I did not have much pain, I was seized by suffering: emotion overcame me and I wept unstoppably to myself. Would we escape it? Would I ever see home again? What would become of us helpless people? All these thoughts were mixed up in my total desolation. The singer was eventually successful in inducing a state of greater quietude amongst us, and here and there someone sang along with him.

The journey ended next morning at Stalino. Here we de-trained and were taken by ambulance through the town to a military hospital. It was very busy despite being Christmas morning. I was taken to a washroom, relieved of my rags and given a warm bath. My splinted leg stayed outside the tub. Then a Russian girl came in, washed off all the filth of the foregoing weeks, rubbed in a stinking anti-lice preparation and dressed me in a night-shirt. Then she brought me carefully to a bed and tucked me in: I weighed scarcely 50 kilos, so light that she could pick me up and carry me in her arms. I had an indescribable feeling of being safe. In the white bed with pillows and coverlet I felt endless gratitude. At a stroke my fate had taken a turn for the better.

After convalescence Joachim Feurich served in the rank of Lieutenant in Italy and was captured by the Americans in April 1945. After the war he became a businessman. He died at Michelstadt on 5 November 1992.

7. ERICH FRANKE:

My Escape from the Pocket on a Motorcycle[1]

Corporal Erich Franke was a motorcycle despatch rider attached to No 1 Section of 2nd Regiment 16 Panzer Division from November 1940 until being taken prisoner in January 1945. He took part in the advance on Stalingrad. He caught diphtheria in September 1942 and was treated in a military hospital at Poltava.

On 23 September I was released from the military hospital and had to report to the Front Draftings office at Kharkov. My orders said: area north of Stalingrad. How I got there was up to me. At first I went by train. Near Losovaya partisans had blown up an ammunition train leaving the stretch interrupted for a couple of hours. I went to the Rollbahn and tried to hitch a lift in a lorry. That evening I arrived at a village in which there was even a cinema. I went in. A Luftwaffe NCO came to sit next to me. We got talking, and I discovered there was a military airstrip here. There were a couple of flights of Ju 52s, therefore transport machines. Where do they go? Answer: Stalingrad and Caucasus! I asked at once if I could go there by air. He brought me to the airfield and showed me to an earth bunker where the orderly officer was sitting. I knocked, saluted and made my request. He hesitated and then replied: 'Each aircraft has loaded six barrels of aviation fuel. If you want to take the risk it's on your own head!' He made me aware of the danger of attack by Russian fighters. I wanted to get to my unit as quickly as possible, however, and this was a rare opportunity.

Next morning at 0600 hrs – it was 29 September 1942 – three Ju 52s took off for Stalingrad, each with their six barrels of fuel, and me tucked in beside them. It all went well: after a two-hour flight we landed at Gumrak airfield, 35 kilometres west of Stalingrad. I was lucky: at a crossroads I flagged down a vehicle from my 16th Panzer Division. The driver of the amphibious vehicle brought me to the immediate vicinity of my panzer regiment. No 1 Section

---

1. This report appeared in *Unsere 16*, issue 184, 47th Year, April 1999, pp. 6–7.

lay in a gully in earth bunkers, eight kilometres north west of the northern suburb of the city – an inhospitable steppe landscape. After reporting to my section commander, Major Graf Strachwitz,[2] I occupied a bunker whose occupant had just gone on leave.

In our sector inside the Northern Boundary there was heavy pressure from the north. We had to keep clearing out the enemy from where he had broken through our frontline. Every day that cost us dead and wounded. By night the light Il 2 bombers – 'sewing machines' as the infantry called them – gave us no peace. The monotonous steppe landscape, the nuisance barrages, the sudden Il 2 fighter-bomber attacks, the need to be alert every second to fight off an attack, the nightly bombing raids and the crouching and lying down in two square-metre bunkers weighed heavily on the nerves. Adding to it all in mid-October cold rain fell. The water ran into our earth bunkers; we scooped it out with tins.

The nights grew colder. A large bucket was converted into a 'stove'. From 6 November it suddenly turned bitter cold. The thermometer fell to -15°C, for us an additional enemy. The main problem was firewood. Lorries drove into the village of Orlovka five kilometres away to fetch beams and planks from wrecked houses. As a motorcycle despatch rider on my official journeys to the regimental Staff I could always make a small detour to Orlovka and fill my sidecar with wood. The cold increased: on 12 November the thermometer sank to -20°C.

On 17 November a senseless attack was made on the village of Rynok in which we suffered losses to landmines. At the end of October I had reported damage to my machine – cylinder and piston – to the section adjutant, Lieutenant Graf Ledebur.[3] Every 10 to 20 kilometres I had to unscrew and clean the sparkplugs of oil. Finally, on 18 November, I had to go to Kalatch on the Don to divisional workshop W3. Luckily they did not start the repair

---

2. Hyazinth Graf Strachwitz (b. Gross Stein, 30 July 1893, d. Trostberg, 25 April 1968). 1921 led a Freikorps in Upper Silesia. 1940, Major, 1942 Lieutenant-Colonel, 1944 Major-General, 1945 Lieutenant-General. He was one of the most highly decorated officers in the Wehrmacht: 1941 Knight's Cross, 1942 Oak Leaves, 1943 Swords, 1944 Diamonds. 1943 German Cross in gold: gold Wound Badge, was wounded thirteen times. 1943/4 joined military resistance to Hitler. After the war military advisor to the President of Syria.

3. Franz Eugen Graf von Ledebur (b. Krzemusch, 13 April 1919, fell Stephanovka, 11 January 1944), final rank Captain, 2nd Panzer Regiment: awarded German Cross in gold, 27 February 1942.

immediately – a fact which three days later was to save a comrade and myself from the Pocket!

In the early hours of 20 November there was an alarm at W3. We were told that the Russians had broken through in the north-west near the Romanian line and were advancing with powerful forces to the south-east. There was an alarm squad, mostly of workshop people, who had little battle experience, and we who had our vehicles in the workshop were incorporated into it. The following night we took up our positions 500 metres north of Kalatch. The bridge over the Don close by was still standing, but the Don highway, thus the western bank of the Don, was in Russian hands.

Two anti-tank guns in the workshop for repair were brought up. At first light on 21 November we heard the endless rattle of tank tracks coming down from the Don height to the bridge. Finally it fell quiet. All infantry and I – there must have been 130 to 150 of us – now knew: this is the lull before the storm. It would be an unequal battle which only a few would survive. Our weapons consisted of rifles, pistols and the two anti-tank guns. The strain on our nerves in these moments was enormous.

Towards 0800 hrs the 'magic show' began with the expected tank attack of twenty to thirty T-34s. The anti-tank gun crews, only two men to each gun, let the tanks come up to 250 metres then opened fire. In a short while they had destroyed six, two were burning. Then one gun received a direct hit, the other was crushed by a T-34. The tank crews had a look and saw that we presented them with no threat and now attempted to grind down our trenches with their tracks. A T-34 was on my trench and did a turn on its own axis. Here the fourteen-day frost came to our aid, for the earth was frozen down a few centimetres. The tanks then went on into Kalatch, followed by the Russian infantry. This was the only chance we had of engaging the enemy for a while with our rifles. Because we were preventing them from moving forwards, they fired mortars at us, inflicting heavy casualties. After that they attacked, and this time we could not hold them off. We fell back 500 metres over the plain to the first houses in Kalatch which offered us some protection.

What I experienced, saw and heard there I cannot set down in words: it was simply ghastly and I shall never forget it. I was one of those to reach the first houses in Kalatch. I went through farms and gardens to the workshop. The roads were controlled by the tanks. As soon as a vehicle showed itself they would fire on it. My motorcycle and sidecar were where I had left them three days previously. I lit a petrol fire in a tin can and put it under the engine block because the oil in the motor housing was so thick from the cold that I could not work the kick-start. At that moment my colleague came to the workshop by a back way. His car was in for repair and not driveable. He asked what were my intentions. 'I am going to attempt to ride through the area of Kalatch conquered by their tanks and then head south along the east bank of the Don. It is a dangerous journey into the unknown, but what else is there for it?'

'Good, take me along,' he said and got into my sidecar. It was an adventurous ride, but the only real way out of the Pocket! Thus I rode along the east bank of the Don southwards past Logovski, Potemkinskaya, Krasnoyarski to a bridge at Zimlyanskaya. Luckily our baggage-train had crossed this bridge two days previously, and seeing the tactical sign on my motorcycle the field-gendarme sentry let me cross too. By signpost shields I found my regiment's baggage-train in a village to one side of the Rollbahn.

On New Year's Eve 1942 we had to leave our quarters in a hurry, for the Russians had begun their move against Rostov with strong forces a few days before. Here my report on Stalingrad ends.

8. OTTO GEMÜNDEN:

The Pilot Who Flew Me into the Pocket also Flew Me Out[1]

Otto Gemünden (b. Ingelheim am Rhein, 30 May 1914, d. Ingelheim, 8 December 2007). He was conscripted into the 8th Anti-Aircraft Regiment at Fürth in 1935 and served on almost all fronts during the Second World War. At Stalingrad he was with the 37th Motorized Anti-Aircraft Regiment of the 9th Anti-Aircraft Division. On September 1942 he was promoted to Warrant Officer and awarded the Knight's Cross on 17 October 1942. In the substantiation it reads: 'On 30 September 1942, Wachtmeister Otto Gemünden distinguished himself with great bravery in the defence of the northern boundary positions north of Stalingrad against massed tanks. By skilful tactical manoeuvring and use of the firepower of his guns he destroyed twenty-one enemy tanks, ten of American manufacture, within twenty minutes using thirty-five rounds. After three men had fallen and another four were wounded, himself wounded in the hand and thigh by grenade splinters, he stood alone to destroy the last three enemy tanks.' As a reward Otto Gemünden was granted special home leave. The Oberingelheim Council awarded him the honour ring of the town. Then he had to return to the front.

On 28 November my return to duty was due, the air attacks on the Reich were increasing constantly and nothing good was being heard from the front – Stalingrad was mentioned a lot then. It was therefore difficult to take my leave, but duty called and I wanted to rejoin my colleagues.

On 5 December I arrived at Morosovskaya to learn that the Stalingrad Pocket had been cut off and was being supplied from there by air. My arrival was reported to General Pickert,[2] and I received permission to fly in at the

1. This report is compiled from the author's *Mehr Luftangriffe in der Heimat – keine guten Nachrichten von der Front* and *Der Pilot, der mich in den Kessel flog, flog mich auch raus* which appeared in the *Rhein-Main Presse* Ingelheim, November 1992, p. 10: also from the author's memoir (typescript pp. 35–44). These reports were placed at my disposal for publication.
2. Major-General Wolfgang Pickert (b. Posen, 3 February 1897, d. Weinheim, 19 July 1984) commanded 9th Anti-Aircraft Division from 25 June 1942 to 27 May 1944, and was afterwards commanding general, III Anti-Aircraft Corps. Decorations: 1943 Knight's Cross, 1944 Oak Leaves: 1942 German Cross in gold.

next opportunity. Being an eternal optimist, it did not occur to me even once that the Pocket might not have an effective strength any longer. For me the priority was to rejoin my comrades.

I was given the choice to fly from Morosovskaya either in an He 111 or a Ju 52. For understandable reasons I settled for the He 111. The same day I was taken to Tazinskaya and arrived in time for a situation conference. That day there was light snowfall, and light fog had been reported over Pitomnik. The commanding officer thought it was best not to fly but await better conditions next day. The pilots were unanimous, however, that they could not leave the men in the Pocket in the lurch, they needed provisions and ammunition, and most importantly the seriously wounded had to be brought out. I got to know a pilot who advised me straightaway to make sure I took along bread and canned food. There was plenty available, and so I packed as much as I could carry inside a canvas sheet. The take-off and flight were easy enough, and an hour later General Pickert received me on Pitomnik airfield.

He took me in his Kübelwagen to the regimental command post. On the way I considered whether I should offer him something from my supply of provisions; after all, it was somewhat unusual for a warrant officer to offer a general a bit of bread! While talking to him I passed a loaf forward which he shared at once with his driver. That was really the first time I was clear about the situation in the Pocket.

In the regimental command post Colonel Wolff[3] gave me a very hearty welcome and with my special provisions I was able to spread a little pleasure around. The same day I went to Major Gaidus. There too I was greeted joyfully, but I perceived a little unease. They were very grateful for the food but they remained poker-faced. After a while Major Gaidus let me know that my No.1 battery no longer existed, having been surprised by a T-34 in a readiness position. Only a few men had survived. These survivors had joined No. 3 battery led by Lieutenant Cablitz.[4]

This news cut me to the quick. Comrades with whom I had been together most of the time, had done everything together, I was not to see them again? I simply could not come to terms with it and for long had the belief that

3. On 12 January 1943 after General Pickert was flown out of the Pocket, Colonel Wilhelm Wolff became his successor as commander of 9th Anti-Aircraft Division and went with it into Soviet captivity on 31 January.
4. Lieutenant Fritz Cablitz (b. Mannheim, 27 September 1917) fell at Stalingrad on 21 January 1943 according to the German War Graves Commission.

somewhere along the way I would meet up with one or other of them. In the general air of depression my promotion to Lieutenant by the Section commanding officer was completely forgotten. When to my great joy over the next few days I saw quite a few of them again, if in poor shape, I felt a lot better.

Our AA battery was sent to the western part of the Pocket at Dmitryevka to defend against targets in the air and on land. We had to watch the expenditure of ammunition carefully, and we were only to fire at worthwhile targets. The front was fairly quiet. Small bunkers were built for the gun crews. These gave a degree of protection not only against artillery and bombing but also against the cold. A small stove could only take steppe-grass which required a lot of effort to collect and kept the men busy, but on the other hand it was not much use because it provided little warmth. For indirect fire we chose an observation post well forward. Additionally the wreck of a KV-1 tank in the open countryside was to a certain extent a safe spot. An artillery spotter had already prepared it: I moved the topmost lookout in and occupied the position with him.

We soon had a telephone line to the fire-direction post, and alternately with Lieutenant Cablitz[4] we occupied the post only by day. That meant walking two kilometres through the snow in the morning, the same back in the evening and we spent the day in the icy colossus. Then a spotter for the howitzers arrived. We calibrated the few markers on the plain and found the ranges. In good visibility we could see the enemy positions on the horizon and were allowed to fire a few nuisance rounds at them. Our footprints between the spotter position and the fire-direction post were seldom recognizable having been swept over. A layer of snow 30 centimetres deep covered the steppe, the telephone cable often helping us to find the shortest way.

Christmas was coming, the provisions were growing ever less and everybody had lice. Even I began to feel the dreadful itching although I washed myself naked in the snow almost every day. The men had to show me where these things like to inhabit most, and so in future we used every opportunity to search the seams for lice. On 24 December the usual sparse rations had a few sweets and six to eight small Christmas trees, expertly folded. They were made of green paper which could be spread out and thin candles attached, and a box

4. Lieutenant Fritz Cablitz (b. Mannheim, 27 September 1917) fell at Stalingrad on 21 January 1943 according to the German War Graves Commission.

of matches was included with which to light them. This day and the next the front fell absolutely silent: we did not even go out to the spotter position. At nightfall I went from bunker to bunker, lit the candles and announced, along with my wishes for Christmas, the fact that our panzers were coming up fresh from the Reich. Although on this Christmas Eve everybody was in low spirits – the men's thoughts were not difficult to plumb – the carol 'Silent Night, Holy Night' was sung by everyone with much fervour.

Over the preceding few days rumours had spread that General Hoth was advancing towards us from the south-west. Earlier at my spotter post I had heard the sound of fighting from that direction. Orders then came that preparations should be made, especially with the vehicles. Only the Henschel tractors, VW Kübel and an Opel lorry were really driveable, however. Over the next few days the front remained quiet. We occupied our spotter post alternately and even with a break now and again. Without being neglectful it was possible to leave it unmanned for a day for we had, together with the artillery, calibrated it and got the range so well that in an emergency they could direct our fire and vice-versa.

On 13 January 1943 at dawn I was making my way to the fire direction post in the KV-1 when on the outskirts of Dmitryevka I passed a mountain of bodies of friend and foe. They had been brought there because the ground was too hard to bury them. When and where they had fallen we could never establish. After about half an hour an enormous blow struck me and I was torn from my seat. With effort I regained my position and raised the periscope only to see approaching at high speed from the horizon Russian tanks with infantry seated on the hulls. At once I opened fire with four guns and the first salvo was very good. The infantry jumped free at once and took cover. They were wearing white camouflage blouses and were almost impossible to make out. When a second shell hit the spotter post I lost consciousness and came to on the floor of the tank: how much time had passed in the interim I had no idea. I climbed back up and looking out saw T-34s passing left and right of me and firing. I left my place and called to my colleagues, but nobody answered. Two lay unmoving in the lateral trenches.

Approaching from the open plain and heading for Dmitryevka, without any cover, a T-34 was a few metres in front of me. I crept up behind it, and as it set off I held on to the upper structure tightly and could easily run in the tank tracks. The Russian infantry was well back and as I was wearing a white camouflage suit over my uniform I was not seen. After about a kilometre – the first houses were almost in sight – I made off to the right where I knew there was a gully, which I soon reached. Totally exhausted I sat down behind the hollowed-out roots of a shrub.

When I came to again I was in an artillery bunker, well down in an offshoot of the gully. Some soldiers were standing around me, and on a stove a large aluminium pot of coffee was steaming, from which I was given a full beaker. To my question how I had got here I was told that some infantry had delivered me, and had long since gone on their way. I studied my map, asked them to show me where we were and saw that I was not too far from the connecting line between the gun position and the limber position. Blood covered my face, and my camouflage suit was bloody, but I was not wounded. The cotton wool padding, greatcoat and camouflage suit had apparently protected me during the shooting and when I fell.

Therefore I set off once more, and had not gone far before finding the telephone cable. In fresh snow or in heavy snowdrifts we had often picked up this cable when leaving the spotter post and followed it, allowing it to slip through our gloved hands. I was finding difficulty in breathing: it took all my concentration to keep awake. After a while a towing tractor passed by without seeing me waving. A second followed with the same result. Finally the crew of a third recognized me, stopped and I was taken on board by our best driver, Corporal Dick. Soon I was in my battery's bunker. It was late afternoon, and all the men were being operated as infantry. Thus I remained alone with the two Russians I had captured with their lorry on the Don and who were watching me very closely. I smoked two packs of Eckstein cigarettes even though I was having difficulty in breathing.

On 15 January 1943 I was taken in the early hours to the regimental surgeon who diagnosed a ruptured lung. My regimental commander, Colonel Wolff, and the surgeon took me to Gumrak airfield and spoke with the senior medical officer at the Army dressing station who would authorize my flight out with the observation that no external injury was visible. The hospital marquees were bursting at the seams with the seriously wounded. The walking-wounded were accommodated in ruined houses and underground bunkers: a male nurse on constant duty made his space available to me, for I was at the end of my strength.

Even in the days following every step I took had to be made with the assistance of a male nurse or another wounded colleague. Once when I left the bunker with the male nurse for toilet purposes there was at the entrance to the marquee a dead steppe-pony, apparently the victim of Russian fire. A number of men were at work cutting out the soft flesh. One of them had succeeded,

52

and he was holding a lump of flesh in both hands, trying to bite into it. It could not be eaten, however, for the blood froze on his hands and face. This awful scene remained in my memory for ages.

Days passed. Neither night or day did we hear aircraft landing and taking off. It was very cold and frequent snowfall interfered with all air traffic. Only the Russian 'nerve saw' dropped a bomb on the area now and again. Our bunker was approximately two metres deep and two by three metres in dimension. The ceiling was railway sleepers and packed earth. There were eleven of us sharing the bunker. On 18 January 1943 a doctor came for the first time but only to ask which of us did not have a flight authority from the senior surgeon: he took the details of the men who did not have one, including myself. He returned in the afternoon but was unable to say if a transport or flight out was possible.

Meanwhile the front was coming nearer: the sounds of battle were clearly heard. I checked my pistol, for I had no intention of being taken alive. As the light faded I stared at a small photograph of my wife Bertl and my son. Now I came to a decision that I would not give in, but make every effort to see them both again. I secured the pistol, got up from my space and announced: 'I am going to the airfield in the dark. If a machine comes, all well and good, if not, I shall die out there.' With a map-case, my photos and a blanket wrapped around me I left the bunker.

Someone shouted after me, 'Yes, you with your Knight's Cross they will take, but us?' I replied, 'If I fly out, you will too!' At that they all followed behind me, one supporting the other. It was bitterly cold. Snow swept the airstrip, which we soon reached: the skies were otherwise clear. In the moonlight I recognized an He 111. A man stood below it. I was well ahead of the others, some of whom had leg wounds. I opened the collar of my greatcoat so that my Knight's Cross could be seen and spoke to the man whom I guessed to be the pilot, asking him if he would be flying out and could I accompany him. 'Of course you can come,' he replied, 'but I am fetching General Hube for Führer-HQ, it can take a while. Keep going to the airstrip, more aircraft are coming. If they don't, come back here!' Where I got the strength I still do not know.

I had gone not 300 metres into the wind when three men came towards me. At arm's length from me the one in the middle said, 'Man, are you still here?' It was the pilot who had flown me into the Pocket at the beginning of December! After briefly considering if he should report to flight control he decided not to, and we went to the aircraft. There it stood, the He 111! The flight mechanic reported the aircraft was fully tanked up, we could take off at once. By now the other ten men had managed to reach us and stood around me. The pilot ordered, 'Open the door, they are coming with us!' Reluctantly it was opened, the first of them were pushed in or up. Then somebody shouted from within, no more, it's full up. The pilot climbed up, directed some into the rear of the fuselage, and with much groaning and whimpering nine men were stuffed in and the door shut. I stood outside with a Captain who had a head wound. We were lifted on to a wing and pushed into the flight cabin. The captain had to stand against the side wall, I was sat on the observer's seat.

Several attempts to start the engines failed. We could feel how weak the starter motor seemed. The flight engineer told the pilot, 'We should get out, other aircraft are coming!' The pilot retorted, 'Get out, we'll crank her!' Two men opened up a mechanism, turned it once or twice, nothing! The pilot called to the wounded captain, behind him was a red knob, he should look to see if it was pressed in, and it was. A few thumps with the fist was enough, and the knob sprang free. More turns of the starting handle combined with the help of the starter motor by the pilot. The left engine caught and the propeller turned, the right one was coupled to it and also ran! A sigh of relief ran through the ranks!

When the two crewmen had got back aboard, the almost cloudless sky was searched and the machine rolled. A soldier with a flag actually stood on the open airstrip waving in one direction. We turned into it, crossed our fingers, and we were getting away very lightly when there was a fighter stood in our path, one wing at an angle upwards. As I was lying in the observer's seat I could see the pilot's face. He leaned back drawing the control stick into his body, his face tense. I was really expecting that we would crash – but nothing of the kind! We must have just passed above it.

Once we had gained altitude the pilot handed me a bar of chocolate and pointed below, where one could make out the Russian lines by their many camp fires. The sight made it absolutely clear to me that the men in the Pocket were done for. To get a grip on myself took an effort: I buried my face in my hands to hide my tears. This pilot had not only distinguished himself by his flying ability, but also by his attitude and character as a man and comrade!

We landed at first light at Novotsherkassk airfield. Without a chance of taking my leave of the pilot, of thanking him for his heroic and self-sacrificial devotion to duty, I was taken by ambulance to Rostov on the Don and examined the same day. Beforehand we seized the opportunity to visit the provisions warehouse. I sat in a corner with a loaf and bread and devoured it without a knife.

A school had been converted into a field hospital. Next day a colonel of the AA artillery in charge of the equipment store visited me. He said I could fly at once to Dnyepropetrovsk, he had a shuttle arrangement with them for the transport of equipment and spare parts. 'But we have to observe the red tape and not be hasty,' he warned. Therefore I had to go first to the senior surgeon, who would examine me for the certificate of non-objection. The doctor told me, 'If you want to die, then you can fly!' I countered this by saying that I had just been flown out of the Stalingrad Pocket and had stood it well, but he was not convinced, and insisted that I went by ambulance train, and lying down. I had to lump it, and on 28 January 1943 I finished up at Warsaw in Reserve Hospital IV.

As we discovered later, all the wounded coming out of Stalingrad were kept out of the Reich proper to avoid the awful events there becoming general knowledge amongst the population. To add to my ruptured lung I got fever and was confined to bed. I shared the large ward with thirty other officers, all out of Stalingrad. On orders of the Führer we were to be given the best possible treatment: so besides cigarettes we got cigars in glass tubes, chocolate and chocolate creams and much else – all of them things which we saw as small miracles, but we were not allowed to smoke and did not wish to: sweets also did not interest us and the mood was irritable. The seriously wounded often groaned all night long. Thus I never forgot a lieutenant whose sexual organs had been shot away: he found comfort in loud prayer and quoting texts from the Bible to himself. After about ten days my fever abated, I felt the improvement, and soon I was appointed spokesman and room senior.

After temporary transfer to the Führer-reserve, Otto Gemünden became a platoon leader with Bewerbungs (Candidates) Regiment Zingst, later battery commander and head of artillery training for military cadets. After his promotion to Lieutenant on 1 June 1943 he was in a military hospital for six months: on 1 May 1944 he was promoted to Captain. In autumn 1944 he served with an anti-aircraft unit in the Burgenland, and in January 1945 in the Ostrau area. After the capitulation he was taken prisoner by the Soviets and spent the next three years in Siberia until his release in June 1948.

9. WILHELM GEREKE:
To the Last Round[1]

Wilhelm Gerecke was attached to No 2 Battery, 171st Artillery Regiment in the 71st Infantry Division.

When in November 1942 the Russian spearheads shook hands on the Don heights at Kalatch, thus closing the Pocket around the Sixth Army at Stalingrad, nobody thought that this would last very long. The first section of our No. 2 Battery had gone on leave and not yet returned. The fire-control position was near the church aiming for the Volga. Battery-officer was Sergeant-Major Grunewald. Our spotter position was the bathhouse,[2] where a Russian regimental and divisional command post had been before we captured it.

The panorama extended far beyond the Volga. In clear weather we could watch the Russians bringing up their artillery. Our battery commander, Lieutenant Wüster, was on leave: the battery was being led by Lieutenant

---

1. This report was published in *Das Kleeblatt* (circular issued for former members of 71st Infantry Division), 135th edition, No 2, 29th Year, April 1985, and 136th edition No 3, 29th Year, July 1985.

2. Lieutenant Dr Wigand Wüster (Letter published in *Das Kleeblatt*, 136th edition, Nr.3, 29th Year, July 1985) located the comfortable observation post of No 2 Battery 'in the ruins of a business premises to the west above the railway property'. The bathhouse (tubs and showers) was in the battery's nearby fire-control point, however. It was a stout construction like a concrete bunker which offered good protection right up to the last minutes of the fighting at midday on 31 January 1943, when the battery was overrun, an island in the passing flood of attackers. Nevertheless the hopeless struggle was continued using infantry weapons without the defenders of the bathhouse thinking about the sense and purpose of what they were doing, or, in their dark despair, accounting for it to anybody.

Hildebrand. Shortly after he became Abteilungs-adjutant,[3] and then Lieutenant Biegel took over the battery.

I was in the forward artillery spotter's position (VB) as radio operator. Every ten days Sergeant-Major Specht and three men went to the VB, in a gully near the Volga. The enemy was opposite us only 15 metres away. Because everything was overlooked, there were communication trenches running from the railway station, and these came under constant mortar fire. The battery was continually combed through; whoever could be dispensed with was transferred to No 1 Battery. This no longer had any guns and was really an infantry company on the Volga.

On 17 December the order came to destroy all non-vital equipment. We took over two guns and marched down to the southern front where panzers had assembled to break out towards Fourth Panzer Army. We had not got far with destroying everything when the order was rescinded. At the end of December/beginning of January, Lieutenant Wüster was flown in. Lieutenant Biegel took over the Staff battery. The Abteilung command post was in the former fuel factory on the road between the airfield and Red Square. Captain Langner was the Abteilung commander.

At the beginning of January I was transferred from the VB-post to the Abteilung command post. At this time the Volga front was relatively quiet. Our artillery would only fire at recognized targets with special permission and then at the most three rounds, while the Russians would open up with a whole battery from the other bank of the Volga in the effort to kill a single man. The ground was snow-covered and a biting frost prevailed, -25°C to -30°C, glorious weather for the Russian air force which was aloft all day.

The former Command Office Centre had been converted to a military hospital and was overloaded with wounded. It was marked visibly with a red cross on a white background but was attacked by Russian bombers and razed to the ground with phosphorous bombs. The fighting in the steppe was getting nearer to the city suburbs, wounded and stragglers streamed into the ruins of the city. Members of all divisions were represented in our command post. The wounded were attended to by our Abteilung surgeon Dr Hengst. We gave these men what we could from our paltry provisions.

On 20 January 1943 the regimental command post was transferred to us.

3. In German artillery practice, an Abteilung was a group of batteries, usually three or four, amounting to less than battalion size [Tr].

Regimental commander was Lieutenant-Colonel von Stumpff,[4] adjutant Captain Schmidt. On 28 January the Russians reached the Volga south of us so that we lost contact with the south. At this time the former GPU prison on the Zariza gorge was full of German prisoners. That same evening Captain Schmidt left. He was intending to break out down the Volga to the Caucasus front with other officers.[5]

On 29 January the canteen stores, of which a remnant was left, were shared out amongst everyone at our command post. What was left of the cold meats had been distributed the previous evening. In the afternoon a German Panzer IV came out on the street and took the enemy mortars and infantry under fire. When the Russians spotted it they fired back with all their artillery, which also put paid to the Abteilung command post. After Lieutenant-Colonel von Stumpf and Captain Langner had fallen,[6] as darkness fell we went to another cellar already occupied by men of other divisions, amongst them what was left of the fighter squadron JG *Udet* under Captain Dr Mundscheit. The most forward line was occupied as a strongpoint so that in the night the Russians bypassed it, leaving us in a small Pocket of our own.

After we had fired off all our ammunition and had made our small arms unserviceable because there was no point in fighting any longer, we surrendered on the morning of 30 January 1943. On reaching the enemy position the fighting troops offered us cigarettes and cigars from our provisions warehouse they had captured. These troops did not steal from us. With the words, 'Woina kaputt, skora damoi!' all prisoners, about 250 of us, were arranged into a column and with one sentry we started off south. When the sentry was relieved after a kilometre and a half, the great shake-down began, in which even the civilians joined in. We were relieved of everything visible. We had now reached the southern arterial road and were headed towards

---

4. Colonel Karl-Lebrecht von Stumpff commanded 171st Artillery Regiment from 1 October 1942, previously its 3rd Abteilung. He was decorated with the German Cross in gold on 3 August 1942.

5. According to Wigand Wüster, this attempt was senseless, an act of sheer desperation. The commander of No. 3 Battery (Captain Siewecke?) also attempted to break out when his battery was overrun. He intended to head west and remains listed as missing.

6. According to Dr Wigand Wüster (letter, as footnote 2 above), Colonel von Stumpf/Stumpff (promoted to a final rank of Lieutenant-Colonel), his adjutant and the commander of No 2 Abteilung all committed suicide at No. 1 Abteilung command post by shooting themselves to avoid capture by the Soviets.

Beketovka. On this road we were overtaken by a Russian motorized unit. Whoever did not jump out of the way fast enough was run down.

After a few kilometres we left the road for the Stalingrad–Beketovka railway line. Here we were fed in a linesmen's house. There was a loaf of bread to be shared amongst eight, and each man got a salted herring. That was our ration for the next eight days. When we returned to the road, a Russian unit awaited us. Here the last of what we owned was taken from us: some men even had their boots taken so that they had to stand barefoot in the snow in temperatures of -30°C. That evening we reached Beketovka Camp and were split up into houses without windows. As they had taken our blankets we had to sleep in the cold on the stone floor. There were 50,000 prisoners at Beketovka Camp. Terrible things went on there because the men were starving. The camp had two captured Opel-Blitz lorries which did nothing all day but remove the corpses to the nearby gullies. There was a kitchen, but insufficient for so many prisoners, so that one got something to eat once a week if one was lucky.

At the end of February we were loaded, 80 to 100 men in a wagon fitted with plank beds. For the necessities there was a 30 x 30cm hole sawn through the wooden floor. There was an oven in the corner, and some logs, and a blunt piece of metal for chopping them up. For rations we received two slices of hard bread and a salted herring again, but on the whole journey nothing to drink. If the train stopped, those who had died on the way were brought out and laid near the railway embankment. When we arrived at our destination and unloaded, we were divided into one of two camps, 'Bauer' and 'Neumann', in the former Volga-German Republic. Whoever could not walk was loaded on to an ox-drawn sledge led by a woman and brought into the camp that way. The women were civilian prisoners who were kept in the Bauer village camp. Bauer was a very beautiful place. Because the inhabitants had been deported, the village had been made into several prison camps. Of the thousand men who were lodged here, often up to thirty per day would die, most of typhus, dystrophy or dysentery. In those first weeks hardly anyone was fit for work. There was no doctor in the camp, only a female Russian nurse who was helpless to prevent the deaths.

In March 1943 Neumann Camp was disbanded; the survivors came to Bauer Camp. The fifty men able to work were given the job of building a collective farm. In September 1943 Bauer Camp was also closed: we, seventy able to work and 150 sick, the survivors of 2,000 men, were now transferred to Volsk Camp.

10. JOSEF GOBLIRSCH:

The Fight for Hill 102 and the Railway Station[1]

Josef Goblirsch (b. Haid/Böhmerwald, 15 March 1921) volunteered for the Wehrmacht in 1940 immediately after obtaining his school-leaving certificate. He took part in the campaigns in France and Russia as a private and NCO with the artillery. As a reserve officer, he was sent to the Don Front in September 1942 with 54th Jäger Regiment of the 100th Jäger Division.

From 13 September 1942 our 100th Jäger Division was withdrawn from the Don Front in preparation for the attack on the east side of Stalingrad. Sixth Army had already forced its way into the northern area of the city on 28 August and reached the Volga the following day. Deputizing for the Company commander, Lieutenant Herbert Maul, who was acting as regimental adjutant, I took over units of the Staff-Company and the mounted platoon to Stalingrad. This included the regimental veterinary group. Much to the amusement of the local population our Staff veterinary officer Dr Hantel had exchanged his horse for a camel: this animal hauled his steppe-pony cart and was satisfied with steppe-grass for fodder. After being detached from the Don Front we reached the eastbound Rollbahn on the first day, this sanded highway went through the Kalmuck steppe to the bend in the Don. Bright sunshine drove the sweat out of our pores. The horses and wagons were covered in dust, our faces like masks, bright grey with black nostrils, lips and eyelids. We chewed our sandy rations between our teeth. Everybody longed for the coolness of night. Until it came, Ju 52s passed above us unceasingly, probably carrying the wounded westwards and bringing in supplies eastwards. They thundered only a few metres overhead of the convoys on the Rollbahn, since this was how best these heavy machines could find some protection against the

---

1. Josef Goblirsch based his typed report on diary entries and sixteen field-post letters from the period in question and placed them at the disposal of the Editor with an accompanying letter on 10 September 2003.

60

Il 2 fighter-bombers. Every unit of the convoy also had a twin anti-aircraft gun ready to fire.

We set out our bivouac for the night to one side of the Rollbahn. For ablutions and while caring for the horses we would run around in swimming trunks, but once the sun set we dressed up warm to avoid freezing to death in the very low temperatures. The tents were erected swiftly: two sentries were enough. Everybody could then rest and sleep. The bitter cold every night soon pervaded the tents. The feet of the sleepers were attacked first. The wool blankets were little help. Continental, warm steppe climate! Thus life in the tents began before one awoke. After rising one made one's way through a tent whose walls were frozen solid with exhaled air. The hoped-for warm slug of tea from the field flask was icy. At least the field kitchens had their fires lit, and hot brown water, which they called coffee, was better than nothing! Our comradely horses stood motionless, their heads sunken. Despite the horse blanket the cold shock of the night had surprised them. The hair of their nostrils had tassels of hoar-frost, even their eyelashes were streaked with white. Their ankle joints were so stiff that they could not be moved until after the sun had warmed them up to avoid tearing a muscle.

In the rosy dawn to the east we saw a thick black cloud of smoke arise, mushrooming out at a great height with a white cap: burning oil refinery at the Volga port. With the mounted platoon ahead of the HQ Company I crossed the pioneer-made bridge over the Don. Like all north-south rivers in Asia the Don also had a steep west bank and a flat east bank. In a riverside meadow on the other side we were shown a place where to bivouac.

During the night motors of the abundant 'sewing machine' Il 2s could be heard unceasingly. Now and again they tossed down a bomb, probably aimed at the Don bridge. As we were told, the aircraft motor would be stopped to reduce speed and the bomb thrown out by hand from the old, lightweight biplanes. Unluckily, a splinter tore the tent of Bandmaster Fülling and took off the head of the tent pole. He struggled out of the tent cursing and began to dig himself a small trench for protection. Early next morning when we were told to ready ourselves to move out, the trench had just been completed! The laughter of those whose had slept their fill annoyed him.

Using the map of Stalingrad, divided up into squares and numbers for providing our bombers with their targets, I informed myself and the Company about the city which lay ahead of us. After one more day on the move we would reach the readiness area of the regiment at the south end of Stalingrad. We were not needed for the attack where we were and so could bring our horses to a settlement and sit 'snug' at tables and chairs outside mud cottages inhabited only by clothes-lice and bedbugs. The lice used to hide themselves in the seams: they carried typhus and the five-day fever also known as Wolhynien or trench fever.

For the first time I saw here the commanding officer, Colonel Pavicic,[2] and several officers of 369th Croat Infantry Regiment of our division when the orders were being distributed. Next day we were transferred about 30 kilometres north to near the city centre on the west side of Stalingrad. On the trek to the high plain between the Don and the Volga we had the muffled growl of battle and the sight of the black smoke from the burning oil refinery in the city port always with us. After passing over a low hill we saw a sea of humble dwellings. Amongst them towered multi-storeyed buildings and factory chimneys: behind them the broad band of the Volga wended its way, glittering in the sun. On the far bank lay a misty plain. Whereas in the south it had been peaceful, over the centre of the city were clouds of smoke through which a giant grain silo protruded. The northern part of the city was wrapped in dark clouds. Burning oil and clouds from bomb-bursts built up a thick layer of smoke over the houses. Above them countless small white and dark puffs drifted: the Russian AA fired at whatever moved in the skies.

As night began to fall we reached the west side of the city. We could make out the silhouettes of houses before the smouldering fires. The heavens were lit by innumerable searchlights: German flak, whose shell-splinters whirred over our heads, fired at the Russian bombers. Whereas the Luftwaffe was master of the skies by day, apparently night was the domain of the Russian air fleets. Also on the far side of the Volga searchlights flashed: many pointed to the targets for their bombers on the west bank by 'nodding' the beam. Our Division occupied the witches' cauldron between the city centre and the northern suburbs, I led my foot-column through the steppe northwards. From the saddle of my horse I photographed the western edges of the 60-kilometre long and up to five kilometres broad industrial city on the Volga. Coming up from the steppe with the Regimental HQ Company, after detouring around the contested western sectors of the city, I approached the endless sea of houses directly on its eastern edge.

The first action our regiment had to undertake was the conquest of the

2. Colonel Viktor Pavicic took over the 369th (Croat) Infantry Regiment from Colonel Mesic in July 1942. On 15 January he had himself flown out: this was hushed-up.

singular Hill 102 which dominated all Stalingrad, the Mamayev-Kurgan.[3] We had taken this height, crowned by two cylindrical water-towers south of the highest point, on 14 September, but lost it again to the Russians on 16 September. Now it was the objective of our Division. We knew it would be a difficult task against a hardened, incalculable enemy. We knew his rigorous manner of fighting from many previous encounters. We also knew the ruthless brutality of the Red Army against itself and its own: whoever hung back, or was wounded, received the coup-de-grâce from a political commissar! The Russian bayonet was intended mainly to kill their own or enemy wounded, only incidentally for close combat. Individual prisoners were tortured to make them talk, then shot dead. Prisoners were relieved of their service books, writing implements, letters and anything usable such as items of clothing, boots and so forth, then taken to an assembly area to be vigorously 'searched' once more by their guards before being abandoned to hunger and infectious disease. The great promises, reports of successes on the fronts and the numerous 'safe conducts' lying around, dropped by aircraft or fired by their artillery in propaganda shells, were believed by nobody.

Our support services and horses were taken to a gully not far from Gumrak airfield, later the main Sixth Army dressing station and landing zone for supply and ambulance aircraft. That was the last we saw of the horses. Probably they all finished up in the nearby field kitchen, for later the provisions supplied by the Luftwaffe were inadequate. Meanwhile they grazed rough steppe grass until cereals would become available from the Stalingrad silo once we captured it. With the Company I occupied well-built houses on the west side of the city near the regimental command post in order to be able to carry out without delay the operational orders of the commanding officer. The Russians knew our movements and made us the target of rocket-salvoes from their Katyushas – called by us 'Stalin Organs' – situated on the Volga island. Outside the houses the air was always 'unhealthy'. When it was calm, great clouds of smoke hung above the city: the stench of burning and decomposition filled the air.

We were soon forced to recognize that even our sturdy, striking, white-washed house was registered as an aiming point and we dug an earth bunker in its shadow. Now the Stalin Organs no longer made us nervous: we heard them fire and would immediately slip away underground. The splinter effect of these rockets was not great, and there were many duds. The Russians tried to increase their splinter effect by welding short iron rods into the head in

---

3. Named after the fourteenth-century Khan Mamaj of the 'Golden Horde'.

order to detonate them about a metre above the actual impact point. This resulted in many comical duds, unexploded rockets on a stick, and depending on the surface waggling ten to fifty centimetres above the ground. The impact was softened by the iron rod and failed to activate the detonator. Later I never bothered to watch them. When preparing a meal in front of the bunkers one night a medical orderly was killed by a splinter and another seriously wounded. Daily we suffered losses from shell splinters.

On our broad road to Gumrak the swollen corpses of dead Russians with laced waists lay between bloated Russian horses, legs extended upright and spread, giving off a vile stench. By night civilians from the supposedly abandoned village crept forth from their hideouts to tear lumps of flesh off these rat-eaten cadavers by the light of fires and flares before vanishing quickly into the ruins. Their houses had no cellars. The Russians did not bury their dead. They threw them into shell-craters or trenches. For reasons of hygiene we buried all the dead we found lying on our side. The German graves were marked by a rifle and bayonet, the Russian graves by a steel helmet on an inverted rifle stock.

At 0300 hrs on 27 September preparations began, and at 0500 hrs the preparatory barrage of our artillery was unleashed, which the Russians answered at once with a crazed defensive fire. A Stalin Organ salvo landed in a gully killing fifteen Jäger and wounding 100 men of two neighbouring companies. There were only minor wounds in my unit. The almost silent conduct of wounded or dying comrades only impressed me at the beginning of the war, not any longer.

At 0630 hrs our Regiment attacked. The first objective was Hill 102 immediately north of us. It had been a favourite excursion spot of the Stalingrad population in earlier times. From this dominating height one could control almost the whole city and the shipping on the Volga. It had been ploughed over by bombs and shells and richly soaked in blood. We could imagine that we were going to be up against the stiffest resistance. The mounted platoon – naturally without horses – and the wheeled vehicle platoon – naturally without wheeled vehicles – had been assigned to the Jäger Company led by myself and known collectively as 'the mounted platoon' now attached to 2nd Battalion, 54th Jäger Regiment. After heavy losses we advanced only 200 metres. The casualties mounted, but around 0900 hrs we reached the first objective, a gully about 100 metres from the water towers. Incessant Russian mortar fire kept our heads down: Stukas and bombing were of little use. At 1300 hrs we were ordered to dig in. The bitter resistance of the Soviet 269th Infantry Regiment prevented any further advance. Cowering in the shell craters and roundish shelter-trenches abandoned by the Russians, attending to small splinter wounds, we awaited with longing the approach of darkness.

In the evening we saw our end closing in. Ten enemy bombers in the east were heading for our positions. Suddenly Luftwaffe fighters appeared and shot half down in less time than it takes to tell it. The rest turned away, still with their bombs, and disappeared over the Volga of which we would have had a good view if we had dared to raise our heads above the parapet of the shell crater in which we were taking cover. Our own artillery did not help us in our plight. Some members of my unit had fallen, others were wounded. The medical orderlies were overworked and exhausted as were we all: shooting – leaping – digging in – orders shouted across the din of battle – our objective reached – supplying ammunition – a shelter for the wounded – renewing severed telephone cables – a bite to eat – a drink of tea from the field flask – shooting dead Russians in their counter-attacks. When night fell we were relieved by a strong Jäger Company to refresh our personnel and psyches. The wheeled vehicle platoon had been shrivelled to ten exhausted men, only 30 per cent of its authorized strength. Next day the remnants of my unit rested in the former quarters behind the former readiness rooms on the road to Gumrak.

We learned that the slopes of Hill 102 facing the Volga and the city quarter behind it had been subjected to a very heavy air raid at 0630 hrs. Stukas dive-bombed with howling sirens: endless sticks of bombs fell from the bomb-bays of He 111s. Our own artillery fired incessantly over our heads at the targets on Hill 102 and the railway embankment east of it. After a long rocket barrage they heard infantry fire and also hand grenades, but despite the greatest effort accompanied by high casualties, neither the water towers nor the hill fell. After two days I received reinforcements – unfortunately inexperienced – while nearby the battle for Hill 102 and the northern section of the railway station raged on with undiminished ferocity. It was mainly the Croats of our division who were able to advance to the railway embankment east of Hill 102 next day.

Soon our entire battalion was disbanded. My company was totally exhausted, the wheeled vehicle section down to ten men. Now we were enlisted to support 2nd Battalion in its attack against the northern section of the main railway station. The aim of this attack was to encircle the Russians defending Hill 102. On 28 September we advanced, mostly in attacks launched from between the burning trains, up to the 'Tennis Racquet', a railway loop. We had artillery and Luftwaffe support to the north on railway property and advanced from one bomb crater to the next. In order to avoid any further disproportionate losses, once we had taken the northern bridge the attack was broken off and we went on the defensive. The same day Hill 102 fell to us so that we could restore the connection to our own units.

I dug in with my company at the northern bridge, therefore at the 'haft' of the famous 'Tennis Racquet' in the industrial quarter. Despite massive artillery support, our attack next day never amounted to much. Then came the order to change the manner of fighting. The enemy was defending at the Tennis Racquet, in and around the ruins of the North main signal box and in the ruins of the Lasur metal factory.

With my preliminary orders I received new maps with the enemy situation marked in. Leading Private Hans Moosburner,[4] acting QM sergeant, constantly concerned for us and the horses, came to me at the command post from the support services in the gully through the constant hail of splinters. He reported that all riding horses were healthy but haggard, and oats were running low. Therefore in the heat of the fighting I wrote him a confirmation that he was authorized to fetch horsefeed with a steppe-pony and cart from the bitterly fought-for and now captured grain silo. By doing so, my signature would have brought me the death penalty or at least 25 years in a labour camp in Siberia had I been taken prisoner.

At 2nd Battalion 54th Regiment my regimental runner, Corporal Franz Rechberger[5] [see his account, No. 30, below] brought me my new mission in writing, to improve the position of the Jäger units of the HQ Company in the main frontline where they now were, by expanding and defending it. My neighbour to the right was our Regimental Pioneer Company under Lieutenant Kühnfels,[6] who had to hold his position down to the banks of the

---

4. Hans Moosburner (b. Bogenberg, 7 December 1919) was wounded in the back in January 1943 during an assault, and after spending the night of 10 January at a dressing station was flown out from Pitomnik to Salsk. After a hospital stay at Rostov he was brought by hospital train to Königswusterhausen via Berlin. Later with the newly reconstituted regiment in Albania, he was captured by the Soviets at the end of the war and after being transferred as a prisoner to the Poles worked as a forced labourer in a mine until the end of 1946. Today he lives at Bogenberg/Danube (oral information to the Editor from Hans Moosburner, 8 March 2011).

5. See Franz Rechberger's account, No. 30 below.

6. Dr Rudolf Kühnfels (b. Reigersfeld/Kosel, 19 August 1917, d. 17 February 1994) was, as a Lieutenant, company commander in the 54th Jäger Regiment. Decoration: Knight's Cross, 9 December 1944.

Volga. My neighbour to the left defending the slope of Hill 102 was Lieutenant Geisberg[7] with his weakened No 4 Jäger Company. The Battalion Commander and his Staff had set up their command post about 500 metres behind the main frontline in a large sewer pipe, approximately 300 metres long. These pipes were tunnelled below the northern marshalling yards and led down to the Volga, on whose western banks the Russians were sitting, therefore in the same stinking, rat-infested pipe equipped with boards, doors and gates as we were. 'Better to be stunk to death than frozen or shot' is an old soldier's adage. In order to prevent the Ivans having any access up from the Volga, the pipe was blocked up to the east.

Despite the good protection against being seen and all bombardments, I would not have spent one day in that stinking sewer, whose rat population easily outnumbered the humans, because all near misses resounded through this concrete tunnel in the most nerve-wracking way. And the Russians did not know what a lull in the firing was. It constantly 'rained' explosive shells of all calibres. Stalin Organ rockets pounded us, and by night there came additionally splinter-, HE- and incendiary bombs dropped by their chattering 'sewing machines'. The 'fragrance' of the constantly burning carbide lamps mixed with the stink of the standing sewage polluted the air they breathed in the 'Battalion Pipe'. They were, so to speak, incarcerated in there, received no fresh air and had no view of how the battle was going outside. The Battalion Commander, a Captain, an officer of the Reserve as was I, was a Professor in civilian life, if I remember correctly.

I was very satisfied with my own command post, close to the enemy. Above, I had cover against bullets though not bombs: a four-axled diesel freight-train locomotive. The distance between each sleeper enabled us to excavate easily, for they were not gravelled over but of loose loam as was all the ground in Stalingrad. Thus every cut with the spade was bound to be rewarded. My command post gave a good view of the surroundings and into enemy territory, moreover we had unrestricted communication amongst ourselves and also good protection against unhealthy air and rain. The steel rails either side provided good storage for rifles under almost complete cover. Because the loam flooring was firm, we could bore holes into it as storage points for weapons, equipment such as radio sets and telephones. A hole in the earth was also good for stretching out, all one had to do was extend the tunnel true

7. Lieutenant Werner Geisberg (b. 24 August 1917) survived Stalingrad and died on 3 September 2009 in Cologne.

to size for the legs. We did not plan for a latrine because getting there would have been too dangerous. Therefore a spade was used. One urinated outside the command post, the major business being performed on a spade, after which the contents would be hurled outside and the spade cleaned with sand.

After his rifle, the entrenching tool was the second most important tool for the infantryman. Contrary to the over-long Russian bayonet it was good for close combat, served as a shovel in underground construction works and for setting up a good weapons store, as an axe for felling trees and hacking off branches to create a field of fire, for winning camouflage material, breaking open doors and windows in village fighting, as a frying pan for cooking meat and preparing egg dishes, as something upon which to rest the report pad, and also, in icy air in the open, for every so-called piece of spade-work in the battle post. What had to be watched out for was to not shower a neighbouring command post when 'hurling'. On the first evening when answering a call of nature I visited the wreck of a half-cylinder car with a steel roof on the neighbouring track. Scarcely begun I heard mortar fire. There was not even time to pull my trousers up properly before I slipped under my protecting locomotive. Just then the mortars landed, and later I saw that the steel roof of my latrine was riddled by splinters.

From my position beneath the axles of the locomotive I had a good view ahead to the underside of the north bridge and further still to the rails of the Tennis Racquet marshalling yard, to the Russian positions and inside the ruins of the Lasur factory. To the right, also to the south, there was a fire-gutted goods train on the inclined track which led over the north bridge. This train marked the right-hand boundary with Lieutenant Kühnfels' pioneer company. It offered a good view and was effective for our snipers and as the changeover position for one of our flanking MGs. On both sides I could survey the area close to me and also look over the flat rising embankment about ten metres away. I could not see Hill 102 nor our positions on the east flank, but I would not have been able to see all the positions in my sector from anywhere else. Thus I was always on call and on the telephone. The lines of the latter were laid on open ground and very often cut by splinters.

Two sleepers further down my runner and telephone operator had dug in, behind them was the medical orderly with a protective hole for himself and one for treating the wounded: behind them again was the company troop leader NCO Kastner with a runner. Below the first and following coaches of the gutted train on the upper track our marksman with a telescopic sight had set up several positions. The decisive position for the entire northern front, the railway and Hill 102 was the northern bridge. About forty metres from my command post the three tracks from the north merged to cross it. If the enemy held this bridge, the right-angled corner pillar to our front, with a flat trajectory and observation posts he could dominate the entire railway territory and 'see into the stomach' of our defences up to the Volga and Hill 102. Accordingly this bridge region not only attracted heavy fire, but also almost daily Russian incursions. They could not make a tank attack. The toppled steel masts littering the railway and the Stuka bomb craters up to eight metres deep made the area impassable for vehicular traffic. On the other hand it was a good place for infantry to hide, infiltrate unseen the world of rubble and make their way from cover to cover.

Our MGs, called 'Hitler-saws' and 'electric rifles' by the Russians, had a lot to do. Especially the two flanking MGs, which were under good cover at the bridge pillars and were the priority of the Russian assault troops. I 'shouted' in vain almost daily for mines to protect our positions. One night the Russians brought a light tank to the burnt-out ruins of the main signal box which our sentries kept under permanent observation, probably an SU-76. Should our MGs fire on it? We pushed our 20mm anti-tank gun from its hiding place directly into the shadow of the dazzling bridge lamps and waited for first light. Then we fired tracer. I had appointed myself loader, and on firing the first round the recoil of the gun threw me backwards into the sand between the tracks. After a few more rounds we ceased fire and pushed the gun back under cover not a moment too soon for the mortar salvoes were on their way. After the smoke from the mortars had cleared to reveal once more the signal box and the tank, we saw that nothing had changed there. Over the next few days the tank remained where it was and never fired. Had our gun been successful? Only the usual high-angled Russian fire, and the flat trajectory fire of rifles and MGs continued to harass us incessantly.

Next day Corporal Franz Rechberger, regimental runner, brought us a weapon we had never seen before. Now we had an anti-tank rifle with an unusually thick and long barrel for the heavy 7.65mm hard-steel bullets. The rifle was fired standing up. For this purpose it was provided with a long bipod to support the business end. When firing it, a second man had to support the shoulders of the shooter against the recoil. I fired it myself a couple of times against tanks without any observed effects – except on my bruised shoulder.

One evening I received a telephoned order from Regiment: 'Goblirsch is to bring one of our female spies with an important mission to within shouting distance of the Russian positions!' I reported my doubts. Our deadly enemies lying only a few metres away could not be trusted under any circumstances! They replied, 'Order from the Army!' And: 'Goblirsch is personally responsible to me for it!'

'Blindfold her?'

'No!'

The next night, I would have to fetch the lady from the same spot in No Man's Land between the fronts where I had left her. Earlier than expected I was called to the battle post. The enemy mortars opened up so furiously that I had to take cover repeatedly in the shallow ditch near the rails before I reached the 'Battalion Pipe'. Meanwhile one had learned to distinguish where the Russians were aiming from the different sounds made when they fired. We old hands therefore knew very reliably if we were the target or some neighbouring company was. Senior visitors and reinforcements had not yet developed this ability and so threw themselves unnecessarily into the ditch.

The sentry outside reported from a pipe covered over with tent canvas and a splinter protection: 'Take care, Herr Leutnant, inside it stinks like a French brothel!' Surely he could not mean the well-known faecal smell? I entered the Pipe and reported myself to the commanding officer. A beautiful young lady, bejewelled, perfumed and dressed in white furs was seated in the miserable light of the carbide lamps.

When it grew dark I set off with the lady. I let her go ahead of me at the water ditch near the rails and caught myself playing with the trigger of my drawn pistol. This caused me to give lively consideration as to whether I should play along with this deadly game or at the next sound of fighting I heard . . . Nobody could blame me for doing that, I thought. Then I drove such 'evil' thoughts from my head. We had reached my own command post: the company troop leader reported from the darkness of his underground billet in a voice which startled the lady: 'Nothing to report!' So now she not only knew the battalion battle post, but also my command post, easy to recognize by the locomotive.

Climbing across mortar and bomb craters, we reached 'shouting distance' as ordered. The lady crouched down in a bomb crater beside some rotting Russians, and I worked my way back. It struck me that the Russians had apparently introduced a temporary ceasefire. Was the lady playing a double game and betraying our positions and command posts to the Russians? Trusting German soldiers! Would the operation cost us our blood? Yes, as feared the whole thing was repeated the next day. The barrages they fired at our command posts were heavier than ever before. The entrance to the Pipe was blocked by rubble created by heavy artillery fire: a telephone pole, probably the aiming point, was felled. But that was not all!

The following night I spared myself fetching the female agent in order not to gamble my life by entering a trap. With our telescopic sights we were unable to see a fur-clad lady in No-Man's Land in the harsh light of the lamps. The heaviest attack on our bridge position occurred in the early hours of the next day before sunrise, a heavy bombardment by weapons of all calibres. Already in the night several companies had infiltrated themselves before our trenches without our poor and too widely-dispersed artillery being able to do anything about it.

As if at a stroke the penetrating, previously pitiful sounding 'Urrah!' was coming nearer. Our four MGs fired for so long that the barrels glowed. The Russians definitely had many dead and wounded, but nevertheless the grey horde was closer. My telephone lines to Battalion and Regiment were shot apart. Our radio reception was so weak that we could hardly hear it above the almost deafening noise of battle.

I loaded my flare pistol with a red star-shell round to request a barrage of fire from the divisional artillery. At that moment standing near my locomotive I saw in the light of battle a number of Russians crying 'Urrah!' and running from under the bridge towards the locomotive, firing long bursts from their machine-pistols. Their commander, who was running ahead of the mob, fired a burst at me. I felt only a heavy blow at my hip, stumbled to one side, which probably saved me from being hit by the next burst, and also gave me a fraction of a second to fire the star-shell at him rather than into the heavens. It hit him in the stomach before he had a chance to aim at me again. He collapsed. His troop now took cover against our rifle fire and once behind the bridge supports they ceased all activity. As I discovered later, a bullet had smashed my Voigtländer camera which I carried throughout the whole war in the left pocket of my blouse.

An old truism states: if the leader is taken out, the group's attack breaks up. In my position some of the enemy dead and wounded lay around: about twenty had broken through, but the others had apparently not followed them. The two MGs at the bridge supports had stopped firing. I had sent off my reserve group to deal with them.

I sent a runner to report the situation to the Battalion commander and requested assistance. The flanking fire from Geisberg's company on my left and Kühnfels on my right had been well aimed at the Russians in the mortar craters at the Tennis Racquet. Meanwhile our artillery had resumed firing, but far too long. We had no artillery spotter post (VB). Finally the battalion commander ordered Lieutenant Kühnfels to send out his reserve group for a counter-attack from my position. I waited in the prepared position to the rear which the Russians had not attacked so far. It was an eternity until the group leader slithered up with his couple of pioneers.

While this was going on, Leading Rifleman Kastner had come with a box of primed hand grenades. He had reached the top of the bridge, free of enemy due to the rifle fire of our brave neighbours, by crawling and creeping over the embankment to get behind the Russians who had broken through. It had been agreed with him that he should remain concealed on the bridge until the beginning of our planned counter-attack, and then drop hand grenades singly on the Russians from above. I saw his hand signal on the bridge, and those of us not wounded and still mobile sprang out from cover with me, running forward, shooting and shouting 'Hurrah', aping them. The Russians were going to fight at first, but soon dispersed in panic when they saw the hand grenades exploding behind them, dropped incessantly from the bridge by the unnoticed Kastner, as if it were a hand grenade barrage. Apparently they were still leaderless and therefore clueless.

The majority of them fled away from us and into Kastner's hand grenades. Whoever got through presumably ran into the machine-pistols of the political commissars. Some discarded their weapons and defected to us. That brought the entire attack to a standstill, for the following groups of the Russian assault troops could not hold out where they were in front of our positions and leapt back from cover to cover into the ruins of the metal works. From the prisoners we learned later that all Red Army personnel, even those wounded, who fled, were shot on the spot by their own soldiers when they returned. Now there stood five young, impressive Mongolian Red Army soldiers who had surrendered, lined up near my locomotive. From their badges they could be recognized as officer candidates, thus elite men. They were guarded by my runner from cover: we asked for them to be collected. They did not want to be transported out because the political commissars had warned them that the Germans first tortured all prisoners before shooting them – just as was the usual Red Army practice.

After the Russian attack was beaten off I went quickly through our position to check on events in general there. All four machine gunners at the bridge, so it would seem, had been bayonetted to death in close combat. Red Army soldiers lay in front of their position, under the bridge there lay other Mongolians, killed by Kastner's hand grenades. Our own wounded had probably been dragged away by the Russians or killed.

One of our machine-gunners, Hans Rothe/Rotte gave a sign of life with a hand. I brought him out of the destroyed nest into the splinter protection of the bridge. He had lost a lot of blood, I unbuckled his steel helmet, laid his head, streaming with blood, on my lower arm and shouted for stretcher bearers. The soldier gasped softly for water. I held my field flask with tea to his mouth, but could not see if he drank any. Then he mumbled his last words: 'Write mother . . . Jesus . . . mother . . . Jesus!' I closed his eyelids. We had lost five dead and had wounded who would all have to be transported back under fire with the help of the prisoners.

The anger of the Russian leader[8] over the failed assault was quickly expressed in a violent 'mortar blessing'. We heard great numbers of them being fired. I crept into my command post under the locomotive and shouted to the prisoners, standing upright waiting for the transport to fetch them, to take cover in the trench. They shook their heads and remained upright in protest until the salvoes rained down. None of them survived. Was it worse than this on their side? Would the Soviet commissars have acted the same?

After the restoration of the telephone lines I complained at Regiment about the inadequate and inaccurate divisional artillery support. In the afternoon Lieutenant Maul[9] brought me some replacements which I shared out amongst the squads. Apart from that he wanted to understand the events of the previous day and the morning.

I told him about the 'lady' and fighting off the assault. Then we observed together through the splinter holes in a railway wagon standing on the adjacent track just before the north bridge. As a result, being a former artillery man and spotter, the artillery commander offered me the job of relief-VB, for he had nobody else who could direct fire. I accepted and at once, in the presence of the astonished lieutenant, gave my first orders, to fire a ranging shell directly in front of our position. The result was a disappointing truth: the first round whistled over and we could hardly hear the explosion, never mind see it. Then I had two detonators loaded for a very visible target, easily seen above the signal box, therefore the range this time was not in doubt! The next

---

8. As became known during a meeting in 1996 at Andorf, this was the former Major and later Colonel Alexander Smirnov. From their mutual enmity there developed later a close friendship. (Note from Josef Goblirsch.)

9. Lieutenant Helmut Maul (b. 18 March 1913) spent his retirement at Plön/Holstein and died there in the autumn of 2010.

impact on the same co-ordinates surprised us by landing immediately before our bridge. I checked the details over with the howitzers and discovered that the barrel linings had been worn out and for some time the guns had been firing 'like a cow's tail'. Dismayed, the lieutenant promised to 'sound out' the Luftwaffe as soon as he reached the regimental battle post. Before he left he suggested recommending Leading Rifleman Kastner, who already held the Assault Badge, the Close Combat Clasp and the Iron Cross First and Second Class, for the Knight's Cross. He had been the decisive participant in the defence of the regiment by recapturing the important corner column.[10]

A few days later the Luftwaffe liaison officer at Division came to me over the radio: 'You are getting twice fifty birds. Give the map square!' I: 'Thank you, map square 60!'

'I repeat . . . remain constantly by your radio, inform me of the exact fall of the first bombs . . . we will report you the time they are coming!'

After about an hour – our positions had just come under artillery fire again – the Luftwaffe reported the ETA as 1130 hrs. The first flight of Stukas arrived. The Russian AA on the Volga island fired at them as if crazed: splinters rained down on our position. Right overhead the first aircraft tipped into their nose-dive. It seemed to us that they were dropping directly towards us, sirens screaming, and we ducked our heads under cover. A few metres above us one after another the machines released four bombs from beneath their wings before turning away into a steep climb. The bombs rustled above us and away directly into the Russian positions in the Lasur factory. At once I radioed the outstanding bomb-aiming.

After another turn came the next approach and dive of the Stukas. This time large HE bombs were released from the fuselage of the aircraft. With a whistle they fell upon the target, which disappeared in the smoke of the explosions. The Russian AA continued to rage from all barrels. Their spinsters whirred into the ground and tinkled on the metal surfaces of the wrecked trains. We were enveloped by thick clouds of smoke. Our eyes burned. It grew dark. The bomb-bursts reverberated through the air and almost deafened us. After a short pause we heard the approach of twin-engined Ju 88s with an ever heavier bombload, but the smoke was so thick we could not see them.

The wind was northerly, and it drove the cloud of smoke over us. We imagined that the targets would no longer be visible to the aircraft and the

10. Together with Lieutenant Kühnfels he received the Knight's Cross at Stalingrad a few days before he fell there (note from Josef Goblirsch).

bombs would simply be dropped into the smoke, below which we now found ourselves. We were almost panic-stricken, because we thought the bomb explosions were coming nearer. Occasionally we saw red flashes through the dense smoke. I shouted into the radio: 'They are bombing too short!' The noise of the explosions was so loud that my cry went unheard, Then, finally, they came again. 'We are finished. No aircraft lost. A soldiers' luck to you, Herr Leutnant. Out!'

Over the next few days their infantry did not attack. Now and again their artillery and Stalin-organs raked us. A shell hit my locomotive. The splinters pierced the oil tank. Long thin threads of oil ran down from above and reached my personal trench. Before I had time to think what to do about it I was standing in a black pool. My uniform was soon drenched and my unshaven face black before I managed to get clear of this black spillage. Taking my odds and ends I went to the personal trench of my runner who was by no means pleased to see me. Dust was being whipped up constantly by explosion and wind and stuck to the oil film on my skin and uniform. It was an awful job trying to wipe it off. We had enough rags, though; strips of uniform torn from Russian corpses were suitable when the need arose, but we were short of water for it.

Early one morning behind our positions and towards the battalion battle post there were violent fireworks from their infantry. We could not mistake the slow hammering of the Russian machine-pistols and the faster reply of ours. Then came the detonations of hand grenades. What was this all about? The Russians had used the open sewage piping at the Volga to infiltrate behind our positions, and had crept out at the railway station end unobserved, pushing up the manhole covers. They had grouped up around our command posts and, where they could, around those of our Battalion, all these presumably having been betrayed to them by the 'Lady'. The raid was probably wiped out by the battalion reserve. In any case I heard nothing more of it. This kind of thing was an almost daily event in Stalingrad.

One night there was a surprise: artillery shells hit our position but with a very dull kind of explosion we had never heard before. So what was this? I crept out from under cover and saw before and behind me flashing fountains of sparks spreading out after each impact. The rain of sparks gave off a white, flashing mist. Phosphorous! Before I could shout 'Gas masks on, shout it through!' I had breathed deeply and was now fighting for breath. I crept back under cover and put the gas mask over my bearded face: naturally without full facial contact it was not gas proof.

Soon a soldier came running down the embankment towards my trench shouting in panic. Phosphorescent patches clung to his whole body and steel helmet. Groaning, he reached out to me from beneath the locomotive his flashing hands, with which he had probably tried to wipe off the phosphorous spray from his uniform. Before I could put his gas mask on him, his cries died down. He suffered a fit of the shivers and fell unconscious. A medical orderly dragged him under cover, where he died a few hours later without having regained consciousness. Because of the heavy bombardment we could not transport him out in time. These facts were kept from his parents.

Later the same morning after the raid with white phosphorous everybody was complaining of chest pains and burning eyes after having breathed in the mist; many were coughing. We vomited mucus and our faeces was watery and whitish-grey. But we had grown accustomed to not paying much heed to such 'trifles': even our increasing loss of strength we put down as normal for our bodies had been weakened substantially for weeks due to the shortage of food.

Many soldiers grew sick suddenly with jaundice, white diarrhoea and a high fever. Many began to hallucinate, fell unconscious and had to be transported out by night. Phosphorous poisoning was not recognized at the time as the cause of the illness and we blamed the deficient, often rotten food, rancid butter and contaminated water. The overworked doctors, most of them surgeons, also failed to identify my pains and sparkling diarrhoea as poisoning during my brief consultations with them.[11]

By 16 October 1942 it was over for me: three shell splinters, two in the head and one in the lower left arm, but not too serious: I hardly needed a plaster. Perhaps I might have held out a few more days and nights in my position, even with shivering fits and fever, if I had not felt the urge for a wash and shave. Therefore I handed over the company to my company troop leader – just for a couple of days, as I thought. When I reported to the Battalion commanding officer in the sewage pipe he sent me off to the main railway station with a 'Get well and come back soon!'

On the wide road to the railway station I was passing a 20mm twin AA gun when an Il 2 tipped down out of the sun to attack it. On the town square the shells of the latter fell in my vicinity. Between two rails of the tramway not on the roadway but only in a substructure I found cover. I was fortunate: between the rails no splinter found me. The Il 2 kept diving and the guns

11. In all the literature ever written about Stalingrad, by 1999 I had as yet never seen anything about this poison gas attack at the metal works (note from Josef Goblirsch).

kept firing: the aircraft lost a wing. Hardly a second later the flak and the aircraft disappeared in a fireball. The shot-off wing fluttered down to the road alone, swaying oddly. I walked on and in Red Square came across a fire-gutted Russian tank. In the regimental command post, in a deeply incised gully, I found only the staff surgeon. He gave me a cursory examination and an injection before sending me, wrapped in blankets, to the nearest lorry for the Army dressing station at Gumrak. Diagnosis: acute inflammation of the liver, suspected inflammation of the heart muscle. On the way I saw Lieutenant Maul on a motorcycle. We waved to each other briefly across the dusty road, which was under fire.[12]

Gumrak was a picture of horror: mountains of amputated limbs, all covered with a layer of calcium chloride: by day air attacks by fighter bombers, by night the 'duty NCO' came with bombs; rats attacking the wounded, recently operated upon: overworked operating surgeons: men wounded in the stomach region, laid out on the barrack floor, 'sorted out' and kept quiet with morphine. I was so apathetic that I no longer took it all in. My filthy splinter wounds were attended to and dressed. I had to take a lot of Prontosil and tea. Every couple of minutes I went feverishly to the ice-cold privy: I passed milky water. Often, especially at night, I failed to get there in time. My liver problem was worsening: my chest and upper torso hurt.

Our Junkers ambulance aircraft landed at and took off from the steppe runway. By night the Russians bombed Gumrak from a great height without doing much damage. On 23 October 1942 an overloaded Ju 52 full of wounded,[13] marked with the Red Cross as an ambulance aircraft, took off from Gumrak with difficulty. It passed above the Don at low level vibrating heavily. Wounded men froze in the rattling corrugated-steel box, moaning and groaning incessantly. Over the steppe we were surprised by three Il 2s which fired at the fuselage. We had no gunner aboard. The pilot shouted into the loading room for a trained MG-gunner. I surged over the bodies of the wounded to the gunner's position and climbed trembling into the icy air stream. A cartridge belt was already there, and I loaded it with numb fingers. The Il 2s came up firing to within a few metres of the tailplane. My tracer went past them. Our ambulance plane with the Red Cross markings was hit again and now there were double-wounded aboard.

---

12. I did not anticipate then that I would take over from him after 13 years at Hammelburg the NCO's Training Company of the Infantry School (note from Josef Goblirsch).
13. The author of this account was aboard.

The pilot dropped the machine low over the steppe, covered with hoar frost or snow and some recently shot down Ju 52s, mostly burnt-out. Now I was ready to shoot. The fighter-bombers came quickly nearer from astern. I saw the MGs of the leading machine flash and fired with tracer at the centre of the target. It turned unimpressed close above my head. I gave the second machine a long burst before it could open up. Without firing it ascended steeply; my tracer had was accurate, ricochets sprayed off its armoured underside. Had I hit him? The third machine turned away prematurely without having attacked.

The fuss all died down and I, almost frozen into a block of ice, climbed back into the aircraft. I heard the pilot's shout of praise before I collapsed back in apathy. Thus we could finally touch down at Taganrog on the Black Sea, the wounded to be attended to and loaded into a hospital train standing ready. I still had shivering fits, diarrhoea and a bad pain in the upper torso. The medical treatment was excellent, the medical orderlies brisk and attentive. Unfortunately I vomited at every attempt to eat and slept through almost the whole journey.

We crossed the new Dnieper bridge to Kiev and then Cracow. The whole train went into the disinfestation station. Everything had been prepared down to the last detail: remove all clothing and personal things and leave the train. Medical orderlies helped with personal care, haircut, shave, steam bath and shower. On the other side of the station was another hospital train. Before we got in and climbed into our drop-beds, each man received back his things disinfested and a new night shirt. Around the neck of each man they hung a plate bearing the rank, name, diagnosis, date of delousing (3 November 1942), military hospital, signed Dr., signature, junior surgeon, duty doctor. I was put in the leading coach in the lower tier near a 'shot in the head' case with only two adhesive plasters. He liked to tell jokes. The bullet had entered between his eye and nose and exited through the back of his head. By a million-to-one chance he had survived what should have been absolutely fatal!

At Breslau, Leipzig, Dresden, Würzburg and Augsburg the train 'lost' one or two wagons. The last remaining wagon in which I lay was unloaded as one of the walking-wounded. On 6 November an ambulance took us to the snowy mountain world, to the attractive military hospital village of Hohen-schwangau, where in the Jäger-house there was already a plate with my name and malady: 'Lieutenant Goblirsch, Jaundice.' The attractive nurses were very attentive. A few days ago Stalingrad and Gumrak, now alpine lakes and Hohenschwangau. I had to deal with that first of all!

After his recovery Josef Goblirsch served with the newly reconstituted 100th Jäger Division in the Balkans and East Prussia, and was sent home in 1945. After a short period as a prisoner of the Americans and Czech forced labour, from which he escaped into Bavaria, he studied paediatrics at Würzburg. He entered the Bundeswehr in 1956, was pensioned off in 1980 in the rank of Colonel. Until 1987 he was Director of the European Institute for Security Questions in Brussels. Authored numerous military studies and publications. He lives today in an old people's home at Bad Boklet.

11. DIETRICH GOLDBECK:

The Last Days of the 160th Anti-tank Abteilung[1]

Dietrich Goldbeck (b. Gumbinnen/East Prussia, 15 April 1914) studied civil engineering at Hanover and Danzig and passed the State examinations in 1939. As a national service conscript he served in the Wehrmacht, first with an anti-tank unit at Goldap, then with the anti-tank Abteilung of the 60th Motorized Infantry Division. [Last section moved to end of account. Tr]

Between 19 and 21 November 1942 when the Russians broke through the north-east corner of the great bend in the Don river, and south of the Stalingrad suburbs of Beketovka and Krasnoarmeysk to encircle Sixth Army, the 160th Anti-tank Abteilung was ordered as follows: No. 1 Company, led by Lieutenant Mähl, had firing positions under cover for its 5cm guns in a strongpoint of at least two guns. These covered the whole breadth of the divisional sector in the Northern Boundary position north of the railway line which ran from Gumrak, in the bend to the east, to the tractor works.

Nos 2 and 3 Companies under Lieutenants Hackert and Creutzburg[2] with 7.62cm self-propelled anti-tank guns were some way to the rear in concealed positions, some of which were heated gun bunkers, ready to move out when the warning was given. The Abteilung and Company command posts were located in a gully about two kilometres south of the railway line near the divisional battle post.

There was quiet in the Division's entire sector: the ground was frozen. Everywhere work was proceeding on the building of winter positions and bunkers. An advance party had already gone to prepare quarters in the resting area on the Donets, for we expected daily the onset of winter. Since October according to a major plan worked out at Division, many men of the Abteilung

---

1. Copy of a report made in 1948: typed text from the unpublished history of the 60th Motorized Infantry Division.
2. Lieutenant Karl Wilhelm Creutzburg (b. Eisenach, 14 March 1914, d. Arsk military hospital for prisoners of war, 26 April 1943).

were constantly being sent on home leave: a notable improvement in morale had occurred, for most had been twenty months or more without leave unless they had arrived with the recent reinforcements. Many soldiers had been hit by the jaundice epidemic which had spread over the whole area from September – which had resulted in my being confined to bed for almost all of October – and were now to be found in military hospitals to the rear. Thus the personnel of the Abteilung went into the final battle much reduced in numbers. The strength must have been between at most 280 to 300 men, perhaps less.

I took part personally in the reconnaissance of the readiness area for the break-out from the Pocket in mid-December and saw that Sixth Army still had considerable panzer numbers available, some of them with experimental 12.5cm and 10.8cm guns – self-propelled naval guns. During this entire period in our sector it had been really quiet – in contrast to the ever-active western sector, where the Russians made frequent tank attacks – and we had kept at improving our winter quarters. Moreover in our rearward area the OT organization had been attempting to lay down new lines of trenches. We had radio contact to elements of the Division amassed outside the Pocket at the great Don bend and at Stalino, these being returners from leave and con-valescents in the rest area advanced parties. Our hopes were not aimed towards the New Year, for nobody conceived an unhappy end to the encirclement. Everywhere preparations were being made for Christmas and, as far as it went, provisions in the supply depots were being readied so that over the festive period nobody would go unsatisfied.

The Abteilung commanding officer, Major Reimann, visited all gun positions in the forward lines on 24 December to distribute cigarettes, chocolate and some brandy before appearing that evening for the happy little Christmas celebration thrown for the command post and communications staffs. For the last time we were carefree, merry and full of hope in thoughts of our loved ones at home, crammed around the glittering little Christmas tree in our bunker. Some letters from home and the chimes of the bell from the German cathedral over the loudspeakers made us forget the bitter reality.

Amazing at this time was the behaviour of the 'Hiwis'[3] who were used as

---

3. Abbreviation for 'Hilfswillige', i.e. Soviet PoWs who had declared their willingness to serve in the Wehrmacht, mostly as drivers, stretcher bearers, cleaners, etc. At first their numbers were not supposed to exceed 10 per cent of the unit's fighting troops, but often it went as high as 30 per cent or more. By the end of the war there were between one and two million Soviet citizens serving on the German side as Hiwis or soldiers.

an auxiliary workforce at Abteilung. Principally in the support services, but also in the unit command posts, chopping wood, building earth bunkers, doing laundry and as vehicle mechanics. They lived in their own bunkers. They were fully in the picture about the encirclement, already a month old, but nevertheless they showed no inclination to rebel despite the lack of inducement on our part, and did their work now as before with the poor rations provided. They were also certain that it was much better to be up with the fighting troops than in the prisoner assembly areas, and their worst fear was the threat of release. Later, in January, there were defectors to our sector, encouraged by shouters. According to the prisoners we took in that manner word had got round along the entire northern front and they were not worried about the 30-kilometre trek to get here. On Christmas Eve when I made a short explanation to the Hiwis at the Abteilung command post about the meaning of Christmas and distributed a small quantity of cigarettes and captured Machorka, they were visibly shocked, and one of them expressed his feelings in a few words of thanks in which he said they knew very well that things were not going well for us, because we were encircled; they were, however, determined to remain with us, even if we went down to defeat! Then they invited me into their tiny bunker for a smoke and to listen to some of their songs.

On Christmas night the Russians made a violent attack on the right side of the divisional sector and made a sizeable breakthrough which could only be patched up with the utmost effort and painful losses. The pressure persisted over the next few days, and at the year's end some small, but in the expanse of the steppe, important hills had to be abandoned. Here our Abteilung suffered losses in men and materials. As we only had left some provisional and unprotected trenches, frostbite further reduced our deteriorating strength. All the same, the situation with us was excellent compared to our divisions on the southern and western fronts, who had been in constant flux since the encirclement began and therefore had had almost no opportunity to dig trenches. These divisions were exposed to the increasing cold of winter and the icy snow storms which swept the steppe. At this time there was lively activity caused by the change in anti-tank gun distributions amongst the various divisions to bolster our defences, but this also caused the provisions situation to become more critical.

On 10 January the Russians began their major offensive to pierce the Pocket at several places after Sixth Army had declined to surrender. In bitter fighting attended by heavy losses our sector held out at first: but eventually, around 15

January, even we had to give up our still-good trenches, especially those in the western part of the divisional sector, in which until then we had withstood the winter well. This was the result of the western front pulling back as far as the railway line at Gumrak after the loss of the airfield at Pitomnik.

Because of losses amongst personnel our No 3 Company was disbanded and its men distributed amongst the other two companies. The former commander, Lieutenant Creutzberg, was detailed to assist the rear services in the ever more difficult task of feeding the Abteilung. The acting CSM, Sergeant Wohlfahrt, maintained the company's personal papers at Abteilung HQ. Despite the terrible situation in which Sixth Army found itself in the narrow area it held, we still believed we could hold out by fighting until Spring! Much material had to be left where it was and destroyed while the casualties became ever harder to bear.

Astounding fighting spirit prevailed amongst all units, who gave everything they had to hold the existing fronts of the Pocket. An airfield at the western suburbs of the city guaranteed us contact with our supply base at Stalino; the wounded continued to be flown out in their thousands. By radio connection to our collection centres at the Donets, we heard from time to time from our leave-takers and convalescents, formed up by Abteilung officers such as Lieutenants Köppen and Ellerbrock, later also Lieutenant König, equipped with new guns for the defence of the great Don bend and mainly attached to 6th Panzer Division. The fighting men were not informed of the overall situation on the southern front and the strategic hopelessness of an imminent relief of Sixth Army: to the very end the idea was spread that the panzer spearhead of the relieving army had crossed the Don at Kalatch and was involved in heavy fighting with the Russians on the western side of the Pocket.

After we had set up the Abteilung command post temporarily in the Tatar Wall east of Gumrak on 15 January, where we stayed several days, the commanding officer told me, returning depressed from a commanders' conference, that we should abandon all hope. There was at least 300 kilometres separating us from the German South Front, and the retreat had not stopped yet, even the Caucasus was threatened with being cut off! I refused to believe it and tried to reassure him.

From that moment on there was increasingly a certain apathy to be observed amongst the senior commanders, although the men, despite un-believable conditions, were still able to fight and in the daily struggles achieved considerable defensive successes. We were unable to house all the wounded, however, while stragglers and apparent deserters loitered aimlessly in the hinterland. A battle ensued when our rearward services west of the Gumrak railway line were not given sufficient notice to pull out. While the withdrawal was prepared with the greatest haste, Lieutenant Flieger, the provisions officer, together with all the men without a specific job at that moment – vehicle mechanics, armourers' assistants – held up the advancing Russian infantry groups at the entrance to the supplies' gully and saved the most important ammunition, fuel and provisions stocks for the Abteilung's last days. For that achievement he was awarded the Iron Cross Second Class on 1 February: a large number of our rearward soldiers and tradesmen who had never previously been caught up in any real fighting, were also decorated for their courage and resolve.

The last, bitter period, the final struggle at the western end of the northern suburb of Barrikady, began. In some two days of rearguard actions, still with a few guns and vehicles, we reached a gully west of Barrikady. Here, bunkers hacked out earlier by some of the supply units formed the backbone of our quickly installed positions for the snows, a few hundred metres west of the bushy slope. By when we moved in, the Stalingrad Pocket was already split into three parts. We were in the northern one, commanded by General Strecker,[4] the commanding general of XI Panzer Corps. Despite all the fearsome battle scenes of these days, in which the wounded and those exhausted by hunger lost contact with their units, and froze in their thousands at the roadside, in the snowy deserts and in abandoned trenches and bunkers, then died or fell into the hands of the enemy, which usually meant the same thing – despite the hopelessness of our situation becoming ever clearer to every individual soldier – we still kept fighting relentlessly. There was hardly anyone now who was not wounded or did not have frostbite. When the Russians attacked, the last man able to fight lay behind his wall of snow and fired with a valour born of despair. The seriously wounded were taken to a large bunker a few hundred metres to the rear, from where the Abteilung commanding officer led the final operations. Nearby were the command posts of the 92nd Motorized Infantry Regiment and the Division. The last vehicles still available to us in working order were quickly destroyed from the air. Our own aircraft

---

4. General Karl Strecker (b. Radmannsdorf, 20 September 1884, d. Riezlern/Austria, 10 April 1973) was an officer in the General Staff in the Great War. On 1 June 1942 he became commanding general, XI Army Corps, with which he entered Russian captivity on 2 February 1943 from the northern Pocket, and was not released until 1955. He was decorated with the Knight's Cross.

were now rarer since the last airfield had been captured. Only at night did the transport aircraft drone over, dropping their loads over our positions, but often to the enemy, and on a marked-out dropping zone at the tractor works.

During these last days it was almost impossible to move about in the open in daylight. The Russian encirclement was now so tight that they could fire at every individual. We had to use the last of the infantry ammunition very sparingly: there was only a heavy gun here and there, or we had no ammunition for one. At night our infantry elements in the gully were brought the essentials in food and ammunition by hand-drawn sledge.

On 30 January there was a terrible bombardment and shelling of our trenches. We heard through the loudspeaker of our Wehrmacht receiver in our bunker that the southern and central pockets had surrendered. Then they played us the *Song of the Nibelungen* to mark our final battle. I still was unable to take it in. Until then we had given all those who fell in our sector a burial, if a makeshift one: now all that stopped. 7.62cm anti-tank shells exploded one after another on the roof of our bunker, which fortunately was strong enough to take it. We could no longer help our wounded. We began to destroy all our papers between them. The last field kitchen was shot to hell: the food for the men in the gully was cooked in instalments. On 1 February the Russians attacked twice after the heaviest preparatory fire and aerial bombing. We warded off the attack with the last of our strength, although several KV-1 tanks were able to manoeuvre unseen between our snow-covered positions. As we saw next morning, when we were led off into captivity through these lines, the Russians had suffered huge losses, the snow was littered with their corpses.

We were done for. During the night Division ordered all units to destroy their weapons and offer no resistance to the expected Russian attack next morning. In this situation nothing remained for us as honourable soldiers but to accept captivity; therefore any action taken out of fear of an uncertain future would be misguided. Strangely the night passed quietly. A distant MG chattered only occasionally. We shared out the remains of our supplies, cooked all night, destroyed weapons and materials and prepared ourselves for captivity as best we thought we should. Shortly before daybreak our colleagues from the forward trenches joined us so as to share the end together. All night they played that death song over the loudspeakers.

Towards six in the morning – it was already fairly light – the Russians came cautiously in files of infantry over the terrain towards us; there was no shooting. At the 92nd's bunker a white cloth fluttered. After a short while infantry carrying machine-pistols and wearing bright white snow smocks appeared at our bunker. Listening to their jarring demands that we should all come out and line up outside, I wrecked our radio receiver with the clawed hatchet and was then one of the last to leave the bunker. Outside they were all lined up – about seventy men, many with serious wounds and frostbite, awaiting in silence the order to march off. The Abteilung commanding officer was able to make a final salute to all in parting. Thus on 2 February 1943 ended the struggle of our anti-tank unit at Stalingrad.

After his release from Soviet captivity in June 1948, Dietrich Goldbeck worked in his grandfather's building joinery firm in Bielefeld, becoming its proprietor in 1982. He was decorated with the Federal Service Cross and lives in retirement in Bielefeld.

12. GOTTFRIED GREVE:

The End in the Northern Pocket[1]

Gottfried Greve (b. Bochum, 12 January 1915) studied theology at Breslau, Leipzig and Erlangen. This was interrupted by his conscription into the Wehrmacht at Stettin, and he terminated his studies in 1951 with the 2nd examination. At Stalingrad he was attached to the 194th Signals Abteilung in the 94th Infantry Division with which he had previously served during the campaign in France.

At the end of October 1942 I was on three weeks' home leave. On the final day of it, 9 November, I heard the Führer utter these measured words in a speech: 'Wherever the German soldier stands, no power on earth can remove him!' Often enough, we bitterly recalled these words when later behind barbed wire in the Tatar steppe we looked towards the West with longing.

On the journey back to the front I began to think really seriously. What would the winter bring? In the first winter of the war in Russia I had escaped captivity by a hair's breadth. Now we were at the Volga, and the fighting was harder than ever. It had been a real consolation, that song 'In all my Days' which the dear, pious house mother had read me in parting after a short stop to see relatives on the return journey to the front. It has a stanza: 'If I am in the desert, I am with Christ, and Christ is my helper in danger: He can protect me in all places, as also here.'

I had to change trains at the great interchange station of Yassinovataya in the Donets basin. Because of the large number of men returning from, and departing for, leave we had to wait three or four days for the connection. On my own initiative I pushed my way into the already overflowing train for Stalingrad without the necessary stamp on my leave pass: as an officer I knew that probably nobody would bother about it. As if that were not enough, I left the train on the Don steppe and, to avoid a two-day train journey, made the last leg aboard an ambulance aircraft for the front, driven by the urgency of

---

1. The Editor received this report in printed form but without any indication of its provenance.

rejoining my people as quickly as possible. Thus I arrived just in time to be encircled with the entire Sixth Army! Had I kept to my orders and waited at Yassi, I would have remained outside the Pocket. Was this of my own choosing, or God's will that I should be inside it? At first I reproached myself bitterly over my precipitate eagerness, and only slowly did I calm down and hold to the realization, 'God sits in the regiment and directs everything well.'

As leader of the horse-drawn platoon of the division's signals Abteilung specially designed for mobile warfare, my people and I initially had a quiet time. We had been forced out of our winter quarters, built with much effort: the Russians occupied them now. So we had to excavate new bunkers in the open steppe. Despite all the worst expectations everybody approached the work willingly and with zeal. On the whole our people remained level-headed and devoted to duty even when the situation looked very desperate. The old and upright Leading Private[2] sent to the airfield to be flown out with a splinter in his skull came back to us voluntarily four days later.

The plan to break out was greeted joyfully everywhere. When everything was ready the Führer-order came through: 'Hold out, you are going to be pulled out from there.' With what excitement we followed the signals from the approaching relief army – alas! Sixty kilometres from the Pocket the advance ground to a halt. At Christmas it was clear: we had been written off! The Pocket was being gradually tightened. In signals we were always well informed about the situation. Soon shortages of the most important necessities began to appear: provisions, clothing, weapons, everything was lacking. The Luftwaffe, which we relied upon to keep us supplied, usually brought less than a tenth of what we needed. The cold became intolerable. Because we had enough horses, at first we felt no hunger: yes, we could supply our neighbouring units and the provisions office richly with horse flesh. I had been so proud of not losing a single horse of the 110 physical stock during our strenuous crossing of the steppe, with little water, which had brought me special praise. Now one horse after another found its way into the field kitchen. It was a pitiful sight, watching our loyal four-legged comrades, who had walked across France and had brought us so many thousand kilometres to the east, grow ever weaker because the only fodder we could offer them was the vermouth herb which grew everywhere. The small, nimble steppe ponies on the other hand would feed on mane and tail hairs if they were hungry.

2. Leading Private = a senior private with equivalent powers to a British lance-corporal but without NCO status.

Christmas came. For the first and only time in the Pocket mail arrived from home, the best possible present. More graphically than the memory can, a letter from the Pocket to my parents on 27 December illustrates how the Christian festival looked with us: 'Since we could not rely on receiving a Christmas package, we baked some "biscuits" from ground wheat. I had been saving an apple, which was then divided into three equal parts . . . From three until seven I went through the bunker, saying a few words here and there; some of the men needed a little comfort but in general they were very well balanced. I could also announce some promotions and decorations which pleased the recipients greatly, and I brought each man a letter from home . . . Despite the snowstorm the circuit brought me much pleasure. At 1900 hrs the festivities in the bunker began. Our small pine tree was adorned. I read to my two bunker colleagues the Christmas gospel and spoke some thought-provoking words. Then the three of us sang Christmas carols, better when louder, but full of joy and fervour. We spoke long of the Homeland, our relations and the near future. It was a rare happy mood all experienced, despite the primitive nature of our surroundings. Before the candle-lit tree I read something from August Winnig's[3] book *Die Hand Gottes* where he describes how he nearly died in a snowstorm in the Harz while on his way home. His description of the forces of nature and his spiritual grasp while it was happening fitted in well with our own situation . . . for our circumstances it was a wonderful Feast which we experienced by God's grace, for which we thank Him from the bottom of our hearts. Not care-less, but trusting in God, our Lord, who still resides in the regiment, I shall look ahead to what awaits us. The winter months which confront us will not be light, but if He, his power and help do not fail us, everything will turn out well. I cannot complain: how many comrades, especially with the brave infantry, have to get through differently. The thought of what they have to suffer shames me again and again . . .' This was the letter to my parents.

On New Year's Eve came the order to disband our worn-out division and incorporate the remnants into so-called 'alarm units', formations cobbled together colourfully from all branches of service, each man equipped with a rifle and a few bullets. Then there ensued a great leave-taking amongst the veterans, many of whom had shared joy and sorrow in the campaigns since

---

3. August Winnig (b. Blankenburg, 31 March 1878, d. Bad Nauheim, 3 November 1956) was a journalist, trade-unionist and author.

September 1939 and now each man, even the simplest, felt: this is the beginning of the end!

On an improvised course, I spent some days with fifteen younger officers of all branches of service re-training for the infantry. So hopeless was the overall situation, one now did as best one could what had to be done. At that time the great Russian offensive started up to the west of us: at the same time the weather got much colder. The Pitomnik airfield, in whose immediate vicinity we lay, fell into enemy hands. That brought the already completely inadequate supply of provisions almost to an end. Unexpectedly I was requested as a signaller by the remnants of a panzer regiment of the remaining battlegroup. My predecessor had not been able to put up with the tension any longer and turned his pistol on himself. Under such pressure, belief in the Führer and Reich could not provide comfort and stability. The closer the end came the more frequent were similar cases. Who would dare to set himself up as judge of those who did it?

My service with the new unit left me no peace day and night. Therefore I had no time to brood: that was a blessing. With only three men I had to maintain in service the telephone lines of our whole sector, which lay under permanent enemy fire. Often everything depended on their being in good working order. One could not think of sleep.

One night – I was alone searching for breaks in the line – on the long walk back I lay down in a snowstorm. Sleep, I must sleep! Two pioneers following my route helped me up, otherwise I should have died a comfortable death in the snow. Later I often used to think: 'If you had fallen asleep then!' One of my helpers fell with a splinter to the forehead: we could not dig his grave in the frozen ground. At that time the impossible was asked of each man. Nobody considered the senselessness of the whole business. Deserts of snow, a couple of ruins, and in snowed-up holes in the ground, men determined to fight to the last breath, starving and haggard, arms and legs frozen, yet would not yield their positions. Before them the numerically superior force, the Russians with their nerve-wracking 'Urrah!' What was being fought for? There was no salvation, the senses would not recognize it but something uncertain and terrible threatened. Thus one fought for the moment, without hope, but with a firm will.

The Russian offensive came to our northern sector, armour against armour, between them everything black from the barking guns. A firm will was no longer any use here: we dispersed and fled back into the rubble of the city. In the evening the small crowd which made up our battlegroup met up in a gully at the northern edge of the city. I found an old telephone line in the snow, connected it up to the field telephone we had saved and received the crushing news: Stalingrad South and Stalingrad Central had surrendered with General Paulus! The order of our Army Corps, which held out in the miniscule northern Pocket until 2 February, was unforgettable: 'Comrades, we have been ordered to fight to the last round. Ordered by God, men!' That was our death sentence.

The next few days in cellars and ruins were hell. We were plastered by guns of all calibres: aircraft bombed us without pause. We crouched down there and awaited the end. Numerous stragglers wandered around, grey-faced, their frozen limbs wrapped in bits of blanket, begging for bread. The daily ration on these last days was 35 grams of bread, 50 grams of tinned meat and 15 grams of wheat grain for soup. We melted snow for water, specks of rubble and splinters being picked out first in our tents. Near our cellar a senior surgeon, a glorious exception, had set up a dressing station where he worked tirelessly day and night. He even cared for my suppurating, stinking hand.

In those days I could only ask God for a merciful and quick death. I ran around outside courting danger, but although colleagues fell at my side, no splinter touched me. It was simply incomprehensible. Then I remembered the psalm which goes: 'If a thousand fall at your side...' Would I even come out of this alive?

On 30 January we heard from a Wehrmacht loudspeaker in our cellar our own obituary, great words of sacrifice and devotion to duty, etc. The effect varied, but was in every case distressing: here wild despair, there resignation, outbreaks of rage, heart-rending laughter, from many others a silent acceptance. That evening two comrades came to us who had fallen into Russian hands. They reported good treatment and plenty to eat. They had been sent back to us. We stared them as though they were some kind of strange animal. The Russians actually treated people humanely, or was it just a trick to obtain our trust? Many were raving with hunger, cold and fear.

On one of those days God gave me a sign that despite everything He had not abandoned me: I stumbled across a field of rubble and found a tin of preserves: it was still half full of lard. I thought of Elias and the ravens. This find meant more to me that just a chance to still my hunger.

On 1 February we kept asking ourselves, why don't the Russians come? We had no more ammunition – now the end had to come! A few tried to cross the Volga to the east. Many were shot dead for their trouble: the remainder joined us in the prison camp fourteen days later, half starved, with severe frostbite. And many saved the last bullet for themselves.

On the afternoon of 1 February a bomb hit our last vehicle, the QM's empty lorry. We dragged our acting QM-sergeant, a fresh young Leading Private with serious injuries, a damaged spine, under the rubble. We laid him on a plank bed in the cellar. He said nothing, his large eyes wandering ceaselessly from one person to the next. Next morning the Russians came – finally! I was the last to leave the cellar, stroked the forehead of the young QM and said some words in parting – for this Earth – but his eyes followed me.

In front of our cellar stood the Russians, machine-pistols at the ready. Without speaking we formed up in a column. Most of us had only the empty haversack and a blanket as baggage, but we felt heavily laden. We headed northwards into the endless snowy desert, a black snake of prisoners stretching to the horizon. Some German reconnaissance aircraft circled above us. That was the final salute from the Reich.

Gottfried Greve was released from Soviet captivity seriously ill in 1948. Until 1978 he was a pastor at Bad Schwartau. He died at Bad Bevensen on 8 July 1984.

13. WILHELM GROSSE:

Men from Supply in the Frontline[1]

Dr Wilhelm Grosse (b. Herne, 4 May 1898, d. Herne 7 November 1974) served in the First World War after obtaining his school-leaving certificate and from 1919 studied dentistry at Göttingen. He practised at Herne. In the rank of major at Stalingrad he commanded the rear services of 16th Panzer Division and its ammunition battalion. When he was flown out of the Pocket he brought with him Dr Kurt Reubner's 'Stalingrad Madonna'. Following his convalescence he resumed his dental practice in Gemünden and returned to Herne at the end of the war. He had his own practice there until 1965. He lived out his retirement in Münster.

The ammunition battalion with its ten convoys, amalgamated at the beginning of November into six large ammunition convoys for reasons of expediency, was between the Don and Volga on 21 November distributed over the Voroshilova camp at Karpova and the area about six kilometres to the west of it. The position was a poor one, but was improved over the course of the next few weeks. It consisted mainly of bunkers: only a very few miserably little houses were available to us.

Since mid-October a sixty-man advance party had been working on our winter quarters at Rubeshyn, a village about 90 kilometres south of Marinovka, where the Regimental Staff (Supply) was accommodated on the Don. Up to 21 November the Regiment had been involved without pause corresponding to the direct involvement of the Division in the fighting. From 25 August until when the Stalingrad encirclement was complete, a total of 6,000 tonnes of ammunition was delivered by our Battalion alone.

This achievement, which made superhuman demands on our drivers, cannot be overstated, particularly since the vehicles were subject to worsening wear and tear daily by reason of the enormous demands made on the lorries

---

1. Excerpt from a letter to Colonel Höfer dated 12 February 1943, published in *Unsere 16*, Issue 107, Year 28, January 1980. The report gives dates which are more or less correct based on Dr Grosse's diary notes.

and the almost complete lack of vital spare parts. The devotion to duty of the drivers was so immense that one is compelled to speak of it again and again. Day and night they brought up ammunition under the most difficult circumstances, and when they had time to rest they spent most of it on the upkeep of their lorries. Returning from each journey unwashed and unshaved they would report at once to the repairs unit to have repairs carried out. It was silent heroism, and one had only the greatest admiration for these drivers. From December the losses rose, for from then on the supply troops were increasingly drawn into the defence of 'Fortress Stalingrad'.

On the morning of 21 November we received the order to prepare for a 300-kilometre move. Nobody suspected to where. The greatest optimists said: 'Aha! 300 kilometres from here are the nearest marshalling yards – we are going to Germany!' People were too happy to believe in this, but unfortunately it was not true. The preparations for the moving out were never concluded. Orders followed hot on the heels of one another and soon news began to filter through that the Russians were attacking at various sectors of the front, mainly to the north of us, with substantial forces.

November 22nd was German Remembrance Day. Very early alarm readiness was ordered: every rearward unit had to prepare to defend itself. The organization of defence in our area, which bordered immediately on the military airfield, was taken over by the deputy commander of the squadron, Major Dr Kupfer.[2] I made available to him some 3.7cm anti-tank guns which happened to be with my workshop platoon. Meanwhile Russian tanks and infantry had appeared between Marinovka and Sowetzki. The fact was, the ring around us had closed, Russian forces advancing from the north and south had met up at Kalatch. I assembled at Voroshilova Camp all Battalion convoys not outside the encirclement at that time. We were about 200 strong with 80 lorries including those used for domestic purposes.

In the course of the afternoon the Battalion received from the Supply Regiment the following order: 'Munitions Battalion is to move to Peskovatka at 0500 hrs on 23 November, break through the enemy perimeter as early as possible.'

---

2. Dr Ernst Kupfer (b. Coburg, 2 July 1907, d. shot down, 6 November 1943). Before the war he studied law and entered the Reichswehr in 1928. 1934 Lieutenant, 1939 to the Luftwaffe; 1940 Major, Stuka pilot. 1941 seriously wounded. 1942 Major; 1943 Commodore, Stuka unit *Kupfer*. Lieutenant-Colonel, 1944 posthumously Colonel. Decorations: 1941 German Cross in gold, Knight's Cross. 1944 Oak Leaves and Swords (posthumously). Over 600 wartime missions.

At 2030 hrs that night a tank and MG attack was launched against our camp. It was pitch dark. Fire was coming from all directions so that nobody could make head nor tail of the confused situation. Here only one thing was decisive for us: not to expose our eighty lorries to destruction. Acting on the orders received from Regiment that afternoon I gave the order to pull out immediately for Peskovatka. Apart from one man wounded and a number of lorries riddled with bullets we arrived without harm at Peskovatka on the dot next morning. Accommodation was quickly-dug holes in the ground. It was cold and misty: during the day there occurred a major build-up of vehicles in and around the location. Russian aircraft machine-gunned us all day, some of our men being wounded. A large number of bombs were dropped.

Towards 0330 hrs on 26 November after a quiet night we were subjected to lively MG and artillery fire. The Russians had crossed the Don and were attacking Peskovatka, this being protected by forces from other divisions already dug-in. The Supply Regiment moved out on the early morning of 26 November to Reference Point 438, two kilometres north of Novo-Alekseyevski. After the confusion of the previous few days one now had the impression that good order and planning had regained hold of our movements.

In the course of the next few days the planned main frontline was set up. After long consideration the western boundary was set well back from the Don to keep us clear of the high river bank. We inhabited an anti-tank ditch whose most recent function had been as a latrine. We lay about four to five kilometres behind the western boundary where we were attacked daily by the Russians whose main interest was the boundary. Artillery, Stalin Organs and aircraft plastered us day and night. We moved our defensive positions several times and were able to increase our numbers there. The Supply Regiment around Point 438 had a fighting strength of 600 men, equipped with thirty MGs and two 3.7cm anti-tank guns. For the latter we had anti-tank HE shells. At 1000 hrs on 4 December we were taken under fire by a Russian tank which had penetrated the boundary. Just by chance a damaged panzer was being towed by a tractor about 100 metres from the Russian. There was a brief exchange of fire: the Russian tank burst into flames, the crew jumped out and were mown down.

After we had laboured at improving the holes in the ground to the extent that they provided protection against snow and storm, we were ordered to leave for Dubininski. Gradually we were noticing the cuts in rations. We were given 200 grams of bread per day and horsemeat. The reduction was bravely borne; at least morale was good. It was simply unthinkable that a whole army would be allowed to go to the dogs here! Certainly, two attempts during December to relieve us failed, but we did not lose heart. The men's bearing was good and often admirable. Want and deprivation would not wear us down! At least it was not so bad for us as for our comrades in the forward defensive line. What we did notice more with each passing day was the plight of the sick and wounded. The field hospitals with their provisional accommodations could only take the worst cases. The rest were rejected, but to where? Most dragged themselves back to their units, suffering from hunger and cold. Nobody gave them extra food, for everyone was hungry. Here and there a poor devil was taken in for a night and given something to eat, but next morning he had to go on his way. Helpless, miserable and filthy he would try to reach his unit dragging himself through the snow and against the icy steppe winds. People cried to see it, but one had to stand by and not help. We experienced similar tragedies daily. However difficult that might be one had to harden oneself: the heart had to be disconnected, one must only think with the head, clear and ice-cold – that was the way of things.

Faces grew thinner, many grew taciturn. Conversation no longer flowed, they played cards when opportunity arose, especially once night fell and the 'Duty Ivan', the Il 2 'nerve saw' had unloaded his bombs. It was so easy for him on moonlit nights against poorly camouflaged bunkers and vehicles! We were back in the hard-frozen earth again when we got to Dubininski on 11 December. Two days later we had expanded the bunkers to provide protection against snow and cold. The latter had increased and temperatures were -20°C to -30°C. Gradually we began to run short of wood which previously we had used to fetch from Stalingrad itself on ammunition deliveries. Now we could only heat the bunkers at set times. There existed a black market in horses and kindling: a horse could be negotiated from mounted units for a wooden beam. Better it was to slaughter the poor animals straight away before they died of starvation, for there was no food to give them.

Christmas approached. Perhaps we shall be relieved then, most thought. Then there would be post and Christmas packets piling up at the gates of the Pocket! Christmas Eve came. There were no packets. The Ju 52s and He 111s brought the odd airmail letter, but that was all. And yet this Christmas festival was such a powerful experience in its own way that man shudders to remember it. Never had I experienced a Christmas with such deep emotion as this one! There was a Christmassy mood in every bunker. The men had fashioned Christmas wreaths from the ugly, grey steppe grasses they had pulled up from beneath the snow. Cigarette papers cut into thin strips, a little cotton wool, here and there a strip of red or yellow cord which had been conjured up from somewhere were the means to adorn these modest grey wreaths. Cakes were baked for everyone from the small stocks of wheatmeal stored here and there in the field kitchens. There was a pack of Schoka-Kola per head from the panzer special supply. Saved-up cigarettes were distributed, and so everybody was blessed with something. Even though it wasn't much, the pleasure was great. For the officers I had had plates made from Russian shell casings, and these had come out very nicely. At 1400 hrs the Staff arrived: I made a Christmas speech.

The days went by, the Russians attacked continually, mostly at the western perimeter although the other fronts had to take it too. Night after night their aircraft dropped their bombs and caused many casualties, but we remained hard and confident.

On the night of 29 December I developed a very painful colic of the kidneys which lasted three hours and was only tolerable with morphine injections. Up to 2 January it had recurred four times with additional inflammation of the renal pelvis. The two doctors treating me, Dr Reuber[3] and Dr Schmidt[4] considered that I should be removed immediately to a hospital where I could receive specialist treatment. This opinion was shared by the senior surgeon of 100 Light Division field hospital, who furnished the certificate of urgency for transport out from Pitomnik airfield.

On 6 January 1943 at 1040 hrs aboard an He 111 I was taken to Novotsherkassk, 40 kilometres east of Rostov. Those final days before being flown out were probably the hardest of my life. On the one hand I now had the prospect of being able to escape the hell of Stalingrad as a result of serious illness: on the other I had to live with leaving my comrades to their fate, for whom I was responsible, and whose affection I had won. I was in such inner conflict that on the morning of 6 January I seriously considered turning down

---

3. Dr (medicine and theology) Kurt Reuber (b. Kassel, 26 May 1906, d. officers' camp, Jelabuga, 20 January 1944). After obtaining his school-leaving certificate studied theology and whilst administering his parish at Wichmannshause also studied medicine at Göttingen. At Christmas 1942 he created the famous 'Stalingrad Madonna', which his commander Dr Grosse took with him when he left the Pocket.
4. Dr Hans-Jürgen Schmidt (b. Berlin, 6 October 1909, d. Krasnoarmeisk camp, 19 February 1943). He studied medicine in Berlin and became a paediatrician, with 16th Panzer Division from autumn 1939.

the opportunity to be airlifted out, and to remain. But what use would I be to anybody in this very infirm state? I was just one more useless consumer of food and a burden on the others, above all at that time, when we had to move out. No – I would no longer interfere with fate!

My colleagues gave me a hearty farewell and we exchanged good wishes for the future. Then the lorry came to take me to Pitomnik airfield.

14. WERNER HALLE:

Advancing to the South of Stalingrad[1]

Werner Halle was a corporal with No 10 Company, 71st Motorized Infantry Regiment, 29th Infantry Division.

The heaviest fighting was behind us. Days, weeks we had been in action without a break. Our main objective was called Stalingrad.

The Russians had established field fortifications between the Don and Volga which had not made it easy to capture this deeply fortified system. Every town, every village, every patch of woodland and obviously every high spot was set up for defence. The terrain had been excavated into a single fortress. We often recognized too late, mostly not until we were almost upon them, the one-man foxholes and bunkers linked by deep communication trenches. The defensive positions were held by large numbers of troops with heavy firepower. We infantrymen experienced their bitter resistance day by day. Yes, the Russians fought with a fanaticism bordering on the impossible. How often in those days had we seen the terror of their Commissars, relentless, daring the utmost and scarcely paying heed to the cost in human life! The Russian losses reached appalling proportions.

We too suffered. No 10 Company of the 71st Infantry Regiment was down to platoon size. We rarely knew our Company and platoon commanders. We had many long casualty lists, for us 'not a good sign'. Every man jack of us – it sounds harsh but it was so – could now conclude from it: which of us is next?

Nevertheless, our objective Stalingrad was not far ahead. Stalingrad lent to us infantrymen, who had fought for days or often a year or more in the East, a consciousness of our strength which always pulled us forwards. Dawn broke. The calendar said 8 September. We were engaged in bitter fighting with the

---

1. This account was published in the journal *Falke*, veterans' newsletter of the former members of 29th Infantry Division, Christmas 1960.

Russians again. Our weapons, artillery and every imaginable gun, rocket and flamethrower was used to reap a grim harvest amongst their defenders. But the Russians would not give in. We received their defensive fire in return. We were fired upon directly by two Stalin Organs in a gully not far from us. There was only one way to survive it: full cover! And already the rockets were hissing and roaring overhead.

The 2cm anti-aircraft gun with which our company had been provided proved its true value here and wiped out the crews and weapons at the shortest range. The way was clear again – but for how long? If we looked up we saw our aircraft, squadron upon squadron, in endless aerial fighting since early morning. It was a proud feeling for us to be supported from the air. Now we stood before a ridge, naturally enemy-occupied. Also here we forced our way into the enemy positions. Always the same picture: dead, wounded and prisoners who crept out hesitatingly from cover. We had got used to it. We looked down from the ridge. Another four to five kilometres, and Stalingrad and the Volga lay before us. A glorious view, this city with its fast-flowing river! It was enveloped in dense smoke and fumes.

After a speedy advance towards evening on 9 September we reached the embankment of the Kuporosnoye–Stalingrad railway line and dug-in. That night we took a lot of prisoners from motorized or horse-drawn units. According to what they told us we deduced that, unaware of the situation at Beketovka, the Russians wanted to send out reinforcements from the city. Yes, even the panzers mixed in with us were under the illusion that Stalingrad was still open. If so we would have been able to take these prisoners without firing a round. That night, for the first time in ages, our field kitchen served us hot food.

The worst was still ahead. To the left and right of us, bitter fighting with the Russians increased hourly. They knew too: they had to fight to the last man. The greatest and final objective was right before our eyes: only a strip 500 to 700 metres long lay between the railway embankment and the Volga. We had to take that strip of land. We ourselves lay with a few colleagues in the gullies which led to the Volga. Our 3rd Battalion of the 71st had set the main frontline here, with neighbouring Battalions to the left and right. In the early morning our troops made numerous major efforts to reach the Volga. These attempts were always brought to a standstill by murderous defensive fire. We suffered heavy losses. Also in the south of the city the Russians put up stubborn resistance. In the streets deep obstacles and barricades had been erected. Between them were steel bunkers, strongpoints, barbed wire fences, concrete bunkers with armoured domes, all so arranged that an attack on one would be resisted from positions on the flanks. In short: every wooden hut was a fortress!

On 10 September 1942 our No 10 Company was handed the following operational orders by our battalion commander, Major Stürber:[2] 'Take Stalingrad-South and reach the banks of the Volga.' For us few infantrymen this was a big mission, probably the most difficult of the lot to date! That night hardly any of us got any sleep. Our Company consisted of only two groups; I was a platoon leader. At daybreak we moved stealthily to our exit positions on the embankment between Beketovka and Stalingrad.

The attack was timed for 0900 hrs. There was still time for a cigarette or two. No wonder that the excitement amongst us was so great! At nine on the dot we heard a droning in the skies: Stukas circled above us, then with screaming sirens they dropped bomb after bomb on the enemy a short distance in front of us. This smoothed our path to the Volga. We buried our heads in the muck: ahead was only smoke from fires and powder. Now the time had come for us, and we stormed the first houses. We were met by heavy defensive fire from the fortifications.

I reached the houses with only a handful of my comrades. Here, left to our own devices, we broke down the enemy resistance in close combat within a radius of about 500 metres, took prisoners and reached the Volga. Finally we could look down – as the first German soldiers in the south of Stalingrad – from the steep bank over the mighty river which at this place was over a kilometre across. At the same time we made good our position and stood ready to defend. How proud we were to have fulfilled our mission! At 1000 hrs we could report to Major Stürber at Battalion: 'Mission accomplished, specified objectives have been reached!' Despite strong counter-attacks we held our positions with only a few men until nightfall before finally two companies of pioneers arrived as reinforcements to help us retain the territory we had won. All the men were splendid in this endeavour. As there were so few of us and each man was needed, I could spare nobody. Thus I sent a ten-year-old Russian boy with an important message to the Battalion command post. After receiving instructions and directions he made the run despite enemy fire. It would not have been possible for any of us to have made it, for we would have gone scarcely a few metres before enemy fire got us.

---

2. Major (German War Graves Commission has him as Lieutenant) Vitus Stürber (b. Hundszell, 6 April 1902, missing in action Stalingrad, 1 February 1943). As commanding officer, 3rd Battalion, 71st Infantry Regiment, awarded Knight's Cross 29 December 1942.

For three days we held off the Russian pressure and maintained our forward position. In the early hours of the fourth day the pressure increased and the Russian hordes advancing from Beketovka seemed endless. Nearer and nearer they came, tightening the bag in which we found ourselves. Despite everything we could do, the incessant attacks by Russian infantry paid off for them and they broke through at about eight in the morning on our right flank. Our pioneers engaged in close combat. We were surrounded, for the Russians now attacked simultaneously from all sides, and apparently no chance remained of making it back to our main frontline alive. We fought bitterly for every tram, every house. Once it was clear that we were surrounded, many of us decided to make for the main German frontline. This was not far but nevertheless seemed impossible to reach.

We sustained heavy losses and only a few men were not abandoned by good fortune. In order to avoid going into captivity with the rest I decided to try for the German frontline with fifteen others. In close combat man to man, we ran the gauntlet and attempted the impossible. Only two men made it, I was one of them! Thus we had to sacrifice our advanced strongpoint on the Volga fighting to the last.

After assembling all remaining men from the rear services and the lightly wounded, and linking up with the motorcycle battalion, led by our Major Stürber we attacked Stalingrad-South next day. We penetrated deep into the city and finally hemmed in the Russians again. Then we were able to restore contact with those already in the city elsewhere. After a ten-day long operation we received our well-deserved pause for rest and were withdrawn.

15. JOACHIM HEIL:

I Flew into the Pocket Without Orders[1]

Joachim Heil was until September 1942 commander of No 13 Company, 211th Infantry Regiment, 71st Infantry Division, subsequently regimental adjutant.

My commanding officer, Colonel Barnbeck[2] had left it up to me whether I should take my home leave in October or December. I chose October /November and thus arrived back as the Pocket was forming. I was accompanied in both directions by our regimental surgeon Dr Arno Scharf who had previously been surgeon to our 2nd Battalion.

At our divisional collection point we met Lieutenant Jensen from the Reconnaissance Abteilung and a leading private with a car from Division. We commandeered the car and went door to door at every airfield and HQ in the attempt to get into the Pocket. On the way we found the village to which our artillery had brought its horses for winter quarters. The veterinary officer who had been appointed village commandant showed us to our lodgings and asked Dr Scharf to help in the surgery because there was a big crowd waiting to be seen and we also treated the local population.

Jensen then brought news following a reconnaissance that the Pocket would be prised open from the south-west over the next few days. We drove to Morosovskaya to make another attempt to fly in. We were told that would be impossible. We would be shot by firing squad if we went in without orders. We kept trying, but met with no success.

---

1. This report is based on two letters dated 7 and 24 July 1982 to Helmut Schröder and was published in *Das Kleeblatt*, 126th edition, Year 1/27, January 1983.
2. Hermann Barnbeck (b. Rösehöfe/Bückeburg, 7 October 1894, d. Minden, 25 October 1944), finished the First World War in the rank of Lieutenant. 1936 Captain, Wehrmacht, 1941 Lieutenant-Colonel, 1942 Colonel. Up to 1 April 1942 commanded 211 Infantry Regiment: awarded Knight's Cross, 20 October 1942. December fell ill: 1944 Divisional Commander's course.

Finally, on 12 December, the chief of staff of a flying corps at Morosovskaya let us drive to the runway bunker in which the pilots waited for instructions. He said he could not order anyone to take us with them. If we found an aircraft which would take us, he would not try to prevent it, but he would deny all knowledge of us. It was a flight of He 111s. The pilots had already flown a mission early that morning. I found a crew with a wounded gunner who were prepared to take me in his place. Unfortunately he had taken his parachute with him and so I would have to fly without one.

Towards 1100 hrs we took off with four bombs and two sacks of mail. I was only allowed to bring my map case and a loaf of bread, everything else had to remain behind and was lost. We dropped our bombs – I couldn't have told the difference between friend and foe, although I was assured by the crew they had hit in the right place. Without an aerial battle, but under heavy AA fire – which however inflicted no damage – we reached Pitomnik. The pilot had promised me he would land without making the prescribed circuit so that I could leave the aircraft before security turned up. We went straight down through cloud and landed. This got the pilot a reprimand. I was able to leave the aircraft without being seen, assisted by our coming to a stop directly before a great crowd of wounded who were to be flown out and immediately surrounded the aircraft.

When the field gendarmes of airfield security turned up I went up to the captain and reported myself as having been sent for by my Division, which needed a surgeon and a landmine specialist. Nobody asked to see our orders. However, I looked like a staff officer, wore no greatcoat, and had a soft field cap and gloves. Nobody in his right mind ran around the Pocket in the cold dressed like that! Dr Scharf came with the third aircraft, Lieutenant Jensen with the fifth. They also had no difficulties. On a timber lorry we then drove into Stalingrad after I had rung our chief of staff, Lieutenant-Colonel von Below,[3] who was initially speechless but then quickly recovered and told us where we should drive. Thus we entered the Pocket. Dr Scharf died later in captivity: I still do not know the fate of Lieutenant Jensen. I was only released from captivity in the summer of 1949.

---

3. Hugo Günter von Below was the brother of Hitler's Luftwaffe adjutant Nicolaus von Below: he fell into Soviet captivity at Stalingrad, 2 February 1943.

16. KARL WILHELM HOFFMANN:

Flying out the Wounded[1]

Karl Wilhelm Hoffmann (b. Werdohl, 14 March 1922) volunteered for the Luftwaffe in 1940 and was trained as a co-pilot. Towards the end of the war he was promoted to Sergeant. On 2 May 1945 he flew a small aircraft from Schwerin to Neuenrade and so escaped Soviet captivity. Until pensioned off he worked for the police department, then as a journalist. He is living out his retirement at Sundern-Langscheid on Lake Sorpe.

About mid-1942 my flight group – or training class, so to speak – of the C19[2] pilot school at Ohlau, where we were re-trained on aircraft exceeding ten tonnes in weight, was transferred to Breslau-Gandau airfield because Ohlau was overcrowded. About mid-August 1942 half the group was suddenly ordered to Wiener Neustadt in Austria: from there we rode with about 340 young pilots from all parts of the Reich in closed goods wagons for twelve days via Lemberg-Kiev and Aleksandrovka to Yassinowataya, where we arrived on 1 September. Here at the front we were to fly the 20,000 kilometres necessary for the pilot's C licence. The giant marshalling yard with its 200 tracks was about 15 kilometres from our destination, Yusovka airfield near the city of Stalino. We 'snotty-nosed kids' – even though we were trained flying personnel – at first refused to walk this 15 kilometres and demanded at least a lorry to take us there. We were told to get stuffed and forced to march there in scorching heat. At that time I was a Gefreiter (airman-private).

At Yusovka, six friends of mine and I from 1st Staffel/1.KG zbV 172[3] were

---

1. This report was faxed by Herr Hoffmann to the Editor on 11 September 2003 as a typescript. The text was added to at various places by oral explanations from the author on 31 March 2011.
2. The letters indicate training on a particular class of aircraft. Normally training would be complete with A and B: C was schooling on heavy aircraft (Author's note).
3. KG zbV = *Kampfgeschwader zur besonderen Verfügung*: Bomber squadron for special purposes.

assigned to the so-called 'Hammer Group'[4] (only after Stalingrad were transport squadrons designated TG 1 or TG 2). This unit belonged to IV Air Corps *Richthofen* at Stalino. We were accommodated in former mineworkers' houses, these being essentially a large living room with a primitive tiled stove in the middle of the room.

Next day I – whose principal preoccupation until then had been to make sure that my various girlfriends in Breslau never met – had my first shocking experience. We had landed in the steppe somewhere near a main dressing station, and my first pilot, a man named Koch from Lüdenscheid, gave me the job of 'loading up', i.e. the seriously wounded. Together with a totally hard-boiled medical corps warrant officer I passed along the line in which the seriously wounded lay on stretchers in the heat of the steppe. Flies swarmed around the dressings: hardly any of the patients seemed conscious. The selection procedure was cruel, but probably necessary. The warrant officer would look at a wounded man and say to the stretcher bearers: 'No, let him be!' If the poor devil was conscious, it seemed to make no difference to him when he heard this death sentence. He would raise the eyelids of another and say, 'This one's dead, leave him!' If a man had a gunshot fracture he would say, 'He's worth it, load him.' Later I saw much worse.

Before Stalingrad was encircled, my pilot warned me about Pitomnik airfield, a grass airstrip. Although it was some kilometres from the Volga, I should not approach it too high because the 'women's AA', a battery served entirely by women on the island in the Volga, according to an infantry rumour, liked to fire horizontally. Our equipment, and therefore also our motors, were kept operational until they gave up the ghost, and so one day it happened that after one of the three motors failed, we had to set down on the steppe. We had no time to radio our location. Because of the endless expanse of the steppe we were searched for over three days by a couple of Fieseler Storks[5] and were found half-starved, for the three-tonne cargo was on top of our rations chest in the fuselage.

Friends in a reconnaissance squadron had observed the developing pincer movement in the Soviet counter-attack right and left of our sharp-pointed

---

4. In Germany there were only five transport squadrons. A squadron had four groups, each with 48 aircraft (Author's note). A Staffel was an 'echelon' or 'flight' smaller than a group but not made up of a specific number of aircraft.
5. Meant here is the Fieseler Storch Fi 156, the standard Luftwaffe courier and liaison aircraft of the Second World War.

Arthur Krüger, Corporal, Danzig Infantry Regiment was amongst the few men of his Company to survive Stalingrad (Chapter 20).

Dr Kurt Reuber, painter of the famous 'Stalingrad Madonna', here seen in a self-portrait, sketched in the Pocket (Chapter 13).

Gert Pfeiffer, Captain, 92nd Motorized Infantry Regiment, 60th Infantry Division (Chapter 26).

Captain Jochen Löser was awarded the Knight's Cross for his involvement at Stalingrad on 26 January 1943. He called his salvation from the Stalingrad Pocket 'a miracle' (Chapter 24).

Friedrich Randhagen, Workshop Company, 2nd Panzer Regiment, 16th Panzer Division, had an adventurous escape from the Pocket (Chapter 29).

Seriously wounded infantryman Otto Schäfer miraculously survived the hell of Stalingrad (Chapter 32).

Eyewitness to the fierce fighting at the Tractor Works, infantryman Helmut Walz was seriously wounded there (Chapter 37).

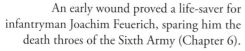

An early wound proved a life-saver for infantryman Joachim Feuerich, sparing him the death throes of the Sixth Army (Chapter 6).

He 111 medium bombers were used as transports at Stalingrad.

Michael Deiml flew eighty-one missions to Stalingrad, fifty-nine bombing raids and twenty-two supply flights combined with flying out the wounded as an He 111 air-gunner and flight mechanic (Chapter 2).

Flown out wounded from the Stalingrad Pocket, Knight's Cross holder NCO Otto Gemünden (seen here later in officer's uniform) realized that there was no hope for his colleagues when he saw the encirclement from the air in mid-January 1943 (Chapter 8).

Despite motorization, horses were indispensable in Russia: here a horse-drawn convoy advances across the steppe to the Volga. (*Sedelmaier*)

Summer 1942: 305th Infantry Division on the road to Stalingrad. (*Grimm*)

100th Artillery Abteilung advancing across the steppe. (*Dr Wigand Wüster*)

View from a trench looking towards the remains of an apartment block, Stalingrad. (*Wüster*)

Surviving chimney-stacks amongst the ruins of Stalingrad. (*Grimm*)

German artillery firing on Stalingrad. (*Wüster*)

Photographs taken by Dr Wilhelm Grosse, commanding officer, Ammunition Battalion, 16th Panzer Division (Chapter 13).
Top: Panoramic view of the damage to Stalingrad.
Bottom: Russian refugees on the Stalingrad Rollbahn, September 1942.

Inside 'Fortress Stalingrad':
Dr Kurt Reuber (centre).

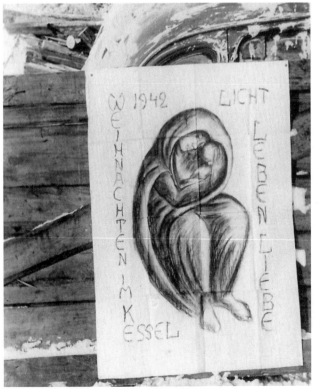

Dr Kurt Reuber's 'Stalingrad
Madonna' photographed
in its position in front of
the bunker. It reads: '1942.
Christmas in the Pocket.
Light Life Love'.

Building bunkers in 'Fortress Stalingrad' with local helpers.

Christmas 1942: the slaughter of the last horse.

Infantrymen at the bitterly-contested Tractor Works.

The Commandant, Zariza Süd, recommends a detour. The sign reads: 'Entering the city is prohibited: sightseers endanger their own lives as well as those of their comrades.'

The Luftwaffe achieved more than was humanly possible with its air bridge to Stalingrad, but available aircraft was in woefully short supply and many German soldiers died of starvation. The above illustration shows Ju 52 aircraft on the Tazinskaya airfield (see map 2) which served as a supply base outside the Pocket. This airfield, and a number of German aircraft, were captured by the Soviets on 24 December 1942.

A Ju 52 at Stalingrad. Whoever managed to get to an aircraft and was not shot down on the flight out were the chosen ones who gave death the slip.

The Univermag department store in the south of Stalingrad under fire: this housed the last command post of the Sixth Army commander, General Friedrich Paulus, whom Hitler promoted to Field-Marshal on 29 January 1943. As Field-Marshal Paulus was expected to shoot himself when threatened with capture. To Hitler's indignation Paulus preferred captivity.

Field-Marshal Paulus leaving the Soviet car in which he was driven into captivity.

Paulus felt himself bound to obey Hitler's order not to capitulate. Therefore he contrived for himself, according to military historian Torsten Diedrich, 'to enter captivity as a private person and transfer responsibility to other commanders in the Pocket'. Conduct unique in military history. In the photo: General Alexander von Hartmann (left) receiving the Knight's Cross from Paulus.

Dead or still alive? Three German soldiers on the brink of life and death.

The appalling end of the Sixth Army. Piles of dead German soldiers at the end of the battle. The deaths continued after the capitulation in the death marches and death camps. Only 6,000 prisoners of war captured at Stalingrad ever returned home.

Hermann Göring, amongst other appointments Commander-in-Chief of the Luftwaffe, celebrated on 30 January 1943 the tenth anniversary of the National Socialist seizure of power, during which he made his bitterly-received 'corpse speech' about the Sixth Army. His arrogant assurance to Hitler that the Sixth Army could be fully supplied from the air contributed in large measure to the tragedy of Stalingrad.

An endless column of German prisoners of war march towards a Soviet death camp where many thousands would die of disease and starvation.

Cameo of a battle in which, in the end, it was easier to die than to live: Sixth Army prisoners of war.

Soviet 'Katyusha' rocket launchers known by the German side as 'Stalin Organs' because the array looked like an organ and made a characteristic whistling sound when fired (Chapter 10).

Hans-Valentin Hube, final rank General, was ordered by Hitler to leave the Pocket to make his report personally at Obersalzberg. He was the only passenger aboard the Ju 52 which flew him out.

spearhead heading for Stalingrad, and had shown us pictures to prove it. We needed no General Staff training to understand whom this was aimed at, and naturally it was also known at Wolfsschanze.[6] We were therefore not at all surprised to learn on 19 November that the Russians had broken through our lines. That evening we were at an airfield not far from Grozny near the Russian oilfields. My cargo, which had not been unloaded the previous evening, had to be pitchforked out into the black mud. It was a pity, for we were loaded to the roof with white leather fur-gloves. Because of our air superiority at the time the Russians had probably waited for a day of bad weather for their offensive.

The three hours to Perelosovskaya – in the Stalingrad Pocket there were still several military airstrips, but not for supply aircraft – we flew at 20 metres altitude. There were some short-range Fw 189 reconnaissance aircraft at Perelosovskaya which to our surprise had heard nothing about the Russian breakthrough. It was foggy, and they had not been able to fly, since there was no point if they could not see the ground. The previous night in the north-east there had been a big ballyhoo, they said, but we should have a quiet meal first; no, in general there were not many wounded. The spoons nearly dropped from our hands and theirs when, passing the barrack-hut windows, came whole parties of walking wounded, hobbling to the airfield over the thin covering of snow. The infantry were still not provided with medical care. The seriously wounded lay outside: as so often with the policy of *sauve qui peut*[7] the much vaunted comradeship was not much in evidence here. We loaded our Ju 52 to the limit with twenty-five to thirty men, for they could all sit up. On the other hand we could only take up to twelve stretcher cases because of the lack of space. As we took off, we saw that the Fw 189s all had their motors running. Two of them which were unable to get off were blown up on the ground. Because our radio operator had forgotten the frequency of the landing beacon at Stalino, where we had a very modern GCA landing system which showed lateral movements off the centreline of the landing path, with our last drops of fuel and our wounded we had to make an emergency landing through a 20-metre cloud base.

After that I made two more flights to Stalingrad. That was more or less when the encirclement had just started, when we could still fly by day and

6. The Führer-HQ at this time was 'Wolfsschanze', located in a forest at Rastenburg in East Prussia.

7. *Sauve qui peut* = save yourself who can.

there were no hair-raising experiences. At Pitomnik airfield it was still relatively routine: it had a radio beacon so that it could be reached flying blind. Naturally now we only took the serious cases: loading was controlled by field-gendarmes, known as 'chained dogs'. I had a few short conversations with the infantry who brought the wounded. They looked at me with their honest blue eyes and said, 'The Führer will soon have us out of here!' On the flight back we used to advise by radio the number of wounded aboard and the level of their injuries. There was never an occasion when we had to wait longer than ten minutes for the ambulances to arrive. My last flight to Stalingrad was on 15 December 1942.

Flying was now the captain's affair: I just had to look-on. I cannot remember defensive fire by the Russians: he probably detoured around the known locations of Russian AA batteries. Neither did we have problems at this time with Russian fighters. The flight from Stalino to Pitomnik was so long that even before the encirclement we had to refuel there from a 200-litre barrel. Now, with the encirclement in place, we had to bring along our own barrel, for naturally there was no more fuel to be had at Pitomnik. In the time remaining I often made longer flights into the Caucasus and the Elista-steppe. I saw the oil drilling towers at Maikop blown up by the Russians. We had to supply an army of 1.5 million there, which was in great danger of being cut off by the Russians at Rostov.

Around 10 December came the absurd order that we 340 co-pilots were to return 'into the Reich' to obtain our blind-flying licences. We were flabbergasted to discover, upon returning to our old pilot training school, that our comrades who had remained behind had heard of the heavy fighting at Stalingrad, but only learned from us that the Sixth Army was encircled.

At least, then: if there is anything positive about the war, I write to my own 'credit account' that I helped to fly out perhaps seventy to eighty of the total of 24,910 wounded to be saved from Stalingrad by air. Amongst the 1,200 men of the flight personnel who fell was my captain. In the Stalingrad operation, 588 of our aircraft were lost, amongst them 280 Ju 52s.

17. GUSTAV KAMINSKI:
At the Last Moment[1]

Leading Private Gustav Kaminski was attached to the signals section of the 60th Motorized Infantry Division.

After my home leave in the autumn of 1942 I reached the railway junction at Tchir. Here there was great disquiet and upheaval without us knowing exactly why. After a lot of looking I found the reporting office of the 60th Motorized Infantry Division and was directed to a collection centre for those returning from leave. From here a large number of us were loaded aboard lorries and driven towards Stalingrad, arriving at Pitomnik around midnight. I was not keen on spending the night there and set out at once on foot for the signals section which was in the immediate vicinity. In the morning I reported to the CSM who informed me that we had been encircled the previous night. At midday he took me forward to my signals troop. The usual radio routine was followed with the restrictions, particularly with regard to supply, which the encirclement entailed.

On a morning between Christmas and New Year we had to fall in. The company commander announced that everyone in our company who was not essential was being transferred to the infantry. A total of fourteen men of Nos 1 and 2 Companies and the light convoy, including myself, had to hand in our surplus equipment as soon as possible. By midday we were in the gun emplacement of a heavy battery of our artillery regiment. There was no ammunition for the 15cm guns and so we were given a short course as machine-gunners.

Next afternoon – we had just been served our meagre bowl of soup – there was an alert. We got into the vehicles at once and were driven towards the

---

1. This report appeared in the unpublished history of the 60th Infantry Division (pp 134–7), the typescript of which was placed at the Editor's disposal. The full name and career of the author were not stated.

main frontline. It was growing dark when I was detached to a company of the 120th Infantry Regiment. On the whole the next few days there were relatively quiet. Late on the afternoon of 14 January 1943 we received orders to make a limited counter-attack to force back the Russians, who had come up fairly close to our position during the night. We had made good progress doing this when suddenly the Russian artillery fired a barrage. A shell splinter tore off the front part of my foot. I just lay there and only with the greatest difficulty later could I drag myself back: the rest of my foot got frost-bitten.

Towards 2000 hrs – I had just got back to our position – I saw that what was left of my foot was almost black. No treatment was available. On the evening of 15 January, still without a dressing, the foot wrapped only in a strip of blanket, I hobbled to the company command post. Even here the doctor could not dress the foot for he had neither gauze nor paper bandages. I was taken to the main dressing station on a sledge. Here they gave me a tetanus injection and a blanket. On the morning of 16 January this dressing station had to be evacuated because Russian tanks were coming. Those unable to walk were loaded aboard lorries; the rest had to walk. Before we set off we were told we had the choice of returning to our unit. The reason for this was probably that no more care was available, either medical or in the way of food.

When we got to Gumrak towards evening there were two of us still in the lorry, all the others having got out on the way there. Originally that had been my intention also, but there was a snow storm and I was faced with hobbling five or six kilometres to my company; and who knew if it was still there? At Gumrak when leaving the lorry we asked where the military hospital was. The driver gestured in the general direction.

We found the hospital – no roof, no windows. A ruin. What we saw in front of, and inside, this 'hospital' was horrific. Dead soldiers lay in the snow before the building and on the floors, or whatever you might like to call them. Inside, the wounded were wailing, praying, singing or just lying there. I told my colleagues I was not going to lay down here, I might as well die outside. So we left, and had got about 30 metres from the building when it was hit by Russian artillery.

Looking for cover I lost sight of my companions and was now alone without knowing where to go next. All I knew was, I had to avoid spending the night in the open. I gathered up my remaining strength and hobbled as best I could back to the village or what once had passed for one. Everything was destroyed there except the railway station. I thought, that could be my salvation, but when I got there I saw that as with the military hospital it was a ruin. Here again many dead German soldiers lay in the snow. I cannot remember what I thought next: I needed to find some kind of roof, and in the ruin I found a door which I could not open. Behind it I heard cries and uproar. I was persisting at this door to the cellar when a field-gendarme took my arm and said I could not go down there. Or did I want to freeze to death like those inside? He advised me it would be better to look for an earth bunker.

Now I stood alone in this inferno. Because of my wound and hunger I had grown very weak but took the advice of the field-gendarme and found an earth bunker where I joined eleven soldiers, of whom apparently only two were still fit, more crouching than lying down. With the help of one of the two able-bodied men, over the next few days twice I dragged myself to the landing strip 500 metres away in the hope of being flown out, but no aircraft came. There seemed no prospect of leaving this witches' cauldron. I was growing ever weaker, for since being wounded on 14 January, like probably almost everybody else, I had lived on biscuit and melted snow. On the morning of 21 January I made the effort alone to get to the airstrip, but again there was no possibility.

That same evening I wanted to try my luck for one last time with the help of a comrade, but by now I had a fever and my leg had swollen so much that I could no longer stand on it. It was all over for me! The others also returned without success from their endeavours to find an aircraft, but wanted to go out again during the night. We all laid down, insofar as that was possible under the circumstances. I could not sleep – my fever was rising.

Towards midnight one of our company left our dugout because, as he told me, he was very hungry and had to find something to eat. The whole time it was deathly still outside – no shooting, no artillery, no motor noises – like the lull before the storm. Then suddenly came the drone of aircraft engines. It sounded like a Russian 'sewing machine' arriving for a night bombing mission. A short while later it fell quiet again. Suddenly it all came to life: somebody came down the steps to the underground bunker shouting, 'Get up, come up quickly, there's an He 111 only 20 metres away which will take us!' How I got out of that bunker I still do not know. I stumbled and tumbled – with a high fever – out into the night and saw an aircraft standing nearby amongst the rubble on the airfield, its motors running. It was a miracle that this machine had landed here at the wrong place, far from the well laid-out regular landing site where in the last few days there had been the most dreadful scenes whenever an aircraft took off or landed. Thus we were the only group of soldiers anywhere near it. The first of our group got aboard while it was still being unloaded. I stumbled, fell and saw my chances to get aboard dwindling – just at this moment when I was so close to the aircraft!

The motors droned louder. I thought it was all up with me – and then occurred a miracle of comradeship: the air-gunner jumped out, ran to me, picked me up across his shoulders, ran with me to the hatch in the underbelly and thrust me inside with a jerk – an act which lasted just seconds as the engines worked up to full power and the aircraft began to roll. The snow sprayed up and the air-gunner swung himself up into the crammed lower fuselage tunnel: his legs were still hanging out as we began to take off! As we rolled I could see the ghostly forms of soldiers running from the regular landing strip towards us. For them it was too late: for us who sat in this aircraft as it took off, it was the luckiest day of our lives. One thing I know: as the machine climbed I exclaimed, 'God be thanked!' That I could be aboard it at all I owed to the selfless act of this still unknown air-gunner who risked his life to bring me – a cripple – into the aircraft. What tragic events must have transpired at Gumrak in the struggle to survive!

I was flown to Novotsherkassk and at the transit hospital there was given medical treatment for the first time since being wounded eight days previously. Now for the first time I began to feel the pain after the frostbite in the stump of my foot began to slacken. The same evening I was flown by ambulance aircraft to Stalino and from there went by ambulance train to Lemberg. Here in February 1943 the front part of my foot was amputated: the whole foot was amputated in July 1944.

18. FRIEDRICH WILHELM KLEMM:

With the Last Aircraft from Stalingrad[1]

Friedrich Wilhelm Klemm (b. 4 February 1914) was until March 1942 commander of 3rd Battalion of the 267th Infantry Regiment. Afterwards, proposed for a General Staff course, he was appointed orderly officer to No.1 Staff Officer(1a) of 94th Infantry Division. When the division was disbanded, as captain with an artillery group he was seriously wounded during a Russian attack at Stalingrad on 17 January 1943. He dug himself an earth bunker and spent a week in it in temperatures of -25 °C, filthy and without food.

The steppe wind blew icy cold over the approaches to Stalingrad. It whipped the dry snow into the hollow faces of the no longer human-looking shapes. It was the morning of 23 January 1943. A great German army lay in its death throes. For the mass of the staggering, haggard and weakened soldiers there was no longer any salvation.

Up to a few hours previously I had been one of this hopeless horde, condemned to defeat. Then the army commander's QM had found me in an abandoned bunker with high fever from a wound, shook me awake and carried me to the Sixth Army Chief of Staff.[2] There I received the authorization to be flown out and orders to go to the last auxiliary airfield at the south-west corner of Stalingrad.

For four hours I moved on two hands and one good leg through ankle-high snow towards my objective. The wound in my upper right thigh caused

---

1. This report was sent to the Editor, together with a letter dated 11 November 2003, as authority to publish the typescript of his unpublished memoir (pp 309–17).

2. Deputy QM, Sixth Army, was Lieutenant-Colonel Werner von Kunowski (b. Lauban, Lower Silesia, 12 February 1907, d. as PoW, Krasnogorsk officers' camp, 10 March 1947). Chief of Staff, Sixth Army was Lieutenant-General Arthur Schmidt (b. Hamburg, 25 October 1895, d. Karlsruhe, 5 November 1987). He entered Soviet captivity with Paulus on 31 January 1943 and was sentenced to life imprisonment. He was released in 1955. Decorations: 1942 German Cross in gold. 1943 Knight's Cross.

me great pain with every movement. Onwards, onwards, my last reserves of will power urged me, but my exhausted body could no longer go on. For months just a piece of bread daily: in the last few days even that was no longer supplied. Additionally the mental burden of this first terrible collapse of our forces. I lay totally spent upon a small snowdrift and wiped the snow from my eyes with the ripped greatcoat sleeve. Was there any point in making this effort? For the Russians a wounded man was put down with the rifle butt. For their factories and mines they needed only able-bodied prisoners.

This morning the Chief of Staff had talked me out of my dark plans. 'Just try to get through to the airfield,' he said while writing my authorization to be airlifted. 'The seriously wounded are still being flown out. You always have lots of time to die!' And so I crept off. Perhaps there was still a chance of salvation out of this great parcel of land turned by man and nature into a witches' cauldron. But how endlessly far was the path for a man who had to squirm along it like a snake? What was that black throng over there on the horizon? Was that really the airfield or a mirage conjured up by an overexcited, feverish brain? I gathered myself together for another three to four metres, and then paused for breath. Just don't lie down! Or the same would happen to me as it had to those past whom I had just crawled. They too would just have wanted to rest a short while on their hopeless march into Stalingrad. But exhaustion overcame then, and the cruel cold saw to it that they would never wake again. One could almost envy them. They no longer had pain nor worries.

After about an hour I reached the airfield. The wounded sat and stood packed close together. Gasping for breath I worked my way to the centre of the square. I pulled myself up against a pile of snow. The snow storm had abated. I looked along the wide road behind the square: it led off into Stalingrad. Individual shapes dragged themselves with great effort to the suburbs. There, in the bug-ridden shacks of this so-called city they hoped to find protection against cold and wind. The mass of the troops seemed to have gone on, but hundreds failed to make it. Their frozen corpses were the milestones along this fearsome road of retreat.

The Russian could have overrun all this long ago. But he was dour, and only went the ordered distance daily. Why should he hurry? Nobody could outrun him any more. Like a giant herd he drove these beaten people towards the city from all directions. The few who perhaps still flew around in Luftwaffe aircraft did not count. The Russian seemed to grant us them. He knew all here were seriously wounded. Near me on a tent cloth were two men. One appeared to have a stomach wound, the other lacked both arms. Yesterday one machine flew out, but since then the snowstorm had made landing impossible, the man without arms told me with a melancholy look. Muffled groans could be heard over the square. Now and again a medical orderly crossed it, but in general here he was helpless to assist.

Exhausted I collapsed on my heap of snow and fell into a restless sleep. The cold soon woke me again. With chattering teeth I looked around me. A Luftwaffe Inspector came across the square. I shouted to him and asked what were the chances of getting a flight out. He replied that three hours ago they had radioed that three aircraft had taken off: they would drop supplies, whether or not they would land was uncertain. I showed him my authority to be airlifted. With a shake of the head he said it was invalid, it needed the signature of the Surgeon-General.[3] 'Go and talk to him,' he concluded, 'it's only 500 metres, over there in the gulley...'

Only 500 metres! Once more this great effort. Every movement meant more pain. The mere thought of it made me weak and I sank back into my half-dozing condition. Suddenly I saw my home, my wife and daughter and bent over them the distorted faces of fallen comrades. Then a Russian ran up to me, raised the stock of his rifle and struck out. Filled with pain I arose. The 'Russian' was a medical orderly who had kicked my wounded leg. There were three of them and a stretcher. They probably had the job of getting the dead away from the airstrip. He had wanted to check if I was still alive. Not surprising, for my shrunken, bloodless face must have looked more like that of a corpse than a living man. The short sleep had given me a little more strength. I got them to describe to me the way to the medical bunker, intending to attempt it. I dragged myself forward with the last of my strength. An eternity it seemed to take before I was sitting in the presence of the Surgeon-General. I reported the incident to him and obtained his signature. 'That ox could have spared you the walk,' he said as he signed, 'the Army signature is enough.' Afterwards he sent me into the neighbouring bunker. The medical orderly wanted to change my dressing, but I declined. A feeling of prickly disquiet drove me from the warm bunker. After strenuously scrambling out of the gully I regained the airfield. I looked for the Inspector and found him still close by my heap of snow. Now my papers were in order,

---

3. The Army Surgeon-General was Dr Otto Renoldi (b. Essen, 9 October 1886, d. Munich, 1 April 1967). He was flown into the Pocket on Paulus' order. On 24 January he became the first German general to be captured, near the Stalingradski airfield (apparently he had got lost while fleeing the advancing Soviet troops). He was released on 9 October 1955.

he said. I chose the path of discretion and refrained from calling him an ox: perhaps it saved my life.

During our conversation the motors of several aircraft were heard droning towards the airfield. Were they Russians or our saviours? All heads searched the heavens. All we could see was shadowy movements in the light cloud cover. From below flares were fired up. Then they came down like giant birds of prey. They were German He 111s, shedding altitude in great circles. Would they drop bomb-casings of provisions, would they land to take a small number of these poor, shot-up men? The blood raced in the arteries, and despite the cold one felt hot. I opened the threadbare collar of my greatcoat so as to look up better. All the efforts and suffering of the last days, weeks and months were forgotten. Up there was salvation, the last chance of going home! In his inner being each man thought the same. Therefore we had not been written off and forgotten, they wanted to help us. How depressing was the sensation of being forgotten!

At a stroke everything changed. First everybody sighed with relief. Next the great airfield was suddenly a-bustle like an overturned ant heap. Whoever could run, ran: to where, even they had no idea. They wanted to be where the aircraft landed. I tried to get up too, but after a first attempt sank back in pain. Thus I remained propped up on my snow hill and watched this apparently senseless frenzy. Two machines came in to land and rolled, heavy laden and springy, to stop 100 metres from us. The third continued to circle. Like a great broad river everybody streamed towards the two landed machines and thickened around them into a dark, billowing throng. Boxes and cartons were unloaded from the aircraft fuselage. Everything was done with great speed: at any moment the Russians might occupy this last German airstrip. Nobody could have stopped them.

Suddenly it grew quiet. At the nearest aircraft a medical officer appeared and announced in an amazingly clear voice: 'We are loading only the seriously wounded able to sit, and only one officer and seven men in each aircraft!'

For a moment there was a deathly hush all around, then the confusion of a thousand voices rising to a hurricane's roar. Now it was life or death! Everybody wanted to be amongst the eight lucky ones per aircraft. This man pushed that man back. The curses of those forced to the rear grew louder: the cries of those trodden underfoot echoed over the square.

The loading officer watched this madness quietly. He seemed used to it. A shot rang out, and I heard his voice again. He was talking with his back to me: I could not understand what he said. I did see, however, how immediately afterwards some of the crowd turned away from the machine and, without a word, sank to their knees where they stood. Other medical officers had been picking out from amongst the crowd those to be loaded.

Totally forgetting my own fate, I sat on my heap of snow. After the many weeks of dozing, this pulsating life had taken me completely under its spell. Before it became obvious to me that now there was no more question of my salvation, a violent gust of air almost raised me from my seat. I turned around in shock and saw just a few paces from me the third aircraft. It had rolled up from behind. A giant propeller almost caught me. Rigid with fear I remained motionless. Hundreds of men were running in my direction from all sides. If there was any chance of salvation, then it was to be found here! The masses collided, were forced under, others trampled them underfoot. That I did not suffer the same fate was due entirely to the death-bringing, still revolving propellers. But now the field-gendarmes held back the crush. The picture calmed slowly. Cartons and crates were tossed out of the machine down to the hard frozen soil. None of the starving men bothered about these indispensable foodstuffs. All waited tensely for the loading. The loading officer climbed on the wing. As silence fell I heard, almost above my head, the decisive words, 'One officer, seven men!' That was all. As he now turned forward to dismount from the wing I recognized in him my Inspector, the man who had sent me off on a wild-goose chase to the Surgeon-General, and he recognized me. With a gesture of invitation he shouted, 'Ah, there you are! Come here!' And, turning away once more, he added in a business-like manner, 'And seven men!'

Discouraged I must have sat down on my snowy seat, but only for a fraction of a second, for then I was up, grasped the wing and went hand over hand to the loading hatch. I perceived how those standing around made room for me dumbly, and the rabble let me pass. My body was wracked with pain. I was lifted into the aircraft. The noise around me became a satisfactory roar: I lost consciousness. It would only have been a few short minutes, for when I came to I heard the Inspector count out 'five'. Therefore five had been loaded. 'Six . . . seven'. A pause. Somebody shouted, 'Sit closer!' and they counted again. We squeezed ourselves in and against each other. 'Twelve', I heard them say after a while, 'thirteen. . . . , fourteen . . . , fifteen.' That was it. The sheet-steel doors were slammed shut. There was only room for eight, and they were taking fifteen.

Fifteen men had been saved from the hell of Stalingrad. Thousands more had to remain behind. Through the steel walls we could feel the staring eyes of those desperate comrades fixed on us. Greet the Homeland for us, their final thoughts must have been. They said nothing, they didn't wave, but turned away and knew that their dreadful fate was sealed. We were flying to salvation, they into years of death-bringing captivity.

The powerful roar of the engines shook us out of our reverie at departure. Had we really been saved? The next few minutes would show. The machine trundled over the uneven ground. The propellers raced at full revolutions. Every fibre of our bodies reverberated with them. Then suddenly the noise cut back. We seemed to be turning. The pilot repeated the manoeuvre. The interior window from the pilot's cabin was pushed up and the pilot shouted inside, 'We are overloaded – some must get out!' Our happy glow was extinguished. Now we faced ice-cold reality.

Get out? What would that imply? The young pilot stared at me expectantly. I was the senior officer, I had to decide who got out. No, this was something I could not do. Who of those aboard, who had just been saved, could I thrust back into that senseless annihilation? Shaking my head I turned to the pilot. The words came drily through my lips: 'Nobody is getting out of this machine'. I heard the relieved sighs of those sitting below me. I sensed that they all felt the same, even if no word of agreement or disapproval was uttered. The pilot was sweating. He looked as though he wanted to protest, but when he saw all the determined faces he turned back to his instrument panel. His colleagues in the cabin must have said to him, 'Try it once more!' And he did! Probably seldom had fifteen men pleaded so earnestly with their God than we did in those decisive moments.

The motors thundered out once more their stormy song. Following the tracks in the snow left by the other two machines, the slim, dull-grey giant hurtled down the airstrip. Suddenly I felt an indescribable pressure in the stomach as the aircraft left the ground. It gained altitude slowly, circled twice above the airfield and then turned away to the south-west.

What was that below us? No longer the grey heaps of the comrades we had left behind? No, those soldiers were brown-uniformed. The Russians were taking the airfield. Only a few minutes more and we would not have got away.[4]

---

4. This could well have been the take-off of the last aircraft to leave the encirclement. An advertisement in the journal *Kameraden* aimed at finally settling this question was not successful. There is additionally a report by Leutnant Krausse (Janusz Piekalkiewicz, *Stalingrad, Anatomie einer Schlacht* [Eltville 1989]) of an aircraft which took off at dusk, but took only nine wounded. A few minutes later Soviet tanks rolled into the Stalingradski airfield. That day only three He 111s are alleged to have landed and taken off: possibly these three here are those meant.

Not until that moment did we understand the stark reality of the situation. It really was salvation from death at the last minute! For just a few seconds the Russians remained visible, then the cloud took us into its protective blanket.

[Transl. note. The He 111 mentioned in Josef Mairinger's account *Sie verreckten zu Tausenden* in his privately published *Meine Jugend in Stalingrad. Erinnerungen*, 1981/82, cf. in this book at p.338, reporting a statement by Sanitätsgefreiter Alois Deimling, medical orderly, was an incident at Gumrak. This airfield fell to the Russians several days before Stalingradski on 23 January 1943 and I have therefore omitted the mention.]

19: WILLI KREISER:

Taken Along as an Air-gunner[1]

Willi Kreiser (b. 25 October 1914, d. Ulm, 5 August 1998) qualified as a businessman before the war. In the rank of Lieutenant at Stalingrad he commanded 1st Squadron, 100th AA Regiment, 100th Jäger Division. At a show trial on trumped-up charges in Soviet captivity he was sentenced to twenty-five years' labour camp. He returned to West Germany as one of the last to benefit from Chancellor Adenauer's negotiations. After that he resumed his pre-war career in Ulm.

At the end of September 1942 we were in action at the Stalingrad Northern Boundary; the Russians attacked relentlessly day and night. Here we received a foretaste of what was to come. At the beginning of October we stood on the western heights of the city and looked down at the massed housing which stretched along the west bank of the Volga. The silver strip of the river could be seen. There was heavy fighting in the city, artillery fire boomed unceasingly, Stukas dive-bombed, large fires smouldered, great oil tanks were ablaze.

Our quarters were empty wooden chalets. The first night the Russians bombed them and we had casualties. For protection against bomb splinters we crawled under the floors, for there were no cellars. Throughout the day Russian heavy guns bombarded us from the other side of the Volga. At our insistence we were transferred from the city boundary to a gully west of it. In its walls we excavated bunkers and awaited our orders. On the night of 24 October advance parties received their instructions. The farther we penetrated into the city, the bigger were the buildings, but also the destruction.

The 24th was a sunny autumn day, and my 26th birthday. As a present a Russian tank fired a round under the chair on which I had been sitting – so, full cover for the rest of the day! At night we returned to our sector of the main frontline: I made my platoons aware of the situation and set up the squadron troop in a splinter trench to serve as my command post. The

---

1. This report appeared at Christmas 1987 in the journal of the 100th Jäger Division.

frontline itself ran along a railway embankment. There was action by day from artillery and the Luftwaffe, by night the assault troops were at large. Stukas dropped their bombs in the nearby factory buildings often no more than 200 metres away, so that we had to constantly let off flares to identify where we were and so avoid being hit.

It was easy to monitor the frontline, but more difficult for our neighbours, because their stretch ran down the middle of the road. One row of houses was in our hands, the Russians occupied the other. Often the front was so serrated that one could easily go astray at night. Therefore on the second night two Ivans arrived in our kitchen with their mess-tins and were astonished to find themselves at the wrong field-post number! Assault troops of both sides felt their way around by night. On X Day there was to be an artillery barrage and Luftwaffe attacks, after which the infantry and pioneers would launch a major offensive, reach the Volga and drive out the last Russians from the west bank.

After an eerie silence, at 1000 hrs on 26 October 1942 the German artillery opened up with a hurricane of fire. We had never experienced anything like it! After thirty minutes, at the word of command, it all stopped. To our rear infantry jumped up out of our trenches, crossed the railway embankment after a brief clash and headed for the Volga. We thought that nobody on the other side could possibly have survived that barrage. After a while our flares rose up at the Volga: now we waited to advance. We had achieved our goal. The Battle of Stalingrad was over? Not by a long shot! Hardly any of the men who formed the advance platoons was ever seen alive again. When the barrage began the Russians had crept into previously prepared cellars and bunkers, let the German infantry pass overhead, and then had come out of their positions to shoot them in the back.

Towards evening I received orders to advance 100 metres under heavy enemy fire and set up a new frontline. This was for the benefit of our platoons retreating from the Volga. However, only one or two men showed up, almost all the others had fallen. I chose a building in the open still in Russian hands, a school. Left and right of it we advanced a bit, then we had to stop and take cover because our own lines were too far behind us. I asked for artillery support against the school, but the HE hit the school walls. I directed my platoons into cover on three sides around the school and set up a command post in a potato cellar.

For the coming day we expected a fresh attack by our troops towards the Volga, but none were available. Therefore we were forced to dig in and hold our positions for weeks – the front had been frozen! The Russians were having difficulties with supply because their shipping could only bring it into the bridgehead on the west bank of the Volga by night and depending on the flow of the river. On the other hand we had to bring up every shell 1,000 kilometres by train and lorry from Germany.

My platoons and their squads built fixed strongpoints. We fetched into them everything we had by way of weapons and ammunition, including Russian MGs with ammunition. Thus in my sector we had three-sided firepower, only in that way could we hold out for weeks. The Russians converted the school into a fortress. They worked at it every night, walling up the windows into small firing ports. We tried to destroy these ports with an anti-tank gun, but failed. Our trenches were often only as far apart as one could throw a hand grenade. Ivan tried to push balled charges tied to long poles into our strongpoints. This went on all night. If I crawled along my trench, the Russians would hurl hand grenades at me. They had noticed that I used to sleep behind a small shed. I heard a light mortar being fired: immediately after, the bomb fell at my feet. It was a dud, otherwise I should not have been here to write these lines.

After the ring closed around us we were in a Pocket. Breaking off from the enemy had been planned, everything prepared for the break-out. Our sector knew exactly what had to be done. At X-hour the squadron was to withdraw from our trenches without making a sound but leaving behind a few men to hold the Russians under MG fire. My Abteilung commander was ordered to the divisional command post. Feverishly we waited for night to fall. Towards dawn the field telephone rang. I picked up the receiver: Hitler had forbidden the Sixth Army to break out of the Stalingrad Pocket! The news was a terrible blow to us all. We had to conserve ammunition and the rations became less in quantity and poorer in quality.

The Russians were growing stronger and left the school to attack us, but we repulsed them in a bloody action. The crew of one of our mortars came to a grisly end. For an hour they had fired one mortar bomb after another at the Russians. Then the mortar captain dropped a fresh one into the tube before the last one had been fired, and all three men were killed.

An order arrived from Division: no officer was to sleep at night – constant alarm readiness! By day I lay on the roof of a ruined wooden house, watching the ever-increasing Russian movements with field-glasses through a crack, and took photos now and again – memories of this sad time on the Volga. Behind the exposed frontline we set up a fortified shortened rear position, for one never knew . . . One night while standing up I observed how the Russians over there were burning a large wooden house. Doing so I forgot that I was illuminated by the reflection. In a small linesmen's hut was a light MG, the gunner had me in his sights. By a hair's breadth a burst missed my head, but removed my cap.

The spectre of hunger rose above our army: the bread rations were less each day. Luckily I was able to offer my men each day a strong meat soup. Our support vehicles had been motorized but we still had a second line, horse-drawn steppe carts, and so I had twelve small steppe horses available for the field kitchen. One evening a messenger brought me a packet from the commanding officer containing the Iron Cross First Class: it was too dangerous for him to come to me himself to award it. It snowed and was cold: in the bunkers ovens were heated, but then Ivan shot at every rising column of smoke. Therefore during the day not only did we have to go hungry, but also froze. With my squadron-troop I had retained my quarters in the potato cellar we had taken over four weeks previously. At the upstairs entrance we erected a baffle to detonate incoming shells. One morning the sentry upstairs was hit by a heavy shell: his last words were for his mother at home. After that I never posted a sentry there.

The Russians attacked again one cold morning. Most of my MG teams were still asleep, overtired and drained by the constant night-time watches. The Russian breakthrough was successful. With my squadron troop in the prepared position to the rear I built up a new one hoping to assemble the remainder of the squadron along this line. In my excitement I forgot the Russian machine-gunner, who this time hit me. One bullet went through my left shoulder, the second my arm. While having these wounds attended to, I ordered my platoon leader to assemble the remainder of the squadron in the new line, but a few minutes later the young lieutenant was hit by a complicated through-and-through in the upper arm. The medical NCO had been shot in the head shortly before while applying a dressing; therefore I radioed for help. Soon the reserve platoon showed up led by a lieutenant, whom I briefed. Then, jumping from house to house, I made for the Abteilung command post. There I found a surgeon who treated me and gave me a morphine injection.

In the evening a Russian PoW was returning me to the squadron rear on a sledge. The morphine had worked: I fell asleep and on a bend fell off into the snow. If the Russian hadn't seen what happened and loaded me aboard again I would probably have frozen to death in the ditch. The divisional main dressing station (HVP) was overwhelmed and so I lived with the squadron rear services and only went there to change the dressing. The services were housed in a gully on the edge of the city, primitive but quiet, and safe from Russian aircraft and artillery. We spent Christmas before a pine branch on which we hung a couple of hand-craft stars. Our thoughts were with our comrades in the advanced frontline and our loved ones at home. Ivan 'cheered up' our Christmas Eve with noisy artillery firing overlong. The wounds to my shoulder were healing, but the shoulder itself was stiff. I was unable to raise my left arm at all and so did all the squadron paperwork with my right. My successor in the forward position, an Austrian lieutenant, had fallen shot through the head: a young infantry lieutenant, who had just been flown into the Pocket, was now in command. From the daily Wehrmacht reports we learned that the German Wehrmacht beyond the encirclement was being forced back ever farther from the Volga westwards, and we were being called 'Fortress Stalingrad'. The supply bases were therefore much farther away too: the slow Ju 52s which were supposed to supply us, and also many He 111s, were being shot down above the Russian Corridor. Soon there were not enough aircraft to bring out the many wounded.

Because my arm could not be treated in the Pocket, I received authorization from the highest medical authorities to fly out. On a bitter cold winter morning in mid-January I decided to try it and took leave of my colleagues in the rear services. Many gave me letters to take to Germany and a few pieces of dry bread for the journey; the most valuable things they had. First I had to go to 100th Division HQ, located in a small village on the edge of the city ten kilometres from the rear services. Two wounded infantrymen heading in the same direction joined me. A Russian 'Rata' noticed us and swooped on us three walkers like a hawk. We were sprayed with MG fire forcing us to disperse. I had to cross a stream and thought the ice would bear my weight. In the middle it gave way leaving me standing above the knees in icy cold water. The 'Rata' flew on. With the last of my strength I jumped out of the stream and reached a small hut which gave me temporary cover. My boots had filled with water: the temperature had been below -25°C and if I did not want frostbite in my feet I had to get out of my wet things.

I set off at a fast pace and reached a farm with a smoking chimney. A German signals unit had quarters inside. They tore the frozen boots off my feet. I undressed and wrapped myself in a couple of woollen blankets. My wet, iced-up clothing went into the oven, the boots hung above it were completely dry in two hours. By reason of this enforced halt I did not reach Divisional HQ until midday, when I found a mood of deep depression. The gentlemen probably saw the hopeless position clearer than the troops! I reported myself off duty and was given a big bundle of letters for Germany, mostly letters of final parting.

In the afternoon I set off for Pitomnik, arriving there after dark. At the edge of the airfield stood a couple of marquees full of wounded. Russian fighters circled overhead constantly, Lords of the Pocket. When our Ju 52s and He 111s landed at night, the runway had to be lit briefly. This was when Russian bombs fell. Startled I thought I heard MG fire. Only a single Ju 52 took off that night, loaded with seriously wounded. Doctors with drawn pistols stood by the aircraft to ensure that nobody unauthorized got aboard. I did not hear any other aircraft land.

The MG fire increased. In the morning the medical orderlies, wearing steel helmets and carrying weapons, entered the marquees and announced that the Russians had reached the perimeter of the airfield during the night, and unfortunately it now had to be given up. A new one was being set up at Gumrak on the city suburbs. We should attempt to get there on one of the lorries always going that way. I clambered aboard a lorry covered by tarpaulin which went off slowly. It was a cloudless day so that the sky above us was full of 'Ratas' which dived eagerly at the lorries. Again and again we had to jump out to seek cover. Because we had not come all that far, I decided to cover the rest on foot.

Ahead was a large snowfield with a Romanian light AA emplacement which had seen off the 'Ratas'. Suddenly I saw to the right an aircraft swoop in and land on the snowfield. I went over to it: it was an He 111 laden with bread and artillery shells. A lorry roared up to take charge of the valuable consignment. In a flash a handful of wounded gathered, begging the pilot to take them. As luck would have it he had landed on a small emergency airstrip set up only that morning. The pilot regretted that he could not take so many but said he thought there would be two other machines coming right away. Therefore I went along the runway a stretch; the second landed 50 metres behind me and the third 10 metres ahead. This latter was the aircraft I approached. The crew got out and an unloading convoy came racing up. I asked the pilot, who said that if I could man the unoccupied third air-gunner's position in the belly, then I could come along. Well, one has to fire with the right shoulder, my left shoulder was the bad one and so I agreed readily. Scarcely had the aircraft been unloaded than the Romanian flak began to shoot at three Russian fighters circling the airfield. Bombs fell in our vicinity: we threw ourselves down. Luckily our aircraft was not hit. The crew boarded hastily. If the aircraft was not to be hit by Russian bombs, it had to take off immediately. I climbed in too: six lightly wounded jumped aboard and were accepted. The He 111 was now full, the access hatch shut and the pilot got up speed. These last twenty minutes will be forever the most decisive of my life. The MG was explained to me by another gunner: I would lie in the plexiglass tunnel, my MG ready to fire.

The aircraft rose quickly. I will never forget the scene below! In beaming winter sunshine lay the ravaged, hapless and fated city. I could see the broad band of the Volga and German soldiers converging on the city centre from all directions. There everything would finally run its hopeless course.

Our three aircraft, which had all lifted off successfully and undamaged, closed up into formation. Soon there were flashes below as we flew through the first Russian AA belt. Left and right of us the exploding shells created small white clouds. What would happen if one hit? None of us had a parachute! The clouds grew larger – apparently we were overflying a large AA emplacement. Then it grew slowly quieter. Undisturbed, our three fast machines held their course to the west. Below us lay the area between the Don and Volga which the Russians had reconquered. I was just keeping a lookout for ground troops when an MG began to chatter above me – a Russian fighter coming up from astern was not a harmless 'Rata' but a British Spitfire!

I fired to get the feel of it and then we got down to business! The other two He 111s were also shooting. Russian tracer swept past us, but the combined defensive fire of all three aircraft held off the Spitfire at a respectful distance. It went through the craziest routine to avoid our bursts of tracer. The air-gunner above me threw down more drums of ammunition. The Spitfire turned away, thank God it was the only one.

After a flight of about two hours over Russian-occupied territory we passed through more heavy AA fire over the main frontline to the west. After about 350 kilometres we were nearing a large city, Novotsherkassk near Rostov. Our machines came gliding in to land. A huge number of Ju 52s were parked around, the supply aircraft for Stalingrad. The ground came closer, our machine touched down in the snow and rolled along the airstrip. Once it had come to a stop the pilot let off a red flare to indicate that he had wounded aboard from Stalingrad. Two ambulances roared up – we had escaped from hell and were saved! The date of my flight to freedom from the Stalingrad Pocket was 16 January 1943.

20. ARTHUR KRÜGER:

The End of the Danzig Infantry Regiment[1]

Arthur Krüger (b. Danzig, 12 June 1920, d. Feltre, Italy, 13 January 2009) volunteered for the Wehrmacht in 1938. From June 1939 he served with a police regiment in 'Battlegroup Eberhart', later in No 8 Company, 120th Motorized Infantry Regiment, 60th Infantry Division in the campaigns in France and Greece. From June 1941 he took part in the campaign in Russia; he was at Stalingrad in the rank of corporal.

Much has been told about the events of the war, of deeds and misdeeds. Many reports are the work of former officers who after the war volunteered for the Bundeswehr. They had obviously not had enough of war and being a soldier. Only seldom does an infantryman speak up who spent years in a frontline trench. We, the so-called 'front-swine', who lay in the filth of the frontline like pigs, had no batman to bring us water to shave and wash. We were proud of our victories and also proud to be German soldiers! We firmly believed in victory. In July 1941, Stalin's order was made known: death to the German occupiers, strike them dead wherever you find them! Thus it was war no longer. They fired like madmen at our medical orderlies, at our ambulances: it was impossible to retrieve our wounded and dead. Young officers who had not the faintest idea about war, the front and the way the Russians fought spoke of Russian sub-humans, of the Führer, of secret weapons and of Final Victory. We few old infantrymen no longer believed in the whole bag of tricks. For us it was clear: we could no longer win the war. Therefore there was nothing left for us to do but sell our lives as dearly as possible.

At the end of June 1942 we were ready again after the battle of Kharkov, and at Kalatch on the other side of the Don we were hot on the heels of the Russians. Our mission was to break through with the panzers and cut off the enemy lines of supply. We went too far ahead: the infantry was left behind.

---

1. Published on the Internet between 2003 and 2008 in various letters and contributions which the Editor arranged in chronological order with the approval of the publisher.

The orders came to form a hedgehog and wait for fuel and the infantry to catch up. As far as you could see there was not a house, a tree or a bush. Only a few Arabian camels which had not wandered off kept us company.

Soon contact was restored. We had fuel and provisions again, and started off afresh towards Stalingrad. We asked ourselves why we had not come up against any more T-34s, only American lorries and tanks: we heard that the Americans were supplying the Russians with war materials through the port of Vladivostok. My group captured a small American tracked vehicle and loaded it with the heaviest parts of our heavy mortars. While our troop began to encircle Stalingrad city, we headed north with 16th Panzer Division and reached the Volga. There we set up the so-called Northern Boundary line and warded off all attacks.

The battles for Kalatch and Stalingrad cost lives. Our companies were mostly only thirty to fifty men in number. Our main frontline had gaps in it: we were waiting for reinforcements. We approached the Russians as closely as possible, often as close as 100 metres to avoid the Stalin Organ rockets which had a 250-metre spread. If they fired at us they would hit their own people. Besides that they had good snipers:[2] moving about by day was suicide.

By night we shovelled like madmen to extend our trenches. The earth was carried off in a tarpaulin and spread behind our position: ammunition and rations were brought up from the rear. We also received replacements now and again, drivers and people from the rearward services, most without experience and poorly trained. Because of the lack of infantry I filled a gap in the front with my ten-man heavy mortar group. Ahead of us was a minefield and the Russians. I had four leading privates in my group, veterans with whom I had served for quite some time. We had calibrated our mortar accurately. As a result of our observations we could hit the enemy anywhere within range.

To our left was No 5 Company command post under whose control my mortar came. To the right lay a heavy-MG group of my company. The rifle company had shortages caused by men being shot in the head. They had rifles with a telescopic sight but poor training. I had one of them pass me a rifle and I killed the sniper. Some men returned from leave and the military hospital. They came to our position with the ration carriers: mentally they were probably still in Germany. Therefore they failed to hear our warning shout, '*Achtung*! Snipers, keep your heads down!' They were never in action again. It

2. The list of the fifty most successful Soviet snipers alleges 15,000 German soldiers as their victims.

made us superstitious: whoever went on leave, died. We didn't need to worry about that any longer because now there was no leave.

The Russians probed the strength of our defences by means of small attacks. Generally we mowed them down. Then we would hear the weakening cries for help of the dying. Three defectors came to our positions. I asked them, 'Why don't you help your wounded?' They replied, 'They only treat those who can keep fighting. Those who get back are helped, those who can't stay where they lie!'

Far behind the Russian lines we heard the rattle of tank tracks every night. We sensed it: something was brewing. Then we heard it: the Russians had broken through in the Romanian sector, the Italian front was tottering. They had reached the Don at Kalatch, and we were surrounded. At first this did not worry us. It had often happened to our division before but we had always managed to get out. I believe that without this hope, without this faith, the battle to the bitter end at Stalingrad would not have been possible. Then we began to grow short of rations and ammunition: we were weak and exhausted. The great strain and inhuman lifestyle had made us old men. Not until 27 November were we informed officially by divisional order of the encirclement. Now the bitter days for us began.

The promised relief never came and we were left to our fate. We felt grim rage: we felt betrayed and sold out. Our enemies promised us death and destruction: the Russian loudspeakers shouted: 'Do you dogs want to live for ever?' and suchlike. If they had not done so,[3] many of us in this hopeless situation would have chosen captivity and not a heroic death. Young men of twenty died of exhaustion; typhus and lice plagued us. Only the wounded still had a chance of escaping this hell. The wish was for a painless death. Some inflicted injuries on themselves in the hope of being flown out as wounded, others cracked, jumped out of the protected position and were cut down by snipers. Only he whose nerve held could survive. Some deserted through panic, hunger and despair. Perhaps they believed they could escape the Pocket this way. They were caught and shot, or were put to clearing landmines with the punishment company.

By God, we no longer believed in a victory and would settle for survival. Until then it had still been possible that he who needed to most of all could go back with the field kitchen: he could sleep a whole night and spend all day cleaning himself of the week's accumulation of dirt clinging everywhere to his

---

3. Namely if the enemy had not promised death and destruction.

129

uniform and body. In the cold the stink was not so bad but the feeling of having lain in the filth like a pig could not be shed. To change one's underwear and write a letter home in peace, those were important activities which at least made us look a bit more civilized. In the evening he would return with the field kitchen, always accompanied by our CSM, and from him we would learn the latest news.

Totally lousy and filthy we lived like rats in our holes, worse than people had it in the Stone Age. Our main occupation was cracking open the largest lice. After crushing a hundred of these pests in a sleeve of my jacket I gave up counting. One evening when the rations were brought a couple of Russians penetrated the trench, ate the contents of a cooking pot, shit into it and then went back to their lines. Apart from stealing the food there were no casualties; this also was war. Obviously at the command posts there were bunkers, heating, water and latrines. If we were not under artillery fire one could move around there freely. Men in the support services had it better. There they were less hungry than we were which probably accounts for there being more survivors amongst them left to tell the tale.

One night a T-34 drove through our lines and came to a standstill. Our senior sergeant Wiartalla smoked the crew out and took them prisoner. With his men, former panzer drivers, he drove into the Russian readiness position and knocked out three of their tanks before returning to the Battalion command post. For this act of heroism he was awarded the Knight's Cross.[4] It was never repeated. I think it happened on the late afternoon of 30 November when we heard the rattle of tank tracks. I counted ten T-34s coming for us. They crossed our trenches and then our anti-tank guns fired on them from the rear. Their infantry followed at some distance in battalion strength, attempting to break through our front. We let them get within rifle range and then all hell broke loose! Their attack failed in our crossfire: our panzers attacked with infantry and so added to our casualties.

I was wounded in the head and left shoulder and carried back to the company command post in the gully near the Battalion command post. There I received first aid from a medical orderly before being summoned to the company commander and our CSM. 'Dear Krüger, we do not wish to lose you from here, but you are lightly wounded and have the chance to get out. You have gone thirty months without leave! You were scheduled to be the first man to go on leave as soon as a replacement arrived for you. Unfortunately

---

4. The author was unable to find this name in the list of Knight's Cross holders.

there is no more leave for anybody. But here is your leave pass, which is valid only outside the Pocket. Here are some letters which you are to hand in at the first post office you come to. As you are a Danziger and will perhaps be going there and we hope, arrive, here is a sealed envelope which you must hand to the Danzig Kommandantur. Report at the dressing station to our divisional surgeon Dr Haidinger!'[5] There I received the very best treatment and was given letters for Austria, Haidinger's native land.

I received precise instructions on how I should behave and went at dawn to Gumrak airfield where I saw the many seriously wounded laid out on stretchers and waiting for their airlift out. Many were left behind to await the next flight. It was impossible for me to get aboard an aircraft and so I waited for two or three days and through two icy cold nights. The priority was the seriously wounded, which ruled me out. I gave up hope.

On the morning of the third day I saw a Ju 52 standing to one side of the runway. I went over to it and had a conversation with the pilot who was a sergeant and ex-infantryman. He said his machine had a wheel in a bomb crater and was waiting for a tracked vehicle to pull it clear. As he could only take seriously wounded, I told him that as a walking wounded I had not obtained authorization to fly out. He went to the machine and when he came back he asked if I could fire an MG, because he did not have an air-gunner. I replied: 'Of course, I am from an MG Company where I was an instructor and group leader!'

'Then I will take you as an air-gunner when I am clear for take-off!' That was my salvation from Stalingrad; it must have been 2 December 1942.

Once his aircraft was full and more with wounded, we took off without a problem and got clear of the encirclement without being noticed. As we were flying over the Don, the pilot said, 'We have to go higher, all hell has been let loose down there!' There was a tank battle in process, but we got clear relatively quickly. We made a safe landing at the destination airfield, where I left the ambulances.

I was one of the last of my company to leave Stalingrad alive. Of my comrades with whom I had been in action, none survived Stalingrad. The others, who were still on the Northern Boundary in January, were crushed beneath tank tracks. Only three from the rearward services survived to be captured captivity: the CSM, the medical orderly and the provisions NCO. Our company commander Lieutenant Kessler and fifty-six NCOs and men

---

5. Dr Haidinger was a junior surgeon and not divisional surgeon.

died the so-called hero's death. The rest perished in Russian captivity. Stalingrad has burnt deep into our soul, can never let us be and has influenced our life. Even today, more than sixty-five years after the event, our thoughts always wander back to where our youth, our hope and our best comrades died.

> *After twenty day's convalescent leave Arthur Krüger was drafted to Stalino in Russia, and later participated in the reconstitution of 60th Division in southern France. He fought in Italy and Hungary in 1945 and was taken prisoner by US forces. He lived his final years at Feltre in Italy and died in his eighty-eighth year as the result of a bad fall.*

21. HANS KRUMFUSS:

To the Bitter End[1]

Hans Krumfuss was a sergeant in No 3 Company, 171st Anti-Tank Abteilung, 71st Infantry Division.

In November 1942, the 171st Anti-tank Abteilung was in a well-developed position at Stalingrad-South on the Volga, the front facing east. The Abteilung command post lay in the Zaritza gully which led to the Volga. Our commanding officer was Lieutenant-Colonel Wildhagen. Our No 3 Company (commander Lieutenant von Alten) was located with all twelve anti-tank guns and MGs at the southernmost part of the front at Minina. Here were also the Company command post with elements of the rearward services, orderly office and CSM: the remainder (harness-master, pay sergeant, fuel dump and the rearward services for the other Companies) lay up to 25 kilometres west of Stalingrad. We were well spread out and had little contact with the other Companies.

The company at Stalingrad was in a suburb still partially inhabited by the civilian population and not too badly battered. With our workshop we had built a bunker at Sovietski and made it habitable with timber fetched from Stalingrad. The local inhabitants were still in their own houses, and we had a good relationship with them.

At the beginning of November Division ordered that all service and fighting vehicles which would probably not be used in action in the coming period were to be dug in and made splinter-proof. The engines, if in need of repair, were to be removed and made capable of being transported: apparently they were to be overhauled in the Reich. Therefore things were on the move! Some of my colleagues dug great pits. My small workshop with two mechanics and

---

1. This report was published in *Das Kleeblatt* (newsletter of 71st Infantry Division) editions 163 and 164, in April and August 1993.

two Russian PoWs began removing the engines. The boards for the wooden trestles we obtained from the ruins of the city.

We finished on 20 November. We loaded our 3.5-tonne Opel to the limit and set off with the other service vehicles of the Abteilung. I was assigned Sergeant Stiller as my co-driver, a colleague from my active service period, which pleased me greatly. The journey would take us to Kalatch, across the Don, past the Marinovka field hospital and the military airfield. After a drive of many hours we reached our destination. I have forgotten its name, but it had a railway branch line. The engines were loaded here. Because November days were very short we had to look round for a billet: we found one very quickly. In it were colleagues from the Northern Boundary strip who told us all kinds of threatening movements. They told us of attempts made by the Russians to break through against the Italian divisions, and of heavy defensive fighting on the northern flank of Stalingrad. A mood of depression prevailed in the billet. My friend Stiller and I took our blankets and tried to sleep in a corner.

During the night we were awoken suddenly by mortar and MG fire. The Russian women in the house shrieked and cried: 'The Russkies are coming!' The two of us naturally went out: in the streets was wild confusion. In the tumult we had a job to find our lorry again, but eventually we found it undamaged. Obviously the best thing now was to get under way, but in what direction? In conversations with the billet fraternity we had heard the word Kalatch mentioned. Maybe the road there would be blocked? Therefore we went south-west to Tchir and from the railway station headed east once more for Stalingrad. Later we discovered that we had taken quite the wrong route: the other lorry drivers had headed west and thus avoided being trapped in the Pocket later. As we drove through Tchir, at the railway station we found a giant warehouse with provisions. In passing by we saw great piles of round cheeses. Later, during the encirclement, we often thought longingly of those masses of food.

We headed for the east. The Rollbahn was quiet although we could hear heavy artillery fire in the distance. We kept up a brisk pace: once at the side of the Rollbahn small groups of German troops appeared, some without weapons and in a desperate condition. To our enquiry they replied that they came from neighbouring units. In the night Russian tanks had suddenly arrived, had set the houses afire and crushed everything in their path. They had only saved their own lives by taking flight. I urged them to come with us to Stalingrad: at this word they refused horror-struck. We described how they could get to the railway station at Tchir where the Russians had not arrived yet. In shock we continued our journey.

Now there also appeared Russian women and children carrying bundles containing all their belongings. They passed us in silence and fearful. From now on we had to be watchful. Finally we saw a signpost for Stalinski: we were there. Unfortunately the Russians were there before us! They had tanks and were firing wildly into the village. The houses were ablaze. Because our rearward services were on the opposite side of the village, we had to leave the Rollbahn and approach it in a great circle from behind. Luckily we were able to do this without being noticed. Sergeant Stiller left to look for his troops. At my own position I found only our Russian 'Hiwis' – led by our mechanic Alex, a splendid fellow. I tried to make him understand that they were free now, his own people had arrived. To my surprise this did not go down at all well and they pressed me to take them with me. When I assented and they got into the lorry, at a stroke another ten were suddenly there!

Meanwhile the situation had become increasingly critical. The Russians were shooting at everything: several vehicles were wiped out at full speed – the poor devils! Now it was time to get the hell out of there. I drove at once into the terrain because the Rollbahn was not safe. It was a ghastly journey: behind us the burning village, ahead the desert steppe. Nevertheless we made it, if the lorry often threatened to turn over. There being no seats, whenever we came to a big hole the Russians would slide around helplessly. How long we kept going like that I have no idea, in any case it seemed to me like an eternity.

Finally the smoking ruins of Stalingrad appeared on the horizon. I had all the Russians get out except my two who remained with me. First I went to the Abteilung command post in the Zariza gorge where I reported to Lieutenant-Colonel Wildhagen. When they heard my report, and that I was the only survivor of No 3 Company rear services to escape the chaos, together with one lorry and two Russian volunteers, they could not believe it. They knew nothing of Stalingrad being encircled. I still cannot believe it myself today that such a state of affairs could happen in our German Wehrmacht! The entire Abteiluing Staff was simply speechless. Lieutenant-Colonel Wildhagen said to me: 'Krumfuss, it cannot be as bad as that, and in a short while the thing will have been ironed out. Return to your unit and report to your company commander!'

I went off to my company where I was received joyfully. The commander, Lieutenant von Alten, gave me a hearty welcome: he said they had already given me up for lost, but the rest of the rearward services had already arrived here. He said the whole situation was completely impenetrable. Our motor pool consisted of only four half-tracks, the field kitchen and my 3.5-tonne lorry. Therefore Lieutenant von Alten made me his company troop leader which I had also been years before.

Apart from the daily artillery fire, at this time the front was fairly quiet. After a few days things became clearer: the Russians had broken through the Romanian lines towards Kalatch: in the north Russian tanks had gone through the Italian front divisions and were heading south. The encirclement was complete when they took Kalatch. Naturally elements of our troops were withdrawn from the Volga front to set up a new defensive line on the western perimeter. Then it snowed, and we had neither winter clothing nor fur boots. It appeared that all stores of clothing were outside the Pocket. The units which had previously inhabited extensive bunkers had now to construct a defensive ring at the western boundary and dig trenches in order to resist Russian pressure. Our company had to pass a platoon of anti-tank guns with half-tracks under Sergeant Taubert on the way to the Northern Boundary. We never saw them again except for Taubert, whom I came across wounded at the end of the struggle in the cellar of a field hospital, a small heap of misery no longer responsive.

Our company now experienced the first rationing of food: daily only 400 grams of bread and an absolute ban on fuel. We had to supply our positions daily with food and ammunition on foot. Russian low level aircraft, so-called fighter-bombers, raked us every day. In our sector was a four-barrelled AA gun. It dared not fire so as not to attract attention to our positions. Things were not going so well with our supply aircraft: it was probably too long a distance for our fighters to accompany them. Many Ju 52s were shot down. At night the 'Duty Corporal' would come: a small Russian biplane. The pilot would see the fires in the chimneys and then dive down to drop small bombs.

At the end of December the bread ration was cut again. Meanwhile the rearward services had not been idle. In front of our noses was the great grain silo; surely there must be something to be had there! With a couple of Russians from our surroundings and a horse-drawn cart we went off to the silo where we found lively activity. We loaded a couple of sacks of corn and then went back. The Russian families offered at once to grind it. They had a large but primitive handmill which needed several men to turn it, which was very strenuous. Now we ground day and night. In the evening the infantry relieved the Russian civilians and it was our turn. The best of it was that we had a master baker in our company: the first oven-fresh loaves we ate with pious respect, for the first time in months! Unfortunately the bread had one great drawback: it tasted bitter. Then the baker discovered that the corn had not been sifted and there was vermouth grain amongst it. But better bitter bread than none! We also supplied the local population with it.

Before Christmas the order came to burn all paperwork because we were going to attempt to break out. General von Hartmann ordered all motor pool and workshop NCOs to report. The meeting took place in an undamaged shed. The general walked along our lines, asking here and there for the senior man, looked at our decorations, was very friendly to us and then announced why he had called us together: we were probably going to attempt a breakout from the encirclement very soon. 'To this end I want you to tell me what the situation is with the vehicles. Have we enough of them serviceable? What is the position with oil and fuel? I get enough reports from the units, but now I want to hear it from you!' We were impressed by the urgency of his words. I had never heard a general speak like that before. He asked a number of us for our opinions. Upon parting he offered each man his hand and looked him in the eyes.

Back at Company I reported to our company commander about the meeting with the general. At that he said with a serious face, 'My dear Krumfuss, meanwhile a new Führer-order has arrived; Stalingrad must be held! The relief army is on its way, but the intention is only to create a corridor for supplies.'

Christmas came; no mail. Our Christmas parcels lay outside the Pocket and were shared out amongst our comrades there. Then we had a tiny pleasure: soldiers from a horse-drawn unit came to ask if they could slaughter two small horses in our kitchen. They had become separated from their unit and had no kitchen facilities of their own. Our CSM allowed it and we were rewarded with a tongue and liver. It was not much, but we enjoyed it nevertheless. On Christmas Eve the Russians fired off at us their version of a carol. It was growing ever colder: the Volga had long been frozen over. Now the Russians could be supplied across the ice. Next came a great disappointment: the Army bulletin reported that Manstein's army had itself been surrounded and had had to fight its way out to the south with heavy losses. A new Führer-order commanded that Stalingrad must be held at all costs to tie down Russian forces and prevent the Caucasus army being endangered. That was the end for us: the Sixth Army was being sacrificed!

At the end of 1942 the Russians put on a great fireworks display, the like of which I shall probably never see again in my lifetime. A glowing ring from north round to south, and a chain of fire on the other side of the Volga. Now we saw our ring of encirclement! What a waste of ammunition – but they had plenty.

On 1 January we heard from our 211th Infantry Regiment that drunken Russians in company strength had attempted to break through our line. Unfortunately they chose the sector where our infantry had a heavy MG company and their 'attack' petered out. Their casualties must have been horrendous. More and more of our stragglers were now arriving from the western front. It was impossible to hold snowholes without winter clothing and they had had to fall back. All units had been split apart. Most men had frostbite to the feet and many had no footwear. Their feet were bound with rags and then strips of tent canvas to protect against the wet: it was a pitiful sight. They had been without rations for days.

Rations were cut again in mid-January. For some time the necessary levels of food had not been met. We had lost Pitomnik airfield, and Gumrak was under threat. A large field hospital was located there, from where the seriously wounded were supposed to be flown out by empty transport aircraft. Division issued a new order: supply, the workshops, administration and so on had to prune their staffs for anybody able to use a weapon and send them to the fighting units. If necessary a short period of infantry training was to be given these people. Therefore we received twenty men, amongst them five staff-sergeants from the field-gendarmerie and a veterinary lieutenant. Lieutenant von Alten passed them to me: I was to make a fighting troop out of them with the help of two NCOs and a senior private. The local Russian population looked on in astonishment. Playing war games struck them as a very strange thing to be doing.

Meanwhile the Russians had made us an offer to accept our capitulation which was turned down on Hitler's order. The Commander-in-Chief General Paulus had his headquarters at this time near to Red Square. Numerous large ruins with undamaged cellars stood round about it. The Square lay in our division's area of command; therefore our company had to make available two anti-tank guns for the protection of the Commander-in-Chief.

More days passed. Romanians began to appear everywhere in our sector. They had already disposed of their weapons, occupied the last of the useable houses and harassed the civilian population. On 25 January we received an operational order. The company commander called the NCOs together and told them to occupy a holding position on the south slope and remain there until the remnants of the neighbouring division, a so-called Light Division with two regiments, showed up and took over. After it did so, we would be returning to our old positions in Stalingrad.

Our small unit was divided into two platoons. Lieutenant von Alten led one platoon, and I led the other. My platoon consisted mostly of newcomers: only two corporals, the acting pay-sergeant Gert Rüppert and armourer-corporal Fritz Meyer were old comrades. After a short march we reached our position, one trench with small bunkers built by the Russians as part of the city defences. It was in a fruit plantation with many small trees. Behind them we could see the roofs of a small village whose name now escapes me. The position was not bad, it had small bunkers everywhere, some with a loam floor. It was a quiet day. Now and again a troop of Romanians came by, of wretched appearance and begging for bread. A major, whom we had not recognized as such, had a schnapps with Lieutenant von Alten and reported that the Russians were hot on their heels and we should keep a good watch.

The first night passed quietly. It had snowed again. Our rations arrived in the morning. It was yesterday's soup, frozen solid and thus requiring us to thaw it. We had less bread because the baker was in the line with us. It had become very, very cold: the only protection for the head was a thin cap-comforter under the steel helmet. The men had made themselves gloves of stitched rags. All in all it was a grim day.

Towards midday we saw a large column approaching from afar. Field glasses gave us reassurance that these were German soldiers. But what a sight! A couple of officers marched at their head. Then came about forty men, armed and still in a tolerable condition. Next at ragged distances troop after troop of men linked together in twos and threes, supporting each other, a woollen blanket around the head, the wounded hobbling on crutches: the entire crowd numbering about one hundred. Lieutenant von Alten and I looked at each other in shock. This was the new holding force, the Light Division? The major approached us and presented 'the remnants of the Division'. The column came to a standstill and the soldiers fell out in rows and fell asleep – a sad sight! Here again many were unshod, rags and bits of tent canvas wrapped about their feet.

The major gave us a tired smile when Lieutenant von Alten passed him the order to occupy the position with his men. He replied: 'You can see for yourself we are in no state to do so.' The sleepers were awoken with the promise: 'Boys, just a couple of hundred metres more there are houses with something to eat.' An NCO of this troop told me they had been two days without food or sleep. After much encouraging and ordering the sad one hundred set out once more in the direction of Stalingrad. Lieutenant von Alten discussed the situation with the NCOs and myself. We reached the decision to wait and see what happened next.

That afternoon it grew misty and we heard heavy MG and artillery fire in the village lying before us. We heard women screaming and saw houses burning. The Russkies were coming! Several T-34s and a pack of infantry came slowly forward. Through our field glasses we saw the latter, wearing long winter greatcoats, felt boots and fur hats. In the belief that they had no enemy to fear, they advanced slowly towards us, shouting and chattering. Lieutenant von Alten ordered absolute silence and to wait until they came into shooting range: he would give the signal to shoot by firing one round. It was for us a hellish feeling, and for most of the men from the rearward services and orderly offices probably the first time in their lives that they had had to shoot at people. Then we opened fire: the Russians were taken totally by surprise and took cover at once. Suddenly a German gun behind us which we had not noticed began to shoot. It was dug in as a flak piece. Now the Russians were uncertain and drew back. Since we were obliged to conserve ammunition, we ceased fire.

After about an hour we suddenly heard the sound of engines: the tanks were coming! Firing ceaselessly they waltzed through the orchard. This meant we had to go, for we had no anti-tank guns. Lieutenant von Alten gave the order: each man withdraw at his own discretion: regroup at the south end of Minina. I was to take them over. He himself wanted to attempt to break through the front with seven men and reach the west. We took leave of each other with a handshake. There was no time to lose.

I had only Corporal Meier with me, the others had gone. Now we discovered the T-34s, with red flags fluttering on their turrets: we made off. Meier fell into a shell crater up to his neck in snow. In the attempt to pull him out, I lost my machine-pistol, which disappeared into the snowy depths. Then we came to a flak gun. The gun captain asked me to give him the range to the tanks from outside. He wanted to engage them with high-angle fire before they got to the orchard. When we replied, the tanks were already there, he joined us with his two colleagues, and we reached the first houses at Minina at our last gasp. The lost crowd of the neighbouring division was already in position. The major said to me, 'Get yourself a gun first, there's enough of them lying around!' Meier and I went into a wooden house occupied by Romanians. There were weapons of all kinds on the floor: the Romanians had given up in their own way. We picked out the guns and ammunition we wanted and then made off in search of the remainder of my Company but none of them was to be seen.

Near our old positions, my faithful Alex ran towards me from our workshop. He trailed a small hand-sledge with my pack containing clean underwear and shaving gear. My joy was great! The CSM had had to relocate our field kitchen and left Alex behind as a signpost. Full of joy I gave him the gift of my pocket watch, which one way or another was bound to fall into Russian hands anyway. We were gleefully received by the rear services. A section of my Alarm Company was also here. They had only one anti-tank and an MG. I passed the remnants of the baggage train to our poor CSM, for whom I felt really sorry. Three months ago he was fresh out of the Reich from officers' training to obtain his front experience with us before being made an officer. Personally I did not want to remain with the rear services and went to our artillery position with a motorcycle despatch rider. To my great surprise, here I met my comrade Stiller who was captain of the last gun. Nearby was an MG with two soldiers. Now my battlegroup still had two sergeants and seven men, and a sentry on the gun and MG day and night. Rations came daily from the kitchen: they consisted of an undefinable thin soup and 100 grams of bread.

Sergeant Stiller and I made a long tour of inspection by day. The wounded, mostly without medication and medical care lay everywhere in the cellars which remained intact. Because the remaining units and stragglers were of no fixed abode and therefore received no rations, they stole from field kitchens and supply units. On a tour through the cellars we came across an old acquaintance: the former driver for our former Abteilung commander. In earlier times he had been a good athlete and a big man. Now he lay here, a heap of misery with two rounds through his lungs. When he saw me he began to cry. He said: 'Here I lie alone and abandoned by everybody!' The bunker doctor was of the opinion he would soon die. It was dreadful and was getting worse: our rations sledge was raided. From now on it was accompanied by two men with machine-pistols at the ready.

A young lieutenant from the anti-aircraft service visited us carrying a large knapsack. He wanted me to tell him how to get through the minefield at the Volga. I explained they were Russian mines and not ours. Moreover snow and much new rubble made it impossible to find them. At that he began to cry: he had left his gun crew and his nerve had given out. We convinced him to remain with us to the end, since we had enough room. When he unpacked the rucksack there came to light many goodies we had not seen for weeks.

Everything was shared out in a spirit of comradeship and we had a real party!

Two days later a captain of the artillery came to us also requesting a guide through the minefield. When he explained that he wanted to take measurements to calibrate his guns I replied that there was no longer any ammunition for him to fire. He acknowledged that I was right, but as an officer he felt obliged at least to try to break out before he went into Soviet captivity. I shook my head. The captain returned with me to the bunker and conversed awhile with the anti-aircraft lieutenant. After that they both packed their rucksacks and took leave of each other with a handshake.

Meanwhile 29 January 1943 dawned. When I returned that evening with a private from the rations distribution I was greeted by long faces. Sergeant Stiller reported that they had been considering our situation and had come to the decision not to go into Russian captivity but rather die. All six were agreed: did I wish to be included? At that moment I thought of General von Hartmann, who amidst his infantry had fought off a Russian attack at the railway embankment and found a soldier's death. I therefore declined, I would not die by my own hand. Accordingly we agreed that I would leave them, if that was how things were.

The food was now almost at an end. We had lost our last airfield a week previously, and the Ju 52s now only came at night. On Red Square an area of terrain had been cleared and surrounded with red lamps. This illuminated square was the aiming zone for low-level parachute drops of supplies and cases. Naturally a lot missed. Anybody who could still run dug through the rubble to find anything edible. On the evening of the 29th a captain came from Division and awarded me the Iron Cross First Class and gave me three Iron Crosses Second Class for three private soldiers.

January 30th came. That evening I went with Sergeant Stiller to the signals bunker where there was a radio set. They were broadcasting a speech by Hermann Göring to mark the tenth anniversary of the National Socialist seizure of power by Hitler. We arrived just at the right time to hear Göring. Verbatim he said: 'The Battle of Stalingrad is now at its end. The Sixth Army has fought heroically to the last man and the last round, and will go down in history as immortal!'

At that moment a boot hit the radio and the voice was silenced. A soldier said: 'The swines are saying we are dead and we are sitting here with 100,000 men still hoping for rescue!' We left the bunker in silence, and Sergeant Stiller said, 'It's all up with us, my dear Hans, do what you can. Should you ever make it back to Germany, don't forget us and tell everybody, how outrageously and senselessly they sacrificed a whole army just because certain senior officers of the German Army paid more heed to the orders of an Austrian senior private than to the lives of 100,000 men!' With that my comrade Stiller took his leave of me. I fetched my few belongings from the command post and joined the two machine-gunners, private soldiers who wanted to continue living as I did.

On the night of 31 January there was shooting everywhere in our positions: hand grenades detonated. At daybreak a Russian shouted into our bunker. 'Kamerad, ruki werch!' We laid down our weapons and walked into the open with our hands raised. The Russians were very joyful and friendly: for them it was a great victory. A young Russian lieutenant said in German: 'War over, Hitler *kaputt*!' Now we were taken to a collection area and searched for weapons. Later a Commissar arrived and ordered me to accompany him. I thought he would shoot me, he held a pistol in my back and ordered me into our command post. There lay my six comrades, each with a bullet wound to the temple and not moving. The Commissar held a finger to his own temple and shouted, 'Durag! Durag!' Later I discovered that this word meant 'Dummkopf'. We returned without speaking to the collection point, where I rejoined the ranks. We marched off into captivity five abreast. The sun was shining, the temperature was -40°C and there was an icy wind blowing.

I thought of home. Today was my mother's birthday. She was 63 years old. The whole family would be sitting and having coffee, and my mother would be saying, 'What is our Hans doing in Russia? It is such a long time since he wrote . . .'

22. FRANZ KUMPF:

As a Telephone Linesman at Stalingrad[1]

Before the war Franz Kumpf trained as a hairdresser. At Stalingrad he was attached to the HQ of the 194th Infantry Regiment, 71st Infantry Division. After the war he opened a hairdressing salon at Flechtorf near Lehre. He spent his retirement at Lehre, and died there a few years ago.

It was before the encirclement. On the advance towards Stalingrad there were less and less of us. I often had prisoners to assist me. One evening I was given an important task. My superior gave me twelve prisoners to set up the telephone connections in the battalion command post. I had great doubts about this and felt insecure. 'I must have a German!'

'Whom shall I give you, seeing I have none!' was the answer. 'And apart from that you have a very good relationship with the Russians.' There was no answer to that. I asked the Russians in their own language, 'Have you water and bread?' A shake of the head and 'Nein' was the answer. I showed them that I also had nothing. 'Let's go, perhaps we shall find water and bread on a dead body!'

After completing the given task I returned to the command post with the prisoners. As I had running sores to my hands, feet and face, I also managed to find some dressings on the bodies we passed on the way. One day I found a pair of cloth slippers and quickly put them on in place of my boots. I wired them to my trousers to keep them on. Always, whenever I spotted a medical orderly I would say, 'Come and help me!'

'I have no dressings,' he would reply. 'But I do,' I would counter. At that he would remove the scabs and apply iodine. Now finally I had relief, and with help I could dress them myself.

Gradually we got closer to Stalingrad. The Russian soldier Alex, a

---

1. This report was printed in *Das Kleeblatt*, newsletter of the former members of 71st Infantry Division, issue 139, Nr. 2 30th Year, April 1986.

telephonist, had long been my assistant: we got on well. He even wanted to have a rifle. I told him, one was enough; if I should be wounded he should take mine to defend us. I even showed him the bullets. It happened frequently that he got no rations. Then I would share mine with him.

One night I had to lay telephone wires at the outskirts of Stalingrad. We had to cross a cobblestoned road. I gave Alex the job of burying the line to protect it against tanks. When he had done that I said he should have a sleep and wait for me. Meanwhile I had to prepare the lines to the command post, but did not have enough cable. I searched around for it desperately and after feeling about in the earth with my bare hands found some Russian connections. Piece by piece with these I patched up the important connection to the command post.

In a happy mood I followed along the cable quickly to my helper Alex. Ducked down in a roadside ditch I looked all around me and shouted his name. I became impatient. I did not think he would have run off, for otherwise he would not have made such a good job of laying the cable between the cobbles: that was something I was not up to physically at that time. Accompanied by infantry fire and flares I kept shouting. A manhole cover opened: I followed the emerging form, rifle in hand, and discovered to my joy that it was Alex. 'Something else I've learnt,' I thought, 'In an emergency go down a drain.'

During my absence Alex had found a Russian kitchen. As he would not let up I said, 'OK, but quick!' He swung himself over a wooden fence and in the next second a canister came back. Quickly opened, it felt like pudding inside. I brought out a lump of it with both hands. It had no specific taste – it was probably millet or maize, the main thing was, something edible. Everything edible and drinkable was a gift from heaven. On the way to our gulley we heard a wounded Russian cry out. I took Alex's arm and said, 'Over there, a Russian comrade!' He talked to him, and then took my arm and said we should go.

Next morning the attack continued. Alex was transferred to another engineering troop. It was already light: the connections to the command post had been severed during the firing and we were now heading into the city. After we had gone on some distance, telephone linesman Gerblich came along with Alex. I saw how exhausted Gerblich looked and called out, 'Let's get into this deep bomb crater!' This would give protection for a short break and gave me the chance to cut up into pieces with my dagger a piece of bread I had found on the way, and share it out. Gerblich said suddenly, 'I am going to shoot this Russian!' I was shocked, for I knew that Gerblich had only come to us a few days previously and already his nerve had gone under the tension in this living hell. I said at once to Alex, 'This comrade will not shoot you, his nerve has gone. I shall speak to the sergeant and today you will be back with me.' I gave him my hand: he had understood. After a brief farewell we each searched for our respective cables, Gerblich towards the Volga and I out of the city.

Whilst proceeding on this venture my comrade Wilhelm Hönnige[2] and I came to an asphalted street with a pavement. We felt greatly insecure here, for fire, steel and barbed wire blocked the way, and we could hear fighting and saw flares here and there. I decided to do a check on the wiring while Wilhelm kept watch. I hung the apparatus around my neck and pressed my service dagger into the earth surrounding a small tree on the pavement. I had just reported finishing my test with a few words when Wilhelm called to me, 'Russians are coming.'

'Don't shoot!' I called back. I could not take cover, being surrounded by paved surfaces and barbed wire. I picked up my carbine, which I had propped against a tree, took off the safety catch and pressed it against my hip, finger on the trigger. In the shadow of the fire I saw the first Russian. The sad outlook was underlined here and there by flares, smoke and a stench. My comrade from the opposing side had come closer and along the middle of the street. He advanced three or four steps, looked around and went on. I thought: so you are very wary too! At every step he took I looked about me. If I was seen he was dead, for I was watching his machine-pistol. A few more steps away I saw the second Russian, I turned myself left and quietly aimed at his body. He took a few more steps and then stopped. I looked for Wilhelm but could not see him. I thought he had probably sought cover at the nearby crossroads close to a kind of traffic cabin. Now another ten Russians appeared, each armed with a machine-pistol. I had decided to defend myself if necessary, but I should definitely not have come out the winner against all these! If they recognized me, at least I could take a few with me. Even today I cannot understand how we could have been so close and they didn't see me. Or did they want to avoid a firefight seeing that I had not fired? We were no more than three metres apart! I might even have spoken to them were it not for their machine-pistols . . .

---

2. Wilhelm Hönnige came from Heilbronn and was probably a wine-grower (information from Hans Kumpf).

The incident was over, I found Wilhelm where I had guessed he would be. We went on, cable in hand. The Russians had made us more cautious. Now I would often stop and examine my surroundings not only visually. I was already used to all bullets, shells, mortars and flares.

What did we see once? A lorry with underwear! For some days I had been without underpants and vest. These had got so filthy and lousy on the steppe that I could no longer tolerate them and threw them away. That was probably a mistake, for my other clothing was in the same condition. At night it was cold and one had the feeling that one was wearing sheet metal trousers. So my find came just at the right time: I put a pair of underpants under my belt. Then I rummaged through the heap to find something that looked like a shirt. What I discovered was not what I wanted since it resembled a jacket but nevertheless it found its way under my belt.

Upon returning to the command post I enquired at once after my comrade Gerblich. They told me that he and his Russian helper had failed to return from checking a line. I asked for some water: telephone-linesman Klaus Neusius handed me his field flask. After a large gulp I had the feeling I had been set alight inside. With horror I discovered that the flask was filled with very strong vodka! It burnt like a fire for some time, because there was no water to be had.

One afternoon Neusius came back with two carbines and said emotionally: 'Wilhelm is lying in the railway station and is probably dead!' I went there at once, grabbed a stretcher and took four prisoners along. Snipers made our journey difficult. Wilhelm lay on his stomach between the rails, the wound was the size of two hands. I put the stretcher alongside him as carefully as I could and with the help of the four Russians transferred him to it in the same position. The steep embankment began a few metres away. The loose sand made it difficult to carry him, and bullets whistled round our ears. Kneeling and crawling we pushed the stretcher forwards. Wilhelm, racked with pain, shouted while rolling, which I had to prevent. I told him, 'Lie still, we are taking you to a doctor!' The shooting kept our heads down all the time, for it was daylight and the enemy could see clearly. Finally we reached the paint house, the regimental command post, where there was a medical orderly. We laid Wilhelm at his feet. Bathed in sweat, I leaned against the wall and looked at the big wound. When I saw flies settling around it, I asked the medical orderly for help. He laid a large pad of gauze on the wound. Wilhelm raised his head: I put a greatcoat beneath it and asked if he felt better. He did not answer – my help was at an end.

Looking for line damage one night I had a grim experience in Stalingrad. I was searching the earth for a cable with my hands. At the same time I had to look up because we had doubled the line on account of the danger of being eavesdropped, setting it up above. Often there would be debris and the like ahead of one's feet, therefore I had made a habit of raising my feet as high as I could. Suddenly I trod on something and went through it. My first thought was: this is a corpse. As I took a step forward I saw a ribcage hanging from my right foot. I kicked it free and continued with my work, finding no time to reflect.

One day I was coming from the Volga with climbing irons on my shoulders, for the lines had to be put up overhead by day. After I had gone through the tunnel to the railway embankment, an open car came towards me and stopped. The occupants wore brown uniforms and swastika armbands. They said they wanted to photograph the Volga. 'Yes, yes, it's just through the embankment. But the enemy has it in view,' I told them. When they heard that, the car turned about at once, and the brave Party men were suddenly gone in a cloud of dust. We alone are here to die, I thought.

Once I had to go to the dentist located in the Pitomnik gully. The practice was in a small wooden hut. I sat in the only room with some colleagues: a chair and a bench were available. On all walls and corners was evidence of bullets which had passed through and the effect of mortar splinters. Soothing music was provided by howling aircraft and MG-fire as the good dentist quietly pedal-started the drill to free us of toothache. He had to perform his delicate work amongst all this shooting! Even today I should like to express to him my heartfelt thanks.

One day I was summoned to the city prison, which housed the command post, to give a haircut to our commanding officer Roske.[3] I reported to his valet, Leading Private Schaberhorn, who had his own cell. Entering this cell I could hardly believe my eyes: there was an array of fruit tarts. I said to Schaberhorn, 'Where did these all come from? We have next to nothing to eat, and here?'

'I brought it from France.'

---

3. Colonel Fritz Roske (b. 20 January 1897, d. 25 December 1956) took over command of 71st Infantry Division, on 26 January 1942 and was promoted to Major-General one day later. He was not released from Soviet captivity until 1955. Decorations: 19 December 1941 German Cross in gold: 20 January 1943, Knight's Cross.

AS A TELEPHONE LINESMAN AT STALINGRAD

'Don't you lie to me, one of these tarts is mine or I'll expose you publicly,' I replied.

'No, I can't, the General's coming.'

'Well, he can eat one tart less, and I shall split it with my comrades.'

I went out and fetched a mess-tin and laundry bag. Once I came back the valet placed a large iron bar across the door so that nobody could observe this trade. He put one tart aside for me and I paid him 20 Marks for it. I ate a quarter of it in great haste with the aid of my dagger, the rest I stuffed into the mess-tin. The senior private now informed the commander that the barber had arrived. Upon entering I reported myself briefly, looked for a chair and said in a friendly tone, 'Please sit here, Herr Lieutenant-Colonel' – the salon was open for business. I requested from him a hand towel for his neck and began my work. While at work on him, Roske ordered me to go with two colleagues to the department store and spend two days there cutting hair. Back with my colleagues I laid my booty on the table; with the help of my dagger I shovelled the tart out of the mess-tin, divided it into four and said they should eat fast otherwise we might have to sub-divide it again. I thought to myself, perhaps this is their last sweet titbit.

Next day I went to the department store as ordered to provide the haircuts. On the way I came under rifle fire. I thought to myself, leave me in peace, I am only going to cut hair. My two comrades had arrived before me: our salon was in the basement. Later this basement was the command post and quarters of Field-Marshal Paulus. This building, of thick concrete, and the way to it I knew very well because telephone wires led there. We had to keep thirty-two lines in commission and so were never unemployed.

On a search for faults in the line I met a small gang of Russian prisoners. They were well dressed: my own clothing was very tattered: parts of my field-blouse were missing, my trousers were worse. It occurred to me I should obtain a pair of good trousers. I spoke to a Russian and said, 'Trousers off!' He gave me a funny look but did as I requested when I took off my own trousers. We exchanged them, his fitted me well except that the brown colour was not quite right.

Now I had put myself in danger. It was not long before an unknown colleague struck me in the back with the butt of his rifle and said, 'On your way, you Ivan!' With this clothing, and two boots each of a different colour I went on leave. Sergeant Mank gave me a docket for a complete new issue of clothing once I got back to the Reich. Between Stalingrad and Germany I was deloused twice. The bus to Stebnitz was crowded with standing passengers

149

while the seats around me were unoccupied. Its good citizens were probably ashamed to be sitting beside such a ragged front-line soldier. I said in a loud voice: 'You can all sit with me in comfort, I might not look all that good, but I am one of the few who ever had the chance to go on leave from Stalingrad in one piece.' At that all heads turned to look at me.

23. HERBERT KUNTZ:

My Last Flight into the Pocket[1]

Herbert Kuntz (b. Dieflen/Saar, 15 February 1915, d. 26 August 1998) was a gifted pilot awarded the Knight's Cross on 14 March 1943 for his service in supplying the Stalingrad Pocket. He was then a Lieutenant. In the summer of 1943 he was appointed Squadron- and Training-leader for the young bomber crews. He flew a total of 450 wartime missions.

January 29th 1943, operational conference with the commanding officer, I/KG 100. 'Pitomnik is, as is known, in Russian hands and is now a fighter base sprinkled with AA guns. Therefore, keep your distance! Our new dropping place, the railway station at Gumrak, has been made into a makeshift landing strip. Landing in the evening will be difficult, taking off from there worse. Every pilot is free to act according to his own judgement!'

Below us, the gutted trams of Stalingrad stood out against the grey snow. The Volga, broad and sluggish, separated the two river banks. Dazzling points glittered here, there, alone and in groups. And at another place shortly afterwards, at the same rhythm, impact after impact. Russian artillery was pounding the shrunken positions of the Sixth Army.

A drama was being played out over Pitomnik. Flight crews, a colourful mixture tossed to the front, hastily conjured up from somewhere, transferred flight instructors, scarcely-fledged trainees and pilots plucked from some operational unit or other circled the airfield in the old Ju 52s. The Russians kept the runway fully lit and fired green flares, the invitation to land. Some machines actually did so – to their cost! Recognizing their mistake, others tried to fly off. Too late, scarcely a single one did. Whatever radio frequency it was that they were using was unknown to us, though it probably was known to the Russians, and so we were unable to call and warn them. For the first and probably last time they saw Stalingrad from the air and confused Pitomnik

---

1. This report was taken from the book *Kampfgeschwader 100 Wiking* by Ulf Balke (pp. 136–8) and placed at the Editor's disposal by Dipl.Engineer Hans Gaenshirt of Freiburg.

with Gumrak. After a tiring flight of several hundred kilometres over enemy territory, harassed by fighters and AA fire, most of them 'greenhorns' at the front, they thought they had arrived safely at the protection of the brightly-lit airfield. Possibly the Russians would even have given them radio bearings over their own frequency.

How should they know that the three tiny green lights here behind us, close to the suburbs of Stalingrad, marked the correct airfield, namely Gumrak? Admittedly, if they had looked closer, perhaps they might have seen the wrecks of Ju 52s and He 111s down below, bordering the narrow runway, laboriously dragged to one side, thus indicating in their own way that from now on German supply aircraft had to land here.

At low altitude I roared overhead, recognized groups of infantry, looking up with growing hope. Tiredly they waved. I still had my doubts about attempting a landing. One had to fly out of it safely, a sacrifice was of use to nobody! Today the runway had been cleared and was about 50 metres broad. The wingspan of an He 111 was 24 metres. Those steel wrecks of aircraft were therefore damned nearly at the runway edge!

The runway was perhaps only 800 metres long, and the He 111 was accustomed to 1,500 metres if taking off full loaded. Landing was, as I have mentioned, at the discretion of the pilot. The decision was quick and uncomplicated. I watched one of my comrades' machines rolling along below, coming to a stop in one piece. At once I banked round on the same course and informed my crew, the radio-operator and flight mechanic, of my decision. The side-wind made the approach awkward; we set down softly in the snow at 100kms/hr. The machine dipped a few times but we ploughed through the snow drifts without the aircraft standing on end. Now we turned off. At once a large number of infantrymen came hobbling towards us. So that none of them should come too close to the propellers I turned the motors off. I should have preferred to let them run: better safe than sorry. Our other aircraft also touched down safely. We quickly unloaded the provisions we had brought – far too little. With about a half-dozen He 111s we represented the entire Luftwaffe of the 'Iron Reichsmarschall'. There was no time to lose. A throng of wounded pressed against the access hatch in the fuselage, silent and resigned. At the beginning, about two months ago at Pitomnik, we could only take six men, that is, by express thoughtless orders. In reality we would mostly take nine, though secretly. Now it was do or die for them. We could not take them all, that much was obvious. We were the last machines to land at Stalingrad.

Whoever remained behind . . . To those indicated by my finger I gave the gift of life. This awful power!

My radio operator Walter Krebs reported he could not take any more, the fuselage was packed. 'Make sure we are not too tail-heavy!' I called to him. I climbed over the wing to my seat in the cabin, my observer, Sergeant-Major Hans Annen, to his. A wounded man had placed himself on the auxiliary seat between the bomb bays and smiled at us, or rather his eyes seemed to. I started up the motors. The ignition chattered comfortingly first time. The excited hubbub in the fuselage was drowned out. 'Are all the hatches shut back there, Walter?' I enquired over the internal telephone. 'No, we can't, wait a bit!' The wounded man between us was forced completely into the cabin. Immediately another took the seat. This one resisted feverishly the constant pressure coming from the fuselage. He failed, and was also forced into the cabin. Mortal fear and the burning hope of being taken along were the driving forces of those pushing at the open underbelly hatch. They had their heads in the fuselage, their feet on the ground, and the motors were running! Nearby one of my colleagues was taking off. His aircraft wobbled up with great difficulty. Now we were the last but one. The wounded in the cabin blocked my view to starboard. Taking off I would be blind that side.

The aircraft which had already left had whipped up the snow to form a drift around the three green marker lamps. At the far end of the runway I see a green light flashing. An infantryman was standing there waving a lamp. He was our aiming point, our entire illuminated flight path. I warmed up the motors more fiercely by increasing the revolutions: I needed all their power for this take-off. Snow flew in all directions.

In the icy wind of the propellers, figures writhed and turned away from us, heading for the nearby last He 111, joining the throng at its fuselage hatch. Russian artillery was firing! I forced myself to be calm, checked once more all my instruments and lever settings and gathered myself for a few seconds. Throttle forward! More than 3,000hp whipped the propellers; we rolled forward heavily. Snow sprayed high, enveloped us and deprived me of all vision. A few seconds passed and we had overtaken our own whirlwind. I had to accelerate the 15-tonne aircraft to over 150kms/hr to leave the ground. Sluggishly the speed indicator increased – too slowly! We already had half the short runway behind us. We were tail-heavy. I trimmed back quickly and forced the control stick forward to get the tail up. Now the speed increased faster. The brave infantryman at the end of the runway was eagerly waving his green lamp. Another salvo of artillery arrived. Would we get up? To abandon the take-off attempt now was too late, we would be bound to crash and break up. Everything gambled on one card! The aircraft vibrated under the roar of the motors, the wheels ploughed through the snowdrifts, the wings took over the weight increasingly. Now! A sharp tug at the elevator control – we were free of the runway. At the last moment the soldier with his green light had had to throw himself clear. I saw his ghostly face. We were flying. Thanks for your help, unknown Leading Private, how calm and devoted to your duty you were! How you must have looked back at us, at me and my Staffel colleague, who followed me up as the last of all to leave Stalingrad – back to the West, towards the Homeland.

We circled above the German positions to reach an altitude of 2,000 metres so as to fly as high as possible above the Russian AA guns. The remainder of the flight was routine. Our destination field was near Rostov on the Sea of Azov, so far had we been forced back after abandoning Morosovskaya on Christmas Eve in the face of Russian massed tanks. We tried in vain to stem their raging attack with bombs and shipboard MGs.

During the night we landed at Novotsherkassk. The wounded crawled through the bottom hatch, another and another, fifteen in all! Frozen, suffering, but saved. None said a word. Why should they? My observer Hans Annen shook my hand. I knew already, after that I would receive the Knight's Cross. A year ago when we were still scuffling with Tommy, against his warships, ports, fighters, AA emplacements and airfields, from London via Malta to Suez, hard but fair, often cocky, believing in our victory, I loved it. Yet in a dull way we felt that the defeat of Greater Germany was unavoidable. Crippling doubts, about whether we had Right on our side. The symbol on the rudder now had a quite different face. As a Lieutenant, however, I had to keep a stiff upper lip and set an example of the military virtues.

For the last time we circled over Stalingrad. Thick fog enshrouded the steppe. A radio beacon, whose invisible rays guided us through it, enabled us to work out our position. Their AA guns were silent. From 2,000 metres I began to bank lower, steering by my instruments, lower and lower. Still no sight of the ground, everything an impenetrable grey. Where should we drop our load? The altimeter read 100 metres, 80 metres, the lowest I dare go because it might not be accurate, set as it was at the air pressure of our distant starting aerodrome. For a second a parcel of grey-white battlefield, burnt out, flitted below us. We were so close to the ground! I jerked the machine back into the fog, into the safety of height. Not until afterwards came the horror of realization. To touch the ground at full speed meant we went up in a blast of flame! We had to drop our cargo, bread, blind. May it have strengthened many a brave infantryman for the long march. Those who remained behind at Stalingrad – all were our brothers! One can never forget them.

Herbert Kuntz survived the war in the rank of Captain (Reserve) and taught gliding until he was eighty-two. His former flight trainee Hans Gaenshirt (also an He 111 pilot) completes the story.[2] 'After a landing at Novotsherkassk we submitted our "battle report". The mechanic fuelled up again, the bomb personnel of the technical staff loaded the machine with the 250-kg provisions bombs [bomb casings filled with provisions. T.] which had to be heaved up into the eight bomb bays. By the time when the crew returned to the aircraft that night, this work would have been completed, the crew – five men – got in and the pilot rolled out to the runway. One usually entered the machine by the under-fuselage tunnel, and wriggled under the radio operator's seat into the narrow corridor (about 50–55 cms wide) between the bomb bays in which the bombs were hung. In the small space under the radio operator's seat meant for the flight mechanic and air-gunner, from where the two lateral MGs could be operated, the wounded had to crouch down and it was very difficult to crawl forward between the bomb bays forward in order to occupy the tiny and impracticable spot in the cockpit.'

---

2. Letter from Hans Gaenshirt, Freiburg to the publisher dated 31 January 2004.

24. JOCHEN LÖSER:

On the Northern Boundary[1]

Jochen Löser (b. Weimar, 3 April 1918) joined the 68th Infantry Regiment at Brandenburg as an ensign in 1936. As a Lieutenant in the 230th Infantry Regiment, 76th Infantry Division, he served as battalion then later regimental adjutant in France, the Balkans and Russia. Subsequently at Stalingrad he fought on the Northern Boundary.

It had become important to defend between Kotluban-Gorge and the northern edge of Stalingrad in order to protect the movements of our panzers, cost what it might. In fierce fighting the Russians were trying to break through this cover. On the evening of 5 September we built our defence, in the middle of the empty and wild steppe, without any reference point, without a tree or a bush. Luckily it was a fine, bright autumn. At night, however, it fell so dark that it was difficult to find one's way and we had to orientate ourselves by the telephone wires. We had the job of identifying the small elevations in the steppe which could be used for our artillery spotters and to maintain contact with our neighbouring divisions.

As regimental adjutant, in the evenings I had to go looking for the battalions. It was so difficult to get one's bearings that we rarely found them and so followed the telephone wires. That turned out to be a stroke of fortune for the commander of 3rd Battalion, who was lying very seriously wounded at the end of this wire. The battle for Stalingrad was not hate-filled, but a battle bitterly contested. I never encountered hate. Thus Russian prisoners carried back Lieutenant Buhl so that he could receive treatment: the telephone line had saved him! The regimental commanding officer, Colonel Abraham,[2] who had won the hearts of his men and knew the name of every man in his

---

1. This report is taken, with the kind permission of the publisher, from the book *Bittere Pflicht: Kampf und Untergang der 76.Berlin-Brandenburgischen Infanterie-Division* by Jochen Löser, publ. Osnabrück 1988.
2. Erich Abraham (b. Marienburg, 27 March 1895, d. Wiesbaden, 7 March 1971) served in

regiment, set his bandsmen to bunker-building. He sent his pioneer platoon back to the banks of the Don to fell trees and prepare cover. His foresight proved itself well-founded next morning when the Russians sent over a very large swarm of fighter-bombers to Kotluban-Gorge, which was easy to make out and carpet-bomb. Happily we had dug some trenches below our tents and took cover in them.

From this day onwards the Russians attacked mostly in the early hours, and after very heavy artillery preparation, with strong forces and individual assault troops, also until late in the night. In our sector we had to bear the attack of at least two divisions daily; but our division repulsed them all. From 7 until 25 September these incessant attacks were very trying on everyone's nerves. Fortunately the Russians always attacked at the same spot using the same plan and mostly at the same hour, apparently on Stalin's personal orders.

Many of us caught the troublesome 'eastern fever': we all had yellow, cheesy faces and were very tired and sluggish. One had to make a special effort to overcome the effects, even at HQ, and hurry forth from the bunker with one's messenger at four or five in the morning, picking up a rifle to help beat off the Russians, who had breached the neighbouring regiment's line in a few places. The company strengths of the 178th Regiment were sometimes down to two men!

The regiment had its command post in the foremost frontline. We had built up a small assault troop from our bandsmen and clerks, whose job it was to sortie out immediately after an attack and take prisoners if the Russian T-34s had abandoned their infantry. That led once to our fifteen officers and men having about seventy prisoners in the command post. When they realized how few we were we had to get them away as quickly as possible. This fighting was a great burden on the division and the regiment: we really did fight to the last round – worse still, until our nerves gave, and there was no question of sleeping. With the exhausted remnants of the 203th Infantry Regiment attached to our regiment, we succeeded in holding the northern perimeter, thus enabling Stalingrad to be supplied and reinforced. The fighting strength of the companies was often only twenty-five men: many of the best had fallen.

the rank of Lieutenant in the First World War. 1935 rejoined the German Army, 1938 Lieutenant-Colonel, 1940 as Colonel, CO of 230th Infantry Regiment. After being flown out of Stalingrad, CO 76th Infantry Division. As Commanding General, LXIII Corps captured by US forces in 1945, released 1947. Awards: 7 March 1942 German Cross in gold, 13 November 1942 Knight's Cross, 1944 Oak Leaves.

My batman, Corporal Max Gens, a gilder from Berlin, who had served me loyally for a year and a half, had his hands full, for he had to alternate between fetching sandwiches for the commanding officer and bringing up SP-guns for me. These three SP-guns under Captain Koch fought stoutly and when all is said and done it was due to them that we held the northern perimeter. The estimated fighting strength of the division was still only 5,000 men, of which 1,000 were 'Hiwis'.

On 29 September the remnants of our division were withdrawn from the northern perimeter: we could scarcely believe it. We were to be 'topped up'. What did that mean? The young soldiers, who had received a pretty basic training in the Reich, fell in: the CSMs of the exhausted units, together with their commanding officers, stood facing them. Lists were brought out and the soldiers assigned. It must have been a strange experience for these young men on the Stalingrad steppe to be included in lists composed by brave warriors of frightening appearance, asked one's trade or profession and then directed to join this group or that. They were all very young and pale-looking and we, without saying anything, were all very doubtful that they would be a proper replacement for the many dead and wounded. Colonel Abraham recognized the difficult situation for these young men. He went along the ranks, spoke to them, personally and man-to-man. I believe that this meeting between the young soldiers and the old commander really did result in their feeling not only at home in the regiment, but also welcome.

The time for rest was short: there was some brief training and on 9 October we were sent to re-occupy the northern perimeter. This time the left flank of our division was on the Don. The weather was still very fine and clear. I was made commanding officer of 3rd Battalion and was pleased to be given a battalion at last. We were given a very favourable position in rugged gorges where we put our command posts and heavy weapons and also some captured mortars with suitable ammunition. We installed the heavy weapons as a battery and had a very good liaison with the 3rd Abteilung of 176th Artillery Regiment whose spotters' positions we shared. The attacks at this time were moderate. Thanks to our 'weapons organization' we were able to quickly ward off the Russians with our heavy guns and thus my battalion had few casualties. The Russians increasingly concentrated their attacks against the left flank of the army on the Don.

On 22 and 24 November orders came from Regiment and Division: we are encircled, the Führer has ordered that Fortress Stalingrad is to be held. As the Germans like to do in the face of such setbacks, we heaped all the blame on our allies. Young officers saw the reason as being the failure of the Romanians to hold firm north of the Don unlike ourselves, who had held firm at the northern perimeter. At the time we did not take such a dramatic view of it: our divisional commanding officer visited me at my command post, briefed me soberly on the situation and said, 'We have often experienced such problems. You have set yourselves up nicely here. You have a quite excellent position. You Brandenburgers will pull through, of that I have no doubt!' We believed him, for we had had similar experiences on a smaller scale but perhaps more hard-pressed than here. Therefore we were fairly relaxed about it all, although we watched less passively as our rations shrank. At this point the fighting was not so hard: in my strip. There were only a few breaches of the line. One night the Russians captured a strongpoint: we counter-attacked by night and under my leadership with SP-gun support won it back. The battalion commander's course scheduled for me in Antwerp and my transfer to the General Staff course were ruled out by reason of the encirclement.

My friend Captain Kulli Müller flew into the Pocket voluntarily to be with his men. On a reconnaissance we got lost in fog, crossed our own narrow frontline to the enemy's side and in the course of this had a serious talk about the sense and stupidity of our mission and the suffering of our men. A day later, once we had found our way back, he went missing – a very brave and exemplary officer and commander. Of the four ensigns from our Brandenburg days he was the last I lost.

Rations were diminishing: every day just two slices of bread and thin horsemeat soup. For the Russians it was the same: they came to our field kitchen at night to raid it. We would chase them off, but never fired at them. There was no firewood in the steppe. The men did have their own small bunkers and trenches, but no wood. They used to crawl forward and raid the Russian stocks of wood which were protected by explosives. That proves how desperate the situation was. We derived special pleasure from the way the pilots of the six fighters stationed in the Pocket looked after us. They flew operational sorties from their base. They had adopted my battalion, and came up every evening to us with something from their rations. Airmen were always better fed than infantry.

Christmas 1942 was behind us and still no information was passed down from the powers that be, leaving us in the dark as to what would become of us. We had ammunition, but not that much. We were unable to receive radio messages because the valves had been removed from our portable receivers:

we were urged: 'Soldiers, hold out! The Führer will get you out of this!' This slogan was in a way symbolic of what was happening to us there. We had fought bravely, loyally and trustingly: now we had all kinds of doubts, not so much because we were exhausted, but because we were deprived of information. An army can only be properly led if one says honestly and soberly and clearly what the situation is. Frequently in Russia it came down the infantry grapevine. But now even the 'grapevine' had run its course and had nothing more to say. For us fighting officers great doubt in the leadership developed not so much because we were encircled and in a crisis situation, but because we had no information.

On 10 January 1943 the Russians attacked with fresh forces and broke through our frontline at our neighbouring 44th *Hoch-und-Deutschmeister* Division. The difficult retreat into Stalingrad for the troops who were located outside the city now began. We drew back several kilometres. We built ourselves makeshift sledges, put the remains of our food into haversacks and had practically only the ammunition loaded in our weapons and not many boxes of it.

During our withdrawal I met two men who belonged amongst the most important personalities and comrades of the division: the commanding officer, Lieutenant-General Rodenburg, attempting to lead his division from the front, and the Catholic divisional chaplain Joseph Kayser who spent his time with the 200 wounded at the main dressing station at Rossoshkatal. It was a very cold and frosty day with a glorious snowscape and bright sunshine. My battalion was about 140 strong, still with three company commanders. We proceeded in file, one company providing security. On the way we went through a small village in the centre of a collective farm. I saw the flag of a dressing station and determined that it was our former main dressing station. This was set up in a large collective farm with stables set out in a cross. My divisional commander was standing at a crossroads holding up a rifle and called me to him. He gave me the job of defending the village, and enlisted my help to round up the many troops all heading for Stalingrad, some fleeing, and incorporate them into the defence. We were not successful: those not from our unit ignored us. They did form up into groups, however, but as soon as our backs were turned they set off for Stalingrad again. I placed only the men of my own battalion around the main dressing station where we took up positions.

That same afternoon, while forming a hedgehog defence with my 239rd Fusilier Battalion in the Bol Rossoshka collective farm with the priest Joseph

Kayser,[3] I had a unique, unforgettable experience: over a hill, glittering in snow and sunshine, hundreds of German soldiers came down the slope and, accompanied by loud shouts of 'Hurra!', stormed the trenches where the Russians had assembled intending to surround the collective farm. They were the surviving artillerymen of the 176th Artillery Regiment led from the front by Colonel Boeck.[4] After having been forced to destroy their guns for lack of ammunition, they made their last attack on foot! Many fell, possibly only one or two returned later to Germany. Colonel Boeck and Captain von Rotzmann[5] were awarded the Knight's Cross in the last days of the encirclement.

During the night we formed a small defensive hedgehog around the village. Suddenly I heard engine noise and saw faintly against the snow in the darkness the outline of a lorry, which shortly stopped in front of me. I thought the driver, who stepped down, was one of ours from the rear. Because my adjutant, Lieutenant Nichtweiss[6] had been wounded through the upper thigh, I wanted to arrange transport out for him and spoke to this driver. We were standing three metres apart when he answered me in Russian, drew his machine-pistol; and squeezed the trigger. A click – misfire! I drew my own pistol, in my excitement forgetting to release the safety catch, and it also failed to fire. We faced each other in silence. Then he turned away, returned to his lorry and drove off. Without getting us involved in a fight, I went back to my bunker. That was proof again that this battle was fought violently but without hate.

Back in my bunker I witnessed a strange scene: my haversack lay on the table and was being emptied by a Romanian soldier (therefore one of our

3. Joseph Kayser (b. Schmallenberg, 22 November 1895, d. Lippetal-Hoverstadt, 24 April 1993): 'Vicar of Stalingrad': fought in First World War then studied mining: Dipl. Engineer. Followed by study of Catholic theology. Ordained into priesthood 1931 Paderborn, 1933 military pastoral care at Höxter, interrogated by Gestapo for anti-State attitude. 1939 Catholic divisional chaplain, 76th Infantry Division. In January 1943 he surrendered the main dressing station to the Red Army and in Soviet captivity joined the NKFD (National Committee for the Liberation of Germany). 8 December 1945 returned to Germany where continued his career as a priest.
4. Wilhelm Boeck (b. Gartz, 15 March 1897, missing since 23 January 1943, declared dead 1953). From 1939 CO, 2nd Abteilung, 6th Artillery Regiment, and later of 176th Artillery Regiment. Knight's Cross 20 January 1943.
5. Fritz Joachim Freiherr von Rotzmann was CO, 1st Abteilung, 176th Artillery Regiment: Knight's Cross 3 January 1943, last promotion to Major.
6. Johannes Nichtweiss (b. Frankfurt/Main, 10 June 1914, d. Rostock, 14 June 1958): joined Wehrmacht 1939. From 1944 lecturer and assistant at anti-Fascist schools: 1949–52 teacher of history, 1956–8 Professor in ordinary for History of the Modern Age, Rostock.

allies), by a Russian soldier whom we had captured, and my batman. When I saw these three sitting there eating so peacefully, the Russian still with his rifle(!), I burst out laughing. We shared out amongst the four of us what remained in the haversack. A small cameo illustrating that hunger and cold were often worse than the enemy.

Now I faced a dilemma: to carry out the orders of my divisional commanding officer and defend the village, or also to head into Stalingrad. I held a short counsel of war with my company commanders who advised me to leave. A member of the artillery radio squad now appeared and told me he had orders to support me in my fight to hold the village. That, and my duty to protect the wounded in the main dressing station, were decisive. In the duel with a Russian rifleman while going from cellar to cellar I received a round stopped by the metal cockade of my soft field cap: like me he was probably no sniper.

Meanwhile the Russians had surrounded us: their infantry lay with light weapons at 300 to 400 metres distance around the village. A number of men with leg wounds had set up a light MG at the exit of the collective farm, took part in the battle and fought bravely. We held out the next day as well, but then took the decision to abandon the struggle. We took the wounded still able to move and broke out – or rather slipped out. The priest Kayser and a doctor remained with the wounded who could not be moved and these were taken prisoner by the Russians.

Thus we came out with thirty to forty lightly wounded, which brought my battalion strength up to 120 men. We crept into earth bunkers but found ourselves in action next morning in the snow and without cover. Each man had about five rounds. My old friend Jupp Holl, until then my telephones officer, was faithfully at my side: my batman, Max Gens, had frostbite in the feet and was to be flown out but did not want to go, preferring to remain with his commanding officer. On 19 January we fought in a thin line, only four to five rounds per man. Under fairly heavy mortar fire I was wounded in the right hand but could not leave the position and so stayed until evening, by when my battalion, the remainder of a whole regiment, was down to two officers and forty men. I was taken by lorry that night to Gumrak airfield and unloaded at the side of the runway. I lay there with Max Gens, who had meanwhile taken the shawl from his legs and wrapped it around my hand.

The sun no longer shone: it was misty. Snow, almost darkness. I watched the first machine, an He 111, a bomber, landing in the slush. It overturned because Russian artillery started up at the same time. An anti-aircraft officer was in charge of the flights out. We waited a day to be flown out, found ourselves a crater and waited to see what happened next. Other He 111s landed. Parcels, loaves, provisions and ammunition were thrown out. Fifty to eighty men then stormed these machines which could take maybe ten to twelve wounded. Field-gendarmes attempted in vain to keep them back. After the first eleven were crammed in, the hatch was shut. The machines took off under artillery fire in the midst of this throng of soldiers, some of whom grasped the wings in their despair, cursing, looking like a pack of crazed animals. Neither Gens nor I saw any prospect of getting into such an aircraft!

Thus we spent another whole day in this crater: a sergeant from my battalion with a leg wound joined us. Finally the three of us succeeded, on the early morning of the third day, 20 January, when less and less aircraft landed and most of the wounded had abandoned hope, to get a flight through the intervention of the young officer in charge of the airfield. The machine had put down some distance from the usual spot, where no others came, and therefore there were no large numbers of people nearby. I crammed my batman Max inside and I got aboard last. Above me was a filthy-dirty NCO bleeding from a neck wound who had to stand upright so as not to bleed to death. I rested with hands and feet against him as I lay in the bomb-bay.

It was a miracle – the aircraft started. We did not see anything else for we were all so exhausted that we fell asleep at once. We were unloaded at Stalino and cared for outstandingly by the Luftwaffe. In the military hospital there I received treatment for the first time. I had a lung infection and almost lost my hand to frostbite. Swiss surgeons[7] operated on it at Cracow to avoid amputation. We Stalingrad-returners were barred from entering the Reich on Hitler's orders so as to prevent us telling of the suffering at Stalingrad, and were brought to the Carpathian mountains instead for our cure.

For his bravery and personal involvement, Captain Löser received the German Cross in gold on 3 October 1942 and the Knight's Cross on 26 January 1943. He spent the next year alternating between military hospitals and studying at Weimar. After General Staff training and promotion to Major, Löser spent the remainder of the war at the Hirschberg War Academy. In 1956 he joined the Bundeswehr and reached pensionable age in the rank of Major-General commanding 1st Panzer Division at Hanover.

7. The Swiss surgeons belonged to the 4th Swiss Medical Mission on the Eastern Front. These missions were a humanitarian gesture to dissuade Hitler from invading Switzerland. The personnel – about eighty – were withdrawn from hospitals at Stalino, Kharkov and Rostov in the face of the Soviet advance and in the last week of the Stalingrad event were active at Cracow.

25. ERICH VON LOSSOW:

Stalingrad Diary[1]

Major Erich von Lossow (b. 31 March 1914, d. Munich, 21 January 1998) joined the Reichswehr as a professional soldier in 1933. From April 1942 he was CO, Signals Abteilung 371th Division.

22.11.42 The Russian broke through at the 20th Romanian Division, attacking from Zaza via Plovitoye and is also operating in the great bend of the Don with strong forces to the south where unfortunately there are only Romanians and Italians. Thus the slogan is being loudly repeated, copying the Italians: 'Avanti – the retreat!' Our Staff officer Ic is of the opinion that only 6,000 Russians and ninety tanks came through. In the afternoon, however, one battalion and one battery were loaded aboard lorries and transported south. In the evening the enemy advanced to Abganerovo, where we spilt so much blood in mid-August and had hard fighting. Seven supply KfZ's with five tonnes of chocolate, coffee, acid drops and other panzer-special rations meant for us fell into his hands. Boo! Our southern supply road and base has been cut off – it is getting serious!

23.11.42 One report after another conflicts. The corps is making an evasive movement, our neighbouring division is withdrawing; we are releasing another Battalion with a battery and anti-tank section to the right. My No 1 Company, lice-infested after just returning from a long stay in trenches in the most forward line, is going back to them. In the afternoon report, the Russian has broken through deep in our back to Kalatch along the Don: to the south of us he is attacking towards Zybenko. Regiment Veith is being pulled out and sent to the interception point near Z. The major pincer operation with the aim of cutting off the German spearhead, whose eastward point is Stalingrad, is

---

1. The diary was kindly made available for publication by Frau Hilde von Lossow. The first section, from 9 July to 21 September 1942 was left out; up to 22 November 1942 there is a gap in which no entries appear.

now obvious to everyone. In the evening Lieutenant Prell as Night Lieutenant heard a conversation between our new C-in-C, General Paulus – we are now attached to Sixth Army – and our commanding general. Both are of the opinion that we should pull back and give up Stalingrad, otherwise we shall be cut off. There is already no longer a telephone connection to the Army Group and through it to FHQ. 'I would be risking my appointment,' Paulus said. He had reported the situation by radio, and thought that the Führer's decision might come early tomorrow. We have to supply ourselves from what we have got in hand: the rations are being cut by half, there is no more mail going out, leave-takers who have already left are unloaded somewhere and fighting troops brought in.

24.11.42 Now for the first time we find ourselves in the Pocket: there is only a very small gap still open to the south-west but we cannot reach it because we are at the opposite end. The army is being supplied from the air by 100 Ju 52s. At 0930 hrs a telex arrived from Corps. I read it as it came in: immediately go to full mobility and cancel all long-range movement plans by all means. Prepare plans for what is to be taken on driveable vehicles. Prepare to destroy all equipment, soldiers' packs, files and motor vehicles which are not to be taken along. Therefore this amounts to giving up Stalingrad and pulling out! We are all contrite: there is nothing worse than the destruction of everything one has built up, and giving up a position one has obtained with blood, sacrifice and enormous effort. We are on the defensive in Africa, the Americans are in North Africa and outside Stalingrad, which has become a byword for bitter fighting, we are supposed to pull back? We do not understand it, for to do so would endanger the Caucasus front and the successes of this summer and autumn. At midday conference with Ia Lieutenant-Colonel Kleikamp[2] about the measures to be taken, afterwards I had the chiefs and officials in charge with me and ordered: we take with us half of the Staff Kfz vehicles, Nos 1 and 2 Companies, most of the companies' equipment. The convoy will move off dispersed, excess personnel to No 1 Company, files and regulations to be prepared for destruction, also all motor vehicles and carts not to be taken along. Destroy defective weapons, issue ammunition to the men, destroy old clothing, issue new. Officers' luggage not

---

2. Helmut Kleikamp (b. Ottendorf, Dresden, 28 April 1901, d. Marburg/Lahn, 6 January 1985). 4 April 1942 Lieutenant-Colonel, Ia, Staff 371th Infantry Division: 1942 Colonel and Head of General Staff Personnel Department at OKW: 1945 Major-General, PoW until 1948. Decorations: 1944 German Cross in gold.

to exceed one trunk. Distribute stores of oats, slaughter all horses not capable of single-horse harnessing and give them to the Hilfswillige to eat, these to travel closed up with the horse-drawn platoon. If any of them takes advantage of the situation or mutinies, shoot dead. Distribute canteen stores. Distribute equipment to company, exchange three small field kitchens for one large one, dismantle parts of the telephone network etc. Everything depends on the allocation of scarce fuel, in total Division only approved fuel for half the Kfz's. A number of the horses are on the other side of the Don in a convalescent home so I shall not be taking all the horse-drawn wagons.

25.11.42 Yesterday in front of the Corps sector, thirteen panzers were destroyed: the Russian is now forcing us to Voroponova, he intends to cut us off completely. He is already attacking the regiment to our right: his American-built fighter-bombers have the cheek to descend to very low altitude to rake us – they killed a horse, some telephone lines were destroyed by bombing. Everybody is working feverishly to restore them: by my reckoning 1,600 telephone conversations. But the front is holding, he is not making inroads. The wildest rumours are circulating: I keep them at bunker-building, give instructions what needs to be done with Christmas in mind and so everything stays on the old track and relatively quiet. Personally I cannot get the idea out of my head that my much longed-for leave is in question since at the moment we have no contact at all to our rear. Not even mail can go, and so my little wife will have to just sit there through December without news of me and that probably requires more strength than holding out here. Perhaps I can give something to the crew of an aircraft landing here and which will be flying back 'over there', but all I have seen so far are Russian aircraft. It gives me great sorrow to have to set fire to my cosy little house, built with such loving care, and all of the books, letters and some of the laundry, and to leave the geese behind or slaughter them. In the evening we are going to discuss what should be saved and taken with us. Previously however we shall drink our fill of the wines and champagne we have set aside.

26.11.42 Some fighter-bombers attacked our command post, bombs fell between the bunkers: no damage. There were some leaflets they dropped with a Soviet special announcement: 'Break through 30 kilometres broad and 70 kilometres deep. German troops at Stalingrad cut off. Kalatch taken, also Abganerovo and with them the only supply routes. Seven divisions wiped out, eleven broken up, 13,000 prisoners, 360 guns captured. The offensive by Soviet troops is being continued.' Although the first part was almost correct, it did not rattle us. The Führer will not leave us in the lurch after he has ordered: hold out! The Hiwis are now given only a quarter of the midday ration, no bread, coffee only once. Since then most of them are working at half speed. In the village the old men laugh at us now that the village commandant has gone: they must have sensed something or have direct information from informers. In the afternoon telephone cables were cut through at five places: nobody has been caught.

In the evening we knew for certain: we are encircled, the enemy succeeded in closing the pincers at Kalatch, the entire Sixth Army is inside the Pocket. For the time being it is a depressing feeling to know that at our backs, left, right and ahead the enemy is entrenched and the concept of all-round defence against the concentric attack of the much more powerful enemy is not going to be successful overnight. Because one cannot tell the men anything, much more uncertainty reigns. The village commandant of Verchne-Yelshanka, belonging to 94th Division, bolted to the rear giving the available food stocks to the population instead of to the infantry billeted there. An Abteilung commander was prevented by our 1a from blowing up his field guns. Things are satisfactorily quiet with us. To my suggestion to give the division the cover-name 'Anvil' for December the 1a countered: 'Hammer would be preferable!' In the end we settled for *Wolfsschlucht* (Gorge of the Wolf).

27.11.42 After a night disturbed by aircraft our first thoughts upon awaking were: encircled, Pocket, cut off from the Reich! And as a logistic consequence: therefore no leave – infantry action instead. The Commander-in-Chief telephoned through the slogan to hold out, the Führer will get us out of this! In the evening we heard the Führer's appeal for ourselves. He said more or less: 'The enemy has broken through at the rear of German troops and is attempting to retrieve the bulwark of Stalingrad. In these difficult hours, alongside mine the thoughts of the entire German people are with you. You must hold Stalingrad, conquered with so much blood, at all costs! What lies in my power will be done to support you in your heroic struggle. Adolf Hitler.' The appeal was made known to the men, it strengthened their self-confidence and reduced the rumour-mongering.

29.11.42 Advent. We have got used to the new situation. 'Our Duchy' is what the men call our enclosed army, which embraces seventeen infantry and two panzer divisions. On the Ic's situation map I see the enemy divisions pinning us down: thirty-seven, divided into six armies. A telex warns us of the possibility of Russian airborne operations. That's all we need! I got rid of my lazy, infirm and unreliable Russians because the foodstock is only enough until 10 December. I approve personally what can be cooked. No 1 Company has meat from slaughtered horses for the first time. It is a real encirclement: the horses get insufficient fodder, die of debility, are butchered and used as food, but that is not in store for my Tanya! No 1 Company has Russian women to bake bread: wheat is delivered. Eighteen loaves daily: it tastes very good. To celebrate the first day of Advent I unwrapped the delightful package my wife prepared for me and in the evening I received my commanders, one of whom I had to send to bed at once with severe jaundice. There was tea, two tarts with pudding and jam layers, baked by a corporal. With the remains of the Munich Advent-wreath I made a new one, binding it with pine, laid out Christmas serviettes and little angels: there were nuts and in the stove an apple stewing in its own juice! Although the candles were lit there was no real joy present. The doctor[3] is very ill, Ziersdorf had to postpone his engagement until Christmas and I have no idea whether letters will arrive or not and the serious wound suffered today by Lieutenant Handwerk, platoon commander in my infantry battalion, has depressed everybody. He had come to the battalion command post for orders and was 10 metres from Captain Wulf when a heavy mortar shell landed. With the words, 'Shit, direct hit!' he collapsed. We broke up at ten o'clock after a Russian aircraft dropped incendiaries and HE bombs 100 metres from my villa, only hitting a bunker of first column with two Hiwis inside, one was killed.

1.12.42 The heavy attacks on 'The Duchy' were beaten off almost everywhere. Our Luftwaffe is active. The enemy is attempting to bisect the Pocket into two halves so that he can gobble us up better. It is not working; our C-in-C Paulus has been promoted to General by the Führer. Lieutenant Handwerk died on the long trudge to the main dressing station: the No 1 officer of the Abteilung; he was always ready for action and had come to Germany from South America to help defend his Fatherland. In faithful fulfilment of this duty he died a hero's death. We cannot go to his grave to pay our respects because of the great distance to the main dressing station. He spent the whole night being transported by horse-drawn wagon because we do not have any more fuel. Otherwise he might have been saved. Apart from him my infantry

---

3. This was assistant medical officer Dr Burkhart Angermann (b. Stettin, 11 August 1917, d. Hagen, 18 April 1990). Studied medicine at Göttingen 1936–42, after that was conscripted into Wehrmacht. End January 1943 Stalingrad, Soviet PoW, released 9 June 1948. Further training in pulmonary medicine, then from 1955–82 general practitioner at Hagen. He was lifelong friends with Dr von Lossow. The Editor knew him personally and published his Stalingrad memories in Vol 1 of *Stalingrad. Zurück aus der Hölle* (Berlin 2006), pp. 39–125.

company has suffered heavy losses. The men mostly received shots to the head, neck and arm. The Russians over there have only a few snipers, but they are very watchful. They have the rifle clamped firmly in place and aimed at the strip of trench past which our relief comes and goes and, because the trench is not deep enough, is overseen from various points in the terrain. If a German steel helmet appears above a depression, the Russian counts off the seconds until he comes into view again and then shoots. I had the trench dug deeper and the MG shifted, but excavation is difficult when the enemy is only 100 metres away. Our men are also too indifferent and earthy. To my question how many Russians he had shot, one of my men told me, 'It is not unlikely quite a few!' And we have one man dead and eight seriously wounded.

2.12.42 At Pitomnik airfield from where the Ju 52s take off there are over 2,000 sick and wounded who want to return to the Reich. In inspections we found that some of them had put on dressings without having a wound, one had even mutilated himself in his panic. So this is what it has come to! But they were not from our division. The Romanians who fled in the south have been spread amongst the regiments: they arrive without weapons or entrenching tools and rob us of our food. The interpreter of a Romanian regiment reported to the staff officer 1a when asked if there were any special occurrences to report: 'The commander was in the forward trench today to observe the morale of the Romanians!' – our dear brothers. Our leave-takers, fifty-six at the last count, and all those transferred elsewhere in the occupied eastern territories will naturally not be coming back under the circumstances: it is a painful loss to us. Thus my adjutant and I cover the roles of paymaster, inspectorate and engineer, none of which we have: moreover the doctor has a bad case of jaundice and lies about lethargically.

4.12.42 669th Regiment has four defectors: they look sick of war and tell us they cannot believe we are still bottled up because the Russians have stopped attacking. At night Pollack on sentry-go was kidnapped by Bolshevists and dragged to their side. The drag-marks can be clearly seen in the snow. A scouting party we sent out received lively fire and returned having achieved nothing. The bread ration has been cut to 200 grams, even at midday we only get half. The horses have no feed, they eat loam and tree bark: one is slaughtered daily. My eleven Christmas geese ate the only duck in the stable one morning after killing it. After that I gave my commanders one goose each as a Christmas present and killed one to celebrate 2nd day of Advent. I have had to lose Lieutenant Helget as communications officer from 669 because the platoon leaders are going into a new battalion formed from supply troops. I am now handling Battalion traffic and installing a radio post and two to Battalion for the connection to the Company! My infantry company has lost three more men to snipers: all shot through the head. Casualties to date sustained by the Abteilung to enemy action: sixteen dead, seventy-three wounded.

6.12.42 2nd day of Advent. It has snowed a lot; the view from my window is glorious and also it is warm, enough to go outside without a greatcoat. In front of the 669th's sector of the line a German voice spoke through a loudspeaker from the Russian trenches: 'Here is soldier Pollack. I am OK, the rations are better here than you have. Come on over!' Then there was a burst of MG fire. Either an interpreter, or the German soldier after torture, or the threat of it. At midday Dummer and I ate the fat goose, a rare delicacy in hungry times, and we were totally filled. Additionally we had the 670th's band which was supposed to have played first of all to the General but which Prell sent to give me a short serenade. The table was decorated appropriately for Advent, two small packets from my little wife pleased me deeply, they were kept back for today although Deblin brought them in November in a big parcel. The forged-iron candlesticks and glazed tiles adorn my hunting-lodge splendidly. Photos bring me closer to the homeland although it is better not to spend too much time thinking about it. My little wife still does not suspect that I shall not be there for Christmas and a fairyland lies between us since weeks ago we lived in anticipated joy and jubilation. But who could guess that we would be encircled here? For Herzl this first Christmas alone will be a very bitter one. I do not reflect too much before setting to work. In the evening a radio message from 'the outside'. 'Rest reassured of our help! Von Manstein, Field-Marshal.'[4] Everybody breathes a sigh of relief, everything looks brighter.

12.12.42 We all celebrate Dummer's 22nd birthday in a nice group. He had been saving some sumptuous delights for now, and so we had potato salad, Debrezin sausage, goose lard, toast, sweet biscuits etc. It was all the more enjoyable with the daily bread ration at 200 grams. Horses are slaughtered on

---

4. Field-Marshal Erich von Lewinski called Manstein (b. Berlin, 24 November 1887, d. Irschenhausen, 9 June 1973). During the fighting for Stalingrad he was C-in-C, Army Group Don and thus Paulus's direct superior. Decorated with the Knight's Cross, Oak Leaves and Swords, on 30 March 1944 he was relieved of his post after he attempted to take command of the Army in the East from Hitler. 1945 British PoW; 1949, Hamburg, declared guilty of war crimes by a British tribunal, served three and a half years at Werl penitentiary where he wrote his book *Verlorene Siege*. Later he took part in the building up of the Bundeswehr.

the conveyor belt: the flesh tastes quite decent if it is made up into meatballs. We are not receiving provisions, fuel or ammunition, too many Ju 52s are being shot down. In the evening Corporal Markmann of the infantry company fell as the result of a mortar attack. The Russians broke through the regiment on the right over a length of 400 metres because the trench complement turned and took to their heels. The will to resist and leadership personalities are lacking. At Aksai, where we found ourselves in August, fighting is raging between the army sent to relieve us against Russians withdrawn from facing our front, and Beketowa.

15.12.42 At 1000 hrs I heard over my monitoring-line to the 1a that I am being given command of Battlegroup Muff, formerly 2nd Battalion 669th Grenadier Regiment. I reported to 1a who told me that Captain Muff is taking over 1st Battalion which will go on the offensive when the 'relief' comes up from the south. There are no more battalion commanders, and so the choice fell on me because the signals section has the most officers and is in the best order. At midday with mixed feelings I packed my trunk, cleared out my pretty little house and put everything into crates: in the evening I wrote to my little wife after taking provisional leave of my appalled officers and giving instructions to Rex and Dummer. In that way in wartime things change from one day to another; from commander of a detachment to the commanding officer of a battlegroup, from the signals corps to the infantry, from a hunting lodge to a hole in the ground, from divisional command post to an infantry trench 30 metres from the enemy. But I hold firm to Bismarck's creed: 'I am God's soldier, and where He sends me there I must go'; I believe that He is sending me and arranging my life as He sees fit.

16.12.42 So now I am also an infantryman. At 0700 hrs I reported to my new regimental commanding officer, Colonel Rüger[5] and then went on to Battlegroup Muff[6] which I am to command. Muff greeted me heartily, brought me up to date and went with me through the trenches. At the entrance to Utech's trench lay a dead soldier; he was from my detachment and had been on his way to Battalion as a runner. The evangelical chaplain was also in the trench visiting the men: he had his gramophone with him and played Bach's Toccata and Fugue. Bolshevik bullets whistled overhead.

---

5. Colonel Dr Friedrich Rüger was commanding officer of the 669th Infantry Regiment, 371st Infantry Division.

6. Captain (final rank Major) Hans-Ulrich Muff (b. Karlsruhe, 1 January 1916, missing since 18 January 1943 between Beketovka and Pestshanka).

17.12.42 During the night a fine mess. At 0400 hrs five Russians slipped through the right wing of the Romanian sector, three remained lying before the Spanish Rider (steel obstacle) while two crawled forward and reached the Romanian command post. Because one of the sentries had just gone off, the other ran after him scared: the Russians jumped in, took the MG off its stand, left their two machine-pistols behind and made off over the embankment in their white snow-suits after throwing a few hand grenades. The Romanians have been court-martialled: a very sorry affair. And these are those highly praised 'auxiliary peoples' and Axis allies so vaunted by German radio! I have about 100 in Battlegroup von Lossow, amongst them Captain Sindjorzano, in charge of the heavy mortar, a good man; and a lieutenant.

18.12.42 At dusk two half-grown Stalingrad youths slipped through the gully near my trenches. They were told to stop, captured and brought to me. They said they wanted to visit their sister in Beketovka. They were 13 years old, totally unkempt and gave an impression of being shifty. They were taken to the Ic at Regiment to whom after a while they confessed they had received fourteen days training from a Russian officer and were given the following questions to answer: 'Where are the Romanians? Where do prisoners work without supervision? What tactical signs are there at crossroads? Where are the telephone-line junctions?' The two boys had just finished this research and were on their way back. A considerable mission to give 13-year-old youngsters! Because they were spies they were shot. For my two sentries I thought about what reward I should give them. In such cases it would normally be leave or special rations but that was out of the question in the Pocket: nothing could be awarded. Finally the Colonel brought me two packs of his own cigarettes. In order to educate people it is important to find some reward adequate and acceptable under the circumstances. Prescribed punishments are also difficult to impose here. If a sentry falls asleep at the MG post the best punishment is a punch in the ribs. In peacetime this would be the offence of 'maltreatment of a subordinate by an officer' and punishable as such. If I shout at the man the Russians will hear me and throw hand grenades or open fire. If I relieve the sentry of his post and lock him up he enjoys a period of peace and quiet. If I give him extra sentry duty I bear the responsibility, if by reason of his being so tired he fails to hear the enemy creeping up and I suddenly find the Russians sharing my trench. If I merely reprimand and warn him as to his future conduct this is nothing new to him and he takes no notice. It is a problem!

19.12.42 My trench is about one kilometre long, starts in the village of Kuporovsno at the end of the spit of land, wanders through the confusion of broken walls, hedges and huts to the railway embankment, passes along it for 100 metres and then reaches open country. To the right is Utech's company with mainly men of the signals detachment, a 5cm anti-tank gun and SWG group to the rear, in the centre a Romanian platoon, left No 6 Company of the 669th, Lieutenant Silberberg and a 3.7cm anti-tank gun: 300 metres to the rear the reserve platoon under Sergeant-Major Giesecke and the Romanian mortar platoon with two Romanian and two Russian 8.2cm mortars under Captain Sindjorzano. At the viaduct is my pioneer-demolition team which can ignite electrically an explosive charge along the track should an armoured train approach. In the railway embankment are the observation posts for my artillery spotters, the IG (infantry-gun) Company and the mortars. Strength of the total position is about 220 men including the Romanians. First Battalion, Captain Ruff, shoots on my right; left behind us is a bicycle detachment and a reserve battalion of 71st Infantry Division in glorious 'Sunday order', i.e. in three ranks one behind the other. These do not have much to fear for we are positioned very well forward like sentries and they can fire well above us. Practically unnoticed by the enemy they are building their trenches at our backs while I alone in the left sector have three casualties daily. My battlegroup is four officers, fifteen NCO's and eighty-five men, plus 120 Romanians. Of those, two officers, eight NCO's, sixty men and five Romanians, therefore 120 men in all, are placed along the trench to hold the southern perimeter of Stalingrad. Behind it there is only an anti-tank gun or battery here and there, and if the Russian passes through these theoretically he can keep going until he gets to Germany – if one did not advance smartly enough. At the bend in the Don, the Russians pushed the Italians farther west so that our 'relief army' was stopped there. Because of that it will probably be the end of January until the Pocket is opened.

21.12.42 Yesterday morning through the scissors-periscope I ogled the Russian observer in the 'Red House' from my observation post. He has knocked himself a hole in the wall of the house, stands in the dark, directs the mortar fire and also does a bit of sniping now and again. My fingers itch to give him a bullet! By begging I got from regiment approval for six rounds and directed the fire with the infantry-gun commander. The first shot was much too short because the barrel was still cold. The next few landed around the house and I think I saw a Russian get his come-uppance while passing through the trench. Unfortunately we are so short of ammunition that one has to ask permission first and only ever fire at a rewarding target. Thus we had to break off without having hit the house. But we enjoyed it!

22.12.42 At night the telephone near me rang. Lieutenant Silberberg of the left sector gave me some bad news. A Russian scouting party had crept into the MG post in the slit trench when the German sentry was in the nearby bunker fetching his gloves. The Russians threw hand grenades; the bunker collapsed, three wounded. They dragged off the Romanian sentry. There was some heavy firing, but they got no glimpse of the scouting party. The Romanian will never be seen again.

24.12.42 Christmas Eve has arrived, but there is no Christmas spirit at all. I spent the whole day thinking of my nearest and dearest who, tucked away at home, will probably celebrate this fairy-tale Feast in a happier frame of mind than I. I have been separated from you seven months: we thought it would be different and hoped to take a few weeks' holiday together. But we must look around us in this hard war and see what remains beautiful, inspirational and good, and not be sad when great demands are made of us. Thus my thoughts go happily again and again to my holy little family despite the missing outer framework. We are alive and are all healthy: it is the wonderful thing about this Feast that we can celebrate with each other three times. Though there is no peace on earth and people delight in warfare, in the evening I read in the Christmas story the laconic words 'Fear not!' and that is my Christmas slogan this year. I have set up a small Christmas table with the Advent wreath, the banner, two small angels and the pictures of my loved ones. In the morning my officers came, bringing me cognac, bread, biscuits, chocolate, cigarettes and a salver with glasses made from protective shell caps – but nice, nothing warlike to see in them! From the General I got my commanding officers' parcel as commander of the signals detachment with Steinhäger, chocolate, cherry brandy and cigars while the Colonel also gave me a bottle as his battle-group commander. Thus the table was soon full. In the afternoon I visited the men in the trench; they stood there as they always did, sentries overtired and filthy, remaining upright only by the greatest effort of will. The joy over the parcel, of which every officer got one, was especially great because it contained foodstuffs and also something to smoke. I noticed with satisfaction that the signals detachment provided for its men much better than the infantry, anti-tank people or artillery did. With our daily ration set at 200 grams of bread, and horsemeat with watered-down soup, that is especially important. The detachment had saved canteen stores from earlier on and now they cooked bread and biscuits from wheat we organized. When I was returning to my bunker-home through the trench the radio was playing carols. I unpacked the letters from my wife and the small bible, and was just going to make myself comfortable when towards 0400 hrs the telephone rang and Utech's excited voice shouted, 'The Russians are sitting in my trench!' So that was our Christmas surprise! Speaking calmly I gave the order to establish where and how many, alert the reserve platoon, the mortars and the artillery spotter and discuss with the Battalion at the right, Captain Muff, how we could make a counter-attack from there. After half an hour we had the picture; six Russians in snow-smocks had crept out of their sappe-trench[7] – about 30 metres away from us – to our trench and jumped in. Corporal Klier of my signals crew went straight to his bunker, raised the alarm and was just reaching for the nearest weapon when he came under machine-pistol fire from a Russian standing in the trench, collapsing with wounds to his upper thigh. The nearest MG-sentry threw hand grenades, forcing the Russians to retire. They were also caught in our MG fire as they jumped back into their own trench. One cried out as though hit, another one was dragged along wounded. They would not come a second time tonight. I had a few mortar rounds fired into their sappe, then it fell quiet. The state of alert was maintained throughout the night since it was probable that the Bolshevists would keep trying to disturb our Christmas Eve. I stayed awake too, drank bean coffee, had a chinwag with Wolter, lit candles, read letters which had reached me by 1 December and dreamed of being in my inexpressibly beautiful paradise in Munich. What large eyes Klaus Peter would make before our Christmas tree, and his inwardly so-loved Mutti would send her thoughts here to Stalingrad, and they would meet with mine with great love, because I cannot receive any mail. I stood at the door to my bunker; it was a starry night. MG rounds whistled overhead; from the trench came the sound of mortars exploding. It was a real war-Christmas; but next year we shall certainly celebrate it at home, and then I shall tell you, my dearest love, of these days when we constantly wished ourselves a 'silent night'.

25.12.42 The night passed peacefully. The afternoon brought us very unwelcome events. Over a period of one or two hours two Romanians defected. One was seen and received a hand grenade for his trouble, which wounded him, the second defector was not spotted because the neighbouring sentry was dozing. Both Romanians arrived in the enemy trenches. As they would reveal our system, I had the relief and meal hours changed etc. and ordered that the company command post was to be manned despite the frozen

---

7. The term *sappe* is derived from the French and means a communication trench for defence and as cover against enemy fire.

ground. Spanish Riders and wire obstructions would be placed around the MG posts to make it difficult for the Russians to get in and the Romanians to get out. That evening another of our Axis brothers refused to stand sentry duty until he received soup. He was sent to Sindjorzano and given a beating. Would that make it any better? On 20 November these people lost everything they owned and had no winter clothing, hardly any good footwear, no rear services and were very hungry. I ordered that the Romanians should receive the same rations as German soldiers and exchanged those Romanians I considered unreliable. Unfortunately an infantryman stole about 200 marks from a bunker, and so there was a lot of ill-feeling on Christmas day.

26.12.42 Boxing Day was much happier. In the morning I ran for an hour and a half to the detachment through crunching snow and a biting east wind. In my house I had a wonderful bath in hot water and had pleasure in putting on clean underwear. These were festive ceremonies for a 'front-swine'. Afterwards my two faithful officers received me with braised goose and peas, red wine and pudding. It was pure poetry and tasted so good served on porcelain plates on a white tablecloth. On the infantryman's horizon, it is here at Divisional HQ that the Etappe[8] really begins. One does not live in constant danger of being caught napping or dragged out of the trench. Dummer gave me a very beautiful wooden candlestick carved by a Russian, I brought everyone a little book which my wife had thoughtfully added to the Advent parcel. After I had spoken briefly to all my officers, unfortunately I had to return from this tightly-welded comradeship, which has become so dear to me, back to my battlegroup.

The Russians over there seemed to have been relieved. The new ones fire at quite new areas. There is an increase in sniper activity: three men fell in one day in the trench when they stood too high. The Russians are getting cocky, we shall have to put the damper on them. But our infantry is overtired and does not have the patience to lie in wait like a good hunter until a Russian shows himself incautiously two or three hours later. We do not have telescopic sights like they do, nor so many people. For some days there has been an increase in the number of swollen legs. Faces look terrible: it is field-nephritis, caused by cold to the kidneys. The sufferers must all leave, twenty-two in four days. Like most of the urgent medical cases, the junior surgeon cannot help here. The diagnosis is not easy to make, it could easily be something else, etc.

---

8. *Etappe* is any area behind the front, here a rear sector for rest and recuperation.

Medical treatment in the frontline here is absolutely scandalous. A wounded man shot through the stomach lay in the regimental operating theatre for two days without being operated on. When I went with the colonel through the trench we found a Romanian lying in the snow with a head wound. I thought, he must be dead, it was night and not a soul around. But he still had the death-rattle in his throat. The medical orderly private said he had given two Romanians the job of transporting the wounded man back. He had not made sure they did so, perhaps they had not understood him, he thought; in any case nothing had happened. So pitiless and indifferent had this soldier become, it was a great pity. The good men are dead, the officers worse than ever, the weariness with war is growing. We are entering year 1943 in the World War. We officers have a colossal job to do, unfortunately not recognized or mastered by them all. But I shall bring some life into the shop! Carrot and stick! Only in that way can one still lead by his personality and not by his shoulder straps!

29.12.42 What is a day in the life of the battlegroup commander like? At 0315 hrs this company commander makes his early report which the adjutant sharing his bunker, Lieutenant Wolter, passes to regiment. If there is nothing special to report, all well and good and one can sleep in until 0400 hrs. If the enemy has started something, first there are long discussions about 'where and how such a thing is possible', and so on and regimental adjutants, drunk with sleep, will then be questioned about it. One can then sleep on until eight or half past, for the mornings are relatively quiet and the air not so unhealthy. After a shave, a couple of slices of army bread will be toasting on the stove-top. Toasting is essential here because bread is generally ice-cold. Other people and the infantry have nothing to spread on it in the morning, unlike myself, whose loyal and caring wife packed two long-life sausages, marmalade and Belgian jam in the food chest. So I have blackberry marmalade on bread: it tastes gloriously fresh from the German woods, and more! But the daily bread ration is 200 grams, that is exactly four slices, and so one cannot go above two for breakfast. Afterwards I talked over with Wolter about the work we need to do today: Silberberg must have a communication trench between the viaduct and his command post. People are killed there every day on the way to fetch food or water, for the Russian snipers see right through the whole gulley and so this company has permanent flanking fire in the back and is as good as cut off. Then we have to lay a barrier of Spanish Riders in front of our trench, arrange for the trenching parties to start tomorrow, expand the artillery observation post, the reserve platoon is to be put to work manufacturing new Spanish

Riders, telephone wires have to be put up, liaise with our neighbour at the left, exchange our sick, transport out the wounded and dead, place the ammunition in safe keeping and so on.

Meanwhile the rays of the sun are stronger today, the snow crunches but one can be outside without greatcoat, pullover and ski trousers and I make my daily rounds dressed accordingly; first to the reserve platoon, outstandingly led by Sergeant-Major Gieseke of my radio detachment, who spends an hour daily in the terrain and an hour instructing on the MG. The Romanians have recommended him for a decoration: the regiment would very much like him as an officer. Until now I have declined the latter because from my experiences in this war I expect much more from an officer than that he simply does his duty. He must be totally clean in character, in times of emergency or panic be an exemplary leader: he must be animated by a holy inner fire and enthusiastic for what is good and combative: he must be able to handle the most difficult situations by his imperturbability and, proud and sure, cultivate a belief in the requirements of destiny, and be capable of dying as a brave soldier. Who of us can do that? Especially amongst our young, hardly educated lieutenants? Therefore the harshest demands are made of the officer, and it helps nobody to make average people into officers. Better that the man remains a good NCO than that he becomes one of those lukewarm, insignificant lieutenants which staff the army today. The infantry naturally sees things differently because the deaths have deprived them of most of their active officers, and they need replacements. Thus with Gieseke I discuss questions of provisions, training, building obstacles and my plan to keep sending men 'for rest and recuperation' from the trench to the reserve platoon 200 metres to the rear. There they at least have water, can delouse themselves easier and have a night's sleep. After six days they return to the trench and make way for other proven soldiers. The colonel, to whom I suggested it, is very taken by the proposal but at the front people never think of such ideas. Everyone in our infantry is so appallingly disinterested and immovable.

I mention, as an example of the pig-headedness of the infantry, that while passing the latrines I saw on the ground near the loo sitting-board a dud Russian mortar bomb, and it had occurred to nobody to remove it even though the latrines are obviously always in use . . . until one night somebody unaware of the relic steps on it! To my enquiry I received the typical assurance, 'Oh, that's been here since we took over the sector!' Then I went to my heavy mortar position and had to reprimand Captain Sindjorzano through the interpreter because yesterday after I gave him fifteen bombs he fired them all off straight away instead of at irregular intervals over a long period of time. Therefore when the bombardment started the Russians took cover and five minutes later when all had fallen quiet they came out again grinning amongst themselves at the stupid Nazis. Sindjorzano made his obligatory deep bows and assured me with southern European gestures and a glowering look that the like of it would never happen again. As with the Italians, no value can be attached to that. The Romanian soldiers standing around gave me a smart salute as I, their *capitano*, passed by. They know that I might give a smart soldier a cigarette or two.

In the deeply-incised gully which leads down to the Volga there have been fresh strikes by Russian mortars, especially in front of and near our own mortar position, and where the evening meal is distributed. Probably the two Romanian defectors betrayed the locations. Water runs through the gully but is presently under a thick layer of ice so that better progress is made by skating than with hobnailed boots. In front of the viaduct where the explosive bullets of Soviet snipers crack I looked for Pioneer Ohmke at the position where he will blow up the railway embankment should the enemy appear over it. I checked the pre-ignition apparatus, peaceably encased in leather instead of being ready to hand, and gave the pioneer a rocket for not knowing the strength of the charge and not having a sketch of where it is located. He will provide these by tomorrow and also report to me daily that the fuse is in order. He was surprised to have been woken up just for that. There is also plenty not right in the observation post up on the embankment. The final part of the way there is overlooked by the Russians so that they watch the changeover of staff and all traffic to the post. There is not much point in having an observation post which the enemy knows all about. I had ordered a trench to be excavated through which one could leave under cover, but I see that no work was done on it last night. There must be a holy stink about their not working in daylight because then their tall fur caps will be visible to the Russians above the embankment. My observation post is permanently occupied either by the artillery or the infantry-gun people and has a telephone installed at the accommodation bunker twenty paces away. The bunker lies under the rails, only the white-painted scissors-periscope projects above them. I stood in there for an hour or two watching the Russian line in front of my sector, the bank on the other side of the Volga, my own trench and the Russian traffic around Beketovka. One has to have a lot of patience at the periscope, lurking like a hunter, but observing is a lot of fun. One learns how to see, and it is never boring: far left are the obstacles of my neighbour, then the notorious

179

gully through which men arrive into the left of my sector: at the end of it is the spit of land. One can see very clearly the shooting slits used by the Russian snipers and their trench system. I discovered a sentry at one of these slits, betrayed by movement. He had ventured too far forward while hidden in the darkness of his roofed-over position. In order to shoot him, one would have to lie on the open embankment but would then be exposed to the murderous fire of the snipers. Once the first trench has been deepened I want to build a shooting position of my own into the embankment. Immediately I rang Lieutenant Jensen, who sent a burst of MG fire in the sentry's direction, at which he disappeared. That was a success, for if one never does anything, those over there get bolder. As it happens, on the spit of land there is some fresh earth on the snow, a newly dug trench and a new bunker visible, and the number of shooting slits has increased. They are digging there every night: what might this portend? There was once a road bridge over the gully, now blown up, and a narrow path overlooked by the enemy along which one can do gymnastics to reach the nearest trench of our neighbour. Below in the gully is a German minefield, but what use it is nobody knows; it was laid at the beginning of October. I asked the pioneers' commanding officer for an exact plan of this minefield and instruction by an officer in the minefield situation ahead of my sector. In the foreground right of the gully is the trench system of my sector, to the left, individual bunkers, MG posts, stretches of trench amongst fallen walls, lattice fencing and the ruins of houses at the edge of Kuperosnoye village. This part of the village is hilly and some 30 to 50 metres away behind a ridge and amongst other fallen walls are the Russians. They have an observation post in the so-called 'Red House' which they occupy permanently and from where they can see into, and fire into, our trench. We still have not managed to hit this house, despite many attempts, and now I no longer have the ammunition to persist with it. Trenches lead into the Red House, I have often seen Russians running through them. Even today there are two Russians there, one behind a window, the other behind a hole made by removing a brick. One would not be able to see it right away, only by assiduous observation of their routes, habits and movements which can last days, just as the huntsman must do from his lair. Behind the village one can see the hulls of two sunken motorboats in the Volga: because the river bank is so high only half of its width can be seen. It is totally frozen over and able to take vehicles. On the far bank one can see the Russians walking about, they have heavy-MG, anti-tank and artillery emplacements there. The distance is about 2,000 metres. Looking along the embankment, behind a central section above the SP-gun is the Russian sappe-trench which goes towards Utech's trench. Before the Russians broke through in October it was German-held and linked to the right flank of my trench system. This part is now half filled in, and there is a Russian with a machine-pistol about 30 metres from Utech's trench: between him and the trench are Spanish Riders. One can see the smoke rising from our own and the Russian bunkers, the whole of my right sector, the neighbouring sector and all the terrain to the right beyond it, the wrecks of Russian tanks, more German trenches, the 'sanatorium' where the Russians are, the Russian pathway to the front, where they make their way on foot, by sledge or lorry with small detachments, and in the background Beketovka, the town which we absolutely had to control to secure Stalingrad and which has now become our doom. It is at Beketovka that the Russians have built a large bridgehead, day and night they bring supplies and re-inforcements there. In order to observe this town I now follow the railway embankment to the 'leather factory' in the left sector, from whose ruined roof one has a view to the south. At Beketovka the chimneys smoke, the factories are at work and the Russians drill as though it were peacetime. Yes, I would not believe it had the infantryman in the observation post not made the scissors-periscope available to me. I see them there on a large snow-covered parade ground in the centre of the town arrayed in squads and companies. It is a shame that we have so little ammunition and cannot fire at them: the range is no more than four kilometres. It allows the Russian to stand down his forward troops every month and rest them in Beketovka, weld them together, delouse them, give them better food and let them recuperate. With us, one issue of uniform has had to last us from July 1942, for the Battle of Stalingrad from September and the nerve-shattering trench warfare from the end of October, all under the greatest deprivation.

When I came down the iron stairway in the leather factory to my horror I saw German soldiers scraping off skin or rind from an old, rotten bovine carcase. It stank to high heaven and was intended to be worked into leather in the summer. When I pointed out it would make them ill, they looked at me without understanding as if to say, then give us something else! As I jumped back over the embankment on my way to the trench, the Russian MG opened up, spraying it, and I ducked down quickly behind the ruins of the factory until I could run to my observation post. Initially I had always stood there on a heap of snow looking through a mousehole – until the snow melted and I saw that I had been standing on a pile of dead Russians! It did not disturb me. Thank God they were all frozen solid and therefore did not stink. So I stood on a skull and by doing so could just reach the mousehole. I could not help them. At 1300 hrs I arrived back at the command post with a giant hunger to find that we had received no bread and the last 200 grams was supposed to have lasted us four days. From now on only 50 grams – one slice – per day! The signs were increasingly evident that harder times lay ahead for us and relief was more improbable. Because the rations do not arrive until 0400 hrs I wrote a letter for home although for some time I have abandoned hope of ever receiving mail. I had collected the last coherent delivery myself on 6 November: since then only an airmail letter dated 1 December – probably some kind of happy chance – had reached me . . .

Here ends the war diary of Major von Lossow. On 3 January 1943, five days after the final entry, under fire in the forward trench he suffered a serious leg wound. On 7 January he had the life-saving fortune to be flown out of the Pocket. Only four men of his signals detachment survived the inferno: von Lossow himself, Dr Angermann as a physical cripple after eight years in Soviet captivity, the 22-year-old adjutant Dummer with a severe wound after years of Soviet captivity and the blacksmith who lost both feet to frostbite. After the war von Lossow studied dentistry and had his own practice in Munich from 1953 to 1983.

26. GERT PFEIFFER:

The Surrender of the Northern Pocket[1]

Gert Pfeiffer (b. Sarow, 8 October 1913, d. Buxtehude, 2 January 1998). 1937 joined Wehrmacht. 3 August 1942 awarded German Cross in gold. At Stalingrad, Captain in 92nd Motorized Infantry Regiment, 60th Infantry Division. Soviet PoW, released 1949, 1955 joined Bundeswehr. 3 May 1962 Lieutenant-Colonel, finally commanding officer, 72nd Panzer Grenadier Battalion at Hamburg. 1971 pensioned off and spent his retirement at Buxtehude.

I experienced the Stalingrad pocket in the open field along the northern boundary. After my third wound healed I returned to my Division in August 1942, was immediately given command of the so-called Divisional *Tross*[2] Battlegroup which meant that the *Tross* was practically under my command and was used twice to repulse breaches of the frontline.

At the end of September 1942 I relieved Captain von Reibnitz,[3] regimental adjutant, 92nd Infantry Regiment, who was taking over at Division in place of the sick IIa. At this time our 3rd Battalion, on the flank of the division in the west bordering with 113th Infantry Division, was reduced on one day of fighting from about 400 men down to thirty, and our 160th Panzer Abteilung destroyed over fifty enemy tanks. The border between the two divisions was the railway line from Stalingrad north-west to Moscow. The Soviet leadership wanted to breach the Pocket from the north-west, and had attacked into 3rd Battalion's sector from a strongpoint and made a deep breach but had not been able to expand the gap because of the German flanking fire from east and west which effectively controlled it. The only all-round battle post in No Man's Land was the former battalion command post where, as one of my first sorties

---

1. This report appeared in *Unsere 16*, edition 179, 46th Year, January 1998, pp 4–6.
2. *Tross*: rearward services including the baggage train, catering and supply, workshops, armourer, smithy, paymaster, medical services, etc, etc.
3. Captain von Reibnitz died in Bonn on 6 November 1994.

one night, I visited the battalion leader, my friend Captain Otto Meyn from Greifswald. It was a ghostly path on which to be alone on a dark night, but I did not want to place the life of a runner in danger. Meyn fell a few days later with his troop. He had declined to move back to a less exposed position farther south.

Our regiment in the Northern Boundary position abutted to the left – west – our sister 120th Regiment on the Tatar Wall and to the right – east – the remains of 16th Panzer Division. It controlled a stretch of front 3.5 kilometres long. The vehicles were dug in as a temporary measure about two kilometres south. Second Battalion led by Captain Hirsch[4] was to the left at the northern edge of a gorge and 1st Battalion led by Major Thurner on a flat slope descending to the north in a predominantly open situation. The companies had taken cover in pairs in anti-tank holes and had no connecting trench. The command posts were mainly in the frontline. With the attached remnants of Nos 13 and 14 Companies of the motorcycle and pioneer units the fighting strength of each battalion must have been around 400 men. The big worries were water, materials for trench building and later also fuel for heating and the field kitchens, for there was no wood in the steppe and the railway sleepers soon went.

After destroying 3rd Battalion the Russians rarely attacked in greater numbers than company strength and only now and again with tanks. Once a Russian tank rammed Major Thurner's command post and it was a miracle he came out of it alive. We had the impression that the enemy was looking for 'soft spots'. Up to 24 December all attacks – with the effective help of our 1st Abteilung, 160th Artillery Regiment south of us – were beaten off, although again and again we lost the anti-tank holes. There were soon no more replacements, for our *Tross* had been finely combed through down to the last sergeant, assistant armourer, cook, lightly wounded and sick, all of which caused us serious problems with catering and so on.

At night Division would occasionally send us small groups which they had weeded out. These unfortunates were all hoping to get better rations. However, every man, from regimental commander down to the Russian prisoners, got the same except that the prisoners were not given a tobacco ration, even if there was one. Relief and warmth was only available at 2nd Battalion: relief was only possible if one fell sick, to which one could succumb

---

4. Captain Hirsch died in the Jelabuga officers' camp in 1943: Major Thurner remains missing.

rapidly. Until the encirclement, losses to sickness had been kept within limits, after that they rose quickly.

The regimental command post lay about 300 metres behind 1st Battalion on the flat slope: at its summit was a rocket battery, a quadruple AA gun and an 8.8cm flak, which at 30 metres' range once destroyed a Russian tank which had broken through. The other gun had shot down a 'Rata' whose pilot baled out, hid out in the difficult terrain and was captured after an exchange of fire. All supporting weapons worked in association, were reliable and effective in action, the rocket launcher being used against identified troop concentrations. We had no latrines and even the colonel had to use the open field. When performing this duty one morning, a Russian troop laying field cables led by a lieutenant came towards us. We retired to the telephone bunker to put our trousers on and then captured them.

Weapons and ammunition came at dawn – for 1st Battalion only at night – brought by one lorry per battalion which then returned with the sick and wounded. This was a major source of friction! Hygiene and health problems including lice increased quickly because we had no laundry facilities. Only the hope that the encirclement was not going to be permanent made the shortcomings tolerable. All the same, the situation at 1st Battalion became increasingly hard to bear. Provisions were cut shortly after the encirclement and by 24 December each man received daily only one slice of bread, one horseflesh meatball and two or three cigarettes.

On Christmas morning I was ordered to the divisional battle post and instructed to reconnoitre the assembly areas selected for the break-out of the division to the south-west. At this time the approach by Army Group Hoth had got to within 50 kilometres of the south-western perimeter where it had been stopped by the Soviets. On the way my Kübelwagen gave up the ghost and I had to force a motorcycle/sidecar rider to take me to the south-west corner of the Pocket at gunpoint.

The result of my reconnaissance was devastating. The majority of our soldiers would never have been able to cross the Pocket on foot carrying arms and ammunition, fight through the encircling troops and then win territory to the south-west! The greater part of the men were already too weak and wheeled vehicles were not available – only a few were in running order. That day both the motorcycle rider and I had had no rations and I had taken from the regimental command post a box with 100 grams Shoka-Kola from the reserve of five boxes stored there openly for message-carriers to prevent them becoming weak at the knees. I knew that all the wounded could no longer be flown out. Break-out and leave the remainder of the wounded where they lay? German officers and doctors would never have been trusted again!

When I reported back that night to the divisional battle post the dice had already been cast. Operation *Wintergewitter*, the break-out from the Pocket, had been abandoned. My crony Reibnitz gave me the details. For the first time in the war I broke down and cried, as much in rage and exhaustion as for my disappointment in the leadership. The soldiers of the Northern Perimeter positions could not have made a break-out that Christmas Day without shame.[5]

Back at my battlegroup command post – where the 92nd Infantry Regiment had been converted into Battlegroup *Finck* by the attachment of remnants – a decision was required whether Christmas Eve tea should have some rum added to it: the last doctor at Regiment did not want to make the decision alone because of the weak condition of the soldiers. I ordered it and the night passed peacefully.

At first light on 25 December when I stepped out of my bunker in unsettled mood I heard rifle fire and hand grenades exploding from the direction of 1st Battalion. I rang them at once but could get no answer. I raised the alarm for the regimental officers, all bunkers, the rocket battery and the AA guns. All had posted sentries for the night and were already aware of what was happening. Then the first soldiers of 1st Battalion, mostly unarmed, came tumbling over the crest of the ridge in front of us. The Russians had attacked them in the early hours with knives and thrown them out – no wonder with this loss of strength! Only a few had managed to save themselves; we never saw their officers again. The artillery barrage came too late.

Colonel Finck, who did not know the regiment, had ordered that the battle post bunkers and neighbouring support weapons were to be held as the frontline. There was no other possibility. After a few days the battlegroup command post at the western end had to transfer to open battle posts in the Tatar Wall because it was no longer possible to direct operations from the frontline.

Some days before the Russians had tapped into our telephone lines and took pleasure in disturbing us at night with threatening and demoralizing heckling, unpleasant for officers and a psychological warfare measure against our telephonists who overheard it. Also weird was 'a man who had changed

5. Meant here is the shame in abandoning the wounded to their fate and leaving behind valuable material.

sides', a giant figure without rank insignia who asked Division not to interrogate him but to simply funnel itself through to the Russians.

We could not remain at the Tatar Wall and pulled back 600 metres into the half-ready rearward command post on which a dozen Russian PoWs and defectors – they were still coming over! – were working under the supervision of an NCO. The command post consisted of enlarged foxholes with makeshift stoves and chimneys, bulletproof and suitable for telephone traffic. Communication via field cables was becoming increasingly difficult, however, because we could no long send out repairmen.

The Russians received the same meagre fare as we did and had to scrape out new holes for themselves each night: once I had heard of the first case of cannibalism I sent them off to the north at night. Meanwhile we had received another batch of 'combed-out' or 'remnant' troops including a few dozen Romanians. The dead we left where they fell, the wounded we brought back. However, we were soon informed that the medical orderlies could only put them in tents on the ice-cold earth and leave them unattended.

In early January 1943 the remnants of an armoured personnel carrier battalion of 16th Panzer Division under Captain Dörnemann[6] nearby to the east undertook a limited attack against a ridge from where the Russians had a commanding view over the Pocket. As unexpected the attack was beaten off. Some of the surviving APCs were transferred to us and gave us protection from a reverse slope.

The Russians advanced from the north only cautiously, but one night after a brief exchange of fire they reached our rearward command post, forcing us to flee the foxholes. The War Diary chronicler, the infirm Lieutenant Linke, and the War Diary were lost, because people ran off blindly in all directions into the dark night. We alerted 2nd Battalion, still in their trench, but then contact was lost and only a couple of men of the battlegroup command post remained together. This must have happened between 12 and 15 January.

The Regiment's last vehicle, a radio car, was still driveable, and took the orderly officer, a lieutenant who had been blinded, to Stalingrad North. He did not survive the surrender of the Regiment, nor did signals officer Lieutenant Harscheidt who had provided outstanding service. From now on we fought our way forward, and with the regimental officers withdrew on foot

6. Heinz Dörnemann (b. 20 February 1910, d. 2001) was commanding officer of 16th Panzer Division's motorcycle battalion: final rank Major. Decoration: Knight's Cross, 28 November 1943.

to Stalingrad North over the abandoned trenches and fragmented remnants of other units, always worried at being surprised by the Russians. What we ate I have no idea! The Staff searched trenches for anything edible and took part in the night searches for provision-bombs dropped by German aircraft. What they found they shared with us, but I never got bread, only salty, fatty, hard sausage, chocolate and acid drops, all suitable to make one constipated or to give one diarrhoea since there was only melted snow for water.

I had had a number of previous experiences of being encircled in Russia but not in winter. None of us had imagined it could be as ghastly as this: hundreds, even thousands of dead, wounded, men freezing to death, famished, some of them crawling towards Stalingrad, often with wounds undressed. I saw the horror of it above ground, what it was like under it is indescribable. There was no medical care, no water, no dressings: I had used my personal 'first-aid dressing pack' somewhere ten days previously: there was no re-issue once expended.

Colonel Finck and I plus one messenger and one radio operator with intact radio set capitulated with the very last elements of Sixth Army early on 2 February 1943. We were totally exhausted, filthy and lice-infested, lying in a hole in the ground somewhere at the western end of Barrikady in the Northern Pocket. I had fired two shots into the radio apparatus. A Russian major armed with a pistol jumped into our makeshift bunker after I had told the runner to fix a strip of white cloth to his rifle and hold it up to be seen. The Russian threw aside the waistbelt with pistol I offered him and commanded: 'Na wjerch' – 'Go up!'

We stumbled a few hundred metres in pairs to a bigger, covered-over hole in the ground, were obliged to enter and received in a not unfriendly manner by a Russian colonel, the commanding officer of a Moscow Guards Regiment, as he informed us later through an interpreter. He invited us to sit in German field chairs and offered us a German field flask with vodka. When Colonel Finck declined, the Russian said we were probably worried about being poisoned, and drank first. Colonel Finck still refused but I took some despite the thick blisters like glacier-burns around my lips. The Russian colonel wiped the bottleneck with his hand and screwed it closed. Soon after an orderly brought two cooking pot covers full of millet gruel, and I ate the lot in my cover. They also served us tea. Through his interpreter the colonel advised us of his displeasure at our causing his unit unnecessary casualties by insisting on fighting to the last round, and in the future we would probably experience worse times than at present, but remain alive and see our Homeland again at the war's end. On the whole he behaved as a correct senior officer in contrast to those we would meet later. With that he dismissed us.

Half an hour later we were plundered and robbed by a Russian *Tross*, and thereafter began the indescribable path of suffering into captivity. Only one in fifteen men made prisoner at Stalingrad survived Soviet captivity: 6,000 of 91,000.

27. PAUL PIEPER:

I Did Not Believe I Would Be Saved[1]

Paul Pieper (b. Georgsmarienhütte, 10 May 1923) completed his apprenticeship as a shoemaker before the war. Conscripted in 1942 he joined 29th Infantry Division and on 19 November 1942, on the same day when the encirclement was complete, he had joined his unit, No 3 Company, 71st Regiment, inside the Pocket at Stalingrad.

On 1 January 1943 during a heavy attack almost my whole unit was wiped out. We were at the western end of the Pocket facing towards the steppe in the open field. I lay with a comrade in a bomb crater about 50 centimetres deep. I had been wounded in the arm – it was stiff and swollen and I could no longer move it: my comrade had been killed instantly.

During daylight one could not leave the position because the enemy shot on sight. Later an unknown medical orderly of our unit inspected the wound, gave me an authorization to fly out and sent me to the nearest dressing station. The doctor there gave me a lattice splint bound with paper dressings: a round had fractured my left elbow joint. Although I was no longer 'fit for the front', despite the splint a rifle was thrust into my hand because the Russians were coming. Some time afterwards I landed up in the main dressing station (HVP) of our unit which was near Gumrak. We lay in a ruin on straw; there we spent a couple of days. There were at least a hundred lying there. It was cold, naturally there was no heating. Once a group of doctors and medical orderlies did the rounds, inspecting the suffering, occasionally asking a patient what was wrong with him. They did nothing whatever, for they had nothing. There was nothing more to eat, and my neighbour said to me, 'We should do something, and leave here!' That probably led to my life being saved.

With this companion I left the dressing station and accompanied him to the airfield to see if there was a chance of being flown out. One could not call it

---

1. The Editor was authorized by the author on 27 June 2003 to edit the material into report form.

an aerodrome: it was just an open field with holes: many soldiers lay around, mostly seriously wounded; I would say thousands! They lay here in the open air with the frozen dead: nobody bothered about them any more. The dead could not be buried. Nobody had the strength to dig into the deeply frozen earth.

I lost my companion who had come with me from the HVP. All day long I did what I could to find something to eat. I almost always slept in the open. I did not want to return to the HVP. I was not always at the aerodrome: I saw aircraft which had been shot down while taking off. Once I saw a Ju 52 which had just got up: Russian fighters appeared and shot it down. There was no point in staying here! The airfield was full of shot-down aircraft and bomb craters. Field-gendarmes guarded a house, I think it had food and parcels, which had come by the field-post. Once I found a field-post packet and went straight to it since it was off to one side.

One evening on the airfield I saw smoke coming up out of the ground. I became curious, went nearer and found a flak unit there. They had built themselves a bunker, a real cellar, in which an open fire was burning. I went inside and found the people wrapped in woollen blankets sitting around the fire. They allowed me to sit with them. Finally I wanted to have a good sleep and did so almost at once. After a few hours they woke me and said two aircraft had landed, I had the authorization to be flown out and I should definitely go. I had already given up, did not want to make the effort any longer and thought to myself, 'It won't be any good, there will be a huge crush again'. Thus I did not believe I would be flown out but went anyway, the flak comrades gave me a blanket and showed me the direction.

It was icy cold and the steppe wind blew my blanket away. Previously I had had to give up my warm clothing. I had been issued a fine warm battledress suit by my unit: the others only had thin greatcoats. Thus I had been well protected, but everything which protected one against the cold had to be given up once one was wounded because the wearer was no longer fit for the front and useless for combat.

I had lost the blanket, I was discouraged and disappointed, but when I got to the aircraft, which I had not reckoned on doing, I noticed that there were hardly any wounded there. Perhaps they hadn't got their dockets to fly! Two bombers had landed, He 111s. It was 20 January 1943. There was no sign of the usual great throng always present on the airfield. Usually when an aircraft touched down everybody would surround it.

The pilot appeared and meanwhile there were about twenty people around, the crew could not take more. The pilot said: 'I hope I can get up with this load! Once you are all inside I shall try it!' We had to get in at the flap through where the bombs used to be dropped. Once we had all climbed in, the flap was secured from the inside. We sat pressed very close together: there were a couple of Romanians too which at first we did not like, but it would have been mean and nasty not to have taken them. The pilot succeeded in taking off. The He 111 was icing up and quite cold inside, for it was an icy night, no luxury flight! Nothing could be seen because it was dark, just one weak light burned on board forward. I do not know how long we were in the air, in any case we finished up at Novotsherkassk.

We could scarcely believe we had come out of it alive; some were crying, others wanted to thank the three airmen. Finally we were brought to a building where they gave us something to eat. That was glorious! Last but not least a Luftwaffe officer came and said, 'Afterwards a machine is flying to Stalino, I am looking for the people to go with it.' Small and modest I sat in the corner and he asked me how old I was. 'Nineteen,' I said. 'Well, then you're coming too!' So in one day I had two beautiful flights.

At Stalino there was a proper hospital where I was treated for the first time in two weeks. A Swiss doctor attended to me, probably the senior surgeon. We lay there in clean beds, and the Swiss doctor came every day to visit, and look at the patients. Those declared fit to travel could go on. We who were not fit said sadly, 'The cup has passed us by!' But after three weeks I was finally on the list and reached Lemberg and from there Silesia. I asked myself then how there could be Swiss doctors at Stalino. This field hospital must have been evacuated in February.

After convalescing, Pieper served in Italy until 1945 when he was captured by British forces and held in Egypt as a PoW until 1948. After that he returned to his trade. He now lives in retirement at Ahaus.

28. EBERHARD POHL:

The Defensive Battle at Baburkin[1]

Eberhard Pohl (b. Sagan/Sprottau, 23 November 1908, d. Ottobrunn, 16 April 1997) commanded 1st Battalion, 134th Grenadier Regiment, 44th Infantry Division. 17 December 1942 Knight's Cross.

First Battalion 134th Infantry Regiment lay in a defensive position on the Regiment's right-hand sector at Chmelevski on the Don, about 60 kilometres from Kalatch. The very high western bank, typical of all Russian rivers, offered excellent observation positions for heavy weapons. What we found unpleasant were the many gullies, *Balkas,* which ran from the river deep into German-held territory. Similarly we disliked the eastern exits of Chmelevski and Simovski on flat land, affording the enemy a good view into the two villages. In the territory opposite, rugged and difficult to survey, the Russians had only weak forces. Nevertheless at night increased watchfulness was necessary along the approximately six-kilometre-long Battalion sector, for it was the practice of enemy scouting parties to cross the river which was only 150 metres wide by boat and surprise our own reconnaissance and the field kitchens which served the strongpoints at night. Thus they kept us on our toes.

The sector was split up into small squad-strongpoints each with bunker, trench and listening post: each squad had two MGs, telephone lines, artillery fireplans etc. The experiences of the first winter had been taken into account in the design and so one could – given normal circumstances – face the winter with aplomb. The weather up to 22 November had been so mild that winter clothing had not yet been issued. The reinforced artillery detachment from 44th Infantry Division's artillery regiment had set up a wide-ranging observation network, and every strongpoint had sketches of the terrain on

---

1. This report was written immediately after the author's return from Soviet captivity in the winter of 1953, edited on 12 March 1962 and published in the journal of 44th Division, Nr. 115, May 1989.

graph paper marked with the main firing lines for the artillery so that each strongpoint could link in and correct. Each man had two blankets: the bunkers were heated and provisions guaranteed by additional culling of the horses.

Since October it had been noticed that the Russians were withdrawing infantry forces from the Don front in our sector and replacing them with motorized Stalin Organ rocket launchers and artillery aimed at our positions. Therefore at Battalion, irregularly during the night, we would lay an artillery barrage coordinating all our heavy guns in the firing plan to thwart enemy preparations for his attacks. From the behaviour of the enemy in front of the 134th, however, one could not draw any conclusions as to his intentions in that respect.

Meanwhile light snow had fallen. Since 19 November from the north we heard the sound of heavy fighting, particularly hour-long massed artillery fire. The divisional artillery detachment knew what was up. We all had an unpleasant feeling. Four weeks previously at an officers' conference I had pointed out the difficult situation of the 'Stalingrad balcony' should the enemy attempt an encirclement with powerful spearheads.

On 22 November strong Soviet spearheads succeeded in meeting up at Kalatch. The Don bridge there fell intact into Russian hands because the German garrison had not been made aware of what was afoot. Without difficulty the Russian thrust had cut through the weakest positions along the German line, i.e. where the Romanians stood in the north and south. By reason of their armament, the Romanians were not in a position to offer effective resistance to strong Russian armour and motorized cavalry units.

Did that all come as a surprise to the military leadership? Certainly not for us! For weeks we had been reporting that Russian troops were being withdrawn from the front for another purpose. Stukas and reconnaissance parties had reported the major troop concentrations north and south of Stalingrad. But nothing was done to engage them, much to our bemusement!

At 2030 hrs on 22 November I was summoned to the regimental commanding officer. According to a prearranged codeword the battalion had orders to move out: taking down of telephone lines, issue of winter clothing, loading up of armoured vehicles – the main part of the rearward services (*Tross*) and the horses was 150 kilometres behind us to the west – and preparations to assemble at the Company assembly points. Only a security occupation force was to remain. On the regimental commander's table was my beautiful birthday cake, which we had been planning to eat tomorrow. Now we would not have the opportunity . . .

At Kalatch the Russians had closed the pocket around us. 44th Infantry Division, cut off from its supply units, was to fight its way across the Don bridges at Peskovatka and Vertyatchi to the east bank and reinforce the Stalingrad battlegroup. One company of the battalion was to remain in the old sectors until 0400 hrs on 23 November and then rejoin the main force. The 134th was to abandon the previous position at once and, following the routes marked on the map, head for Vertyatchi.

The men were informed, everything necessary ordered and, without any blowing up of bunkers or trenches, on the night of 22 November in light snowfall the units set out in the direction indicated. The men were moody; they all knew what it meant in winter warfare to leave good positions. What would we find over there, how would the situation shape up? It would have been easy for us that night to have forced open the weak ring and re-established contact with our forces in the west, but nothing was done. Dawn came. We must have marched 20 kilometres, occasionally bombed by the 'Rollbahn crows', when suddenly from the north-west, troops approached us dressed in olive-green uniforms – with neither weapons nor vehicles, the officers ahead in automobiles. Because visibility was poor and we could not yet recognize who they were, for safety's sake I had the MGs brought up. It was our Axis allies, the Romanians! As though panic-stricken, this mob poured over the Don crossings towards Stalingrad.

In the area around Vertyatchi I was detailed to occupy the bridgehead by the later traitor, General von Lenski.[2] It was all blocked up on the bridges and the Russians were awfully near. Therefore it was decided to counter-attack. The attack had to go through a valley with the support of 16th Panzer and the artillery. There was no snow on the ground, it was damp and there was little cover. Therefore we had to reverse our camouflage suits. This took over an hour. Then we started off – it went well at first, but we had to spend the night in the open with only blankets to protect us against the weather. I climbed up on a panzer, but left it very quickly because of the cold.

---

2. Arno von Lenski (b. Czymochen/East Prussia, 20 July 1893, d. 4 October 1986). Ended First World War in rank of Lieutenant-Colonel. 1938 Colonel; September 1942 commanded 24th Panzer Division as Major-General. In Soviet captivity member of German pro-Communist collaborationist organizations NKFD and BdO. 1944-1945 studied Social Science at the Krasnogorsk Anti-Fascist School. 1949/1950 deputy Chairman, National Democratic Party in the DDR: 1952 Major-General, Volkspolizei: 1958–67 member of the People's Chamber, DDR.

Meanwhile the traffic over the bridges was now flowing smoothly and we could occupy the envisaged bridgehead position. The ice over the Don was not thick enough to cross the river away from the bridges. Next day, 25 November, we blew up the bridges and occupied the former Russian trenches on the east bank to defend the troops moving towards Stalingrad. The enemy was sitting as high as a house in the positions above us on the west bank and we received his blessings at first hand. Individual panzers and SP-guns were stationed along the roads leading to Stalingrad to protect the troops pulling back to the east. The 134th received from the divisional commander the order to set up a new defensive position facing west based on a line on the map about five kilometres west of Baburkin. From now on Sixth Army would supply the Division.

I drove ahead and could not find the way because the steppe was covered with snow. As far as the eye could see there was no mark by which to orient oneself, and so finally I joined up with the commander of the artillery detachment on a sector of terrain to which some of the troops had repeatedly had to set up a front to hold the advancing enemy. The divisional commanding officer appeared and designated a totally barren, flat area of territory without any cover whatsoever as my new main frontline – the nearest village was five kilometres farther east of me – and he pointed out how easy it was to follow because it was lined with telegraph poles. I was speechless. I explained that one could not defend here in a snowy desert without the immediate proximity of a village. We had no explosives to burrow into the earth. He shrugged his shoulders. The Army had ordered this line. It was another one of those moments in which one despaired of the military leadership. And as always: the regimental commander had to suffer the consequences and, relying on the relationship of trust with his veterans, find some practicable way to transform the impossible into the possible.

I was extremely annoyed that so little had been learnt from the 1941 winter. My assumption that the Army must have prepared some trenches for a front facing west – that finally they had identified the overall situation including 'Stalingrad island' – was falsely drawn. That one could not defend the line ordered was obvious. My repeated suggestions, to run the main frontline along the western side of Baburkin, were rejected. With regard to the neighbours, who were in a similarly unfavourable position, one could change nothing without uniform leadership.

After all the men and vehicles had arrived and the mood of despondency sank even lower once they had cast eyes on the new 'position', we got to work. No matter how tired we might be, we had to be ready to defend as quickly as possible. The first thing I did was saw down the telephone poles which the enemy would have used for range-finding purposes. Companies were given their own sectors and work began at digging into the frozen earth, insofar as that was possible with the tools available. Within 24 hours we had dug down 50 centimetres. At the right-hand end of the line was Hill 124.5. This small mound was perhaps three metres high, but in this flat terrain even dominated Pitomnik aerodrome 18 kilometres away. It was the magnet which attracted all observer posts. That it provided no life insurance was self-evident. We sank slit trenches into it and put the artillery spotter posts and No 13 Infantry-Gun Company atop it. The right-hand neighbour, our 2nd Battalion, had only brought up weak advanced parties into the new sector because the mass of the battalion would have to engage the advancing enemy.

On the night of 1 December everything was at last where it had been ordered to be. *Tross-* vehicles and the kitchens had been shifted into Baburkin village meanwhile: the battalion command post was behind the main frontline halfway along 250 metres to the rear of No 1 Company. Before we at Battalion HQ got into the earth we erected tents against the cold. After setting up the telephone and radio-telegraphy network we tried to get underground as quickly as possible. After organizing the defence and trench drainage with my adjutants and some runners, I had scarcely laid down in my tent when an enemy mortar bomb fell in the battalion's sector, hitting the signals' staff tent. We had two dead and four wounded – a crying shame which created panic. Naturally all the wire connections went to the devil. The companies were calling out into the darkness, asking what had happened. I set up a shelter for the wounded with my able medical officer Dr Apfelthale[3] in a small depression. Because we could not keep vehicles or horses in this open country, we had to telephone Regiment for a vehicle. They sent horse-drawn carts: the drivers had great difficulty in finding us at night.

Baburkin village had long since been dismantled. There was no house nor bunker standing. It had been occupied by rearward army units whom we forced out eastwards for lack of space. On the morning of 1 December there was an artillery bombardment, the like of which we had never experienced before. For four hours Stalin Organ rockets hissed, shells howled, the air

---

3. Senior Surgeon Dr Erich Otto Apfelthaler (b. Vienna, 23 August 1916), qualified 23 November 1939, Battalion surgeon, 1st Battalion, 134th Infantry Regiment. No further details known. His brother Senior Surgeon Dr Hans Apfelthaler (b. 30 June 1914), qualified 1940, features in Hans Dibold's book *Arzt in Stalingrad.*

trembled and from the skies a curtain of fumes and smoke separated friend and foe. Losses were high, because we had still not got underground properly. Weak enemy attacks were beaten off: unfortunately during these one of my most capable company commanders, Knight's Cross holder Lieutenant Vormann,[4] fell while firing at the Russians.

Over the next few days we worked like galley-slaves to dig ourselves in. Anti-tank defences and a complete network of observation posts of all weapons branches were set up, AA guns readied on the most favourable reverse slopes, additionally the infantry-guns of my dear comrade Lieutenant Jordan. A company of Romanian reinforcements arrived, at which I was not delighted. Finally I could spread the companies somewhat farther back. Wood, steel sheet and so forth was driven up by night from Baburkin and gradually the tiny trenches with their makeshift overhead cover gave the men at least a basic protection. There was no washing or shaving possible unless snow was used.

By 4 December everything was going better. The Romanians had slotted into my units: their company commander spent his time in the rear with the *Tross* and was only ever seen at night when arriving to take note of the casualties. He got double rations, one from us and the other from a Romanian supply base. The field kitchen drove up with our hot food by night to a spot about 400 metres behind the line, but only if it was not too bright – and how we cursed those Stalingrad nights! A bowl of horsemeat soup, 300 grams of bread per head, and that was it. On 4 December the Russians launched a major attack with massive artillery preparation and flamethrower tanks. Assault troops sat on the tank hulls until shot dead, but the enemy force crushed Captain Schida's[5] 2nd Battalion and wiped out one of my own companies, both on my right. The company commander, Captain Schmidt, was wounded. It was the typical picture of a major battle. Everywhere, including behind us, enemy tanks cruised with their death-dealing weapons; other tanks were burnt-out, having been hit by our anti-tank gun fire: all telephone wires were shot down or driven under tank tracks: anti-tank guns crushed, radio telegraphy nullified. Here our own men were running back, there Russians with MGs and machine-pistols ran

---

4. Lieutenant Johann Vormann (b. 15 September 1912, fell per German War Graves List 1 December 1942), commander No 10 Company. Decoration: Knight's Cross, 10 September 1942.

5. Major Roland Schida (b. Buchweiss, 6 August 1911, fell Baburkin, 4 December 1942), from 1 October 1942 CO 2nd Battalion, 134th Infantry Regiment.

firing towards us. Our own and enemy shells exploded amongst us.

At my battalion command post everybody was firing. Cold-bloodedly we killed every tank commander who stood up in the hatch to gain his bearings, and with accurate fire cut down anyone who came too close. In times of the greatest danger every round must count! The situation had developed in such a way that we saw no other solution. According to the rules, the soldier on the defensive had to continue doing his duty until his last breath in order that by his obstinacy he tied down enemy forces and gave his side freedom of movement. But not all was lost yet! From Baburkin the regimental commander had seen what was afoot and had sent up an SP-gun detachment under Major Bochum[6] and a company of pioneers. At the last moment they had received fuel and the chase began. Help arrived just in the nick of time. We succeeded in recapturing Hill 124, but my adjutant Lieutenant Pfisterer, whom I had expressly ordered not to involve himself in this action, fell. The self-propelled guns took out a number of enemy tanks. Naturally during all the manoeuvring the last lengthy pieces of my telephone cabling went to the dogs, but they could be replaced.

As it grew quieter I attempted to survey the situation. At 2nd Battalion, my right-hand neighbour, there was nobody left, the commander and most of his men having fallen at their posts. Some stragglers found their way to me later. The Russian tanks took off some prisoners when they retired westwards. No 1 Company to my right was almost completely wiped out; there were serious losses at Battalion: the left flank was still intact. I saw that I would not be able to hold the little height, it was too exposed. I therefore decided to establish a frontline about 250 metres east of it on the reverse slope in order to expose the mound to our sniper fire and so prevent the enemy using it for observation purposes. I shortened the front to the right, closed up to the 113th Artillery Division detachment and placed in a central position projecting towards the enemy a strongpoint with four MGs. To my left everything remained unchanged.

On 5 December we heard once again the sound of enemy armour. No attack was forthcoming, however, apparently they were towing away their wrecked tanks. The previous day for the first time we had used hollow-charge limpet-mines with good results and without loss to ourselves. My battle post now lay in the battalion frontline: having regard to the tense situation I did

---

6. Gerhard Bochum, CO 177th SP-gun Abteilung. 4 October 1940 Major, 1 April 1943 Lieutenant-Colonel, survived Soviet captivity.

not want to change it at the moment. After I had succeeded in bringing back some order to affairs, I sent my signals leader to a small depression about 500 metres behind me where two wrecked T-34s stood. He was to investigate the possibility of setting up a battalion command post under the tanks. He came back with the report that the tanks were manned. I gave him some people to smoke out the crews with hand grenades. After the first one went off they surrendered. With frostbite, jet black, wounded and afraid of being shot, they climbed out of their inhospitable hiding place. I gave up my intention of bringing the command post out of the line having regard to the morale of the men.

For a change we had a chance to watch an aerial dogfight. So long as Pitomnik aerodrome remained in our hands we could expect our fighters to show up occasionally. The Russian pilot baled out over his own positions but our people moved fast and grabbed him. At dusk I had him brought to me. My hole in the ground was covered by a steel sheet: in the far corner there was a small hearth made out of some stones; a piece of sackcloth concealed the entrance. A Hindenburg lamp flickered to one side: one had the feeling it would go out at any second. I looked at the airman. I knew from earlier cases that in winter Russian airmen wore wonderful felt boots. This man had only woollen cloth wrapped around his legs. Where were his boots? He said he did not have any. I did not believe him and suspected that he had been bullied and relieved of them. Therefore I sent a runner, who was wounded on the way, to the Company which had captured the airman and had the commander write me a note confirming that the shot-down pilot had not been wearing boots when captured.

Combat activity returned to normal. The Russian infantry had lost its will to attack. There was hardly 100 metres between the two sides. We still thought that a relief force was on its way to us from the west and that therefore there was some point in holding out. Captured German recognition flares which the Russians fired off on the Don heights reinforced this assumption. Occasionally at night some of them turned up at our field kitchens with a mess tin. Both sides wore white camouflage suits, but theirs were cleaner.

On 7 December I received from the divisional commander the order to train men in the rearward services – *Tross*, construction Battalion, artillerymen and so on – so as to be available to cover our losses in infantry. Here was a sight for sore eyes! Men whose rifles had not been cleaned for years, who had never fired a shot in anger in the war, who assured me they were very short-sighted. I consoled them that they would soon meet the Russians so close that they would not need spectacles to see them. A small training detachment taught them close combat. Naturally we always used live ammunition.

On 7 December I was awarded the Knight's Cross. That evening I received a small packet wrapped in dirty brown paper. On the paper General Paulus had written in pencil a few words of recognition. The packet contained some Army bread and a tin of herrings in tomato sauce. On 10 December a telephone call came from Regiment and immediately afterwards a Kübelwagen arrived with the order that I should go to Battalion at once. The battalion was pulling back to Baburkin. I drove as if demented for the battalion position. What had happened, and how had it come about?

I had appointed Captain von H[7] as my deputy. Before the encirclement he had gone on leave and had been flown in upon his return. He had brought with him a sack filled with Christmas presents. I thought I had made the wrong choice in appointing him, I had never held him in special esteem; he seemed to me to be something of a poseur and play-actor. When it came to recommending awards and decorations I had always put him low on my listing until my regimental commander remonstrated with me on the subject. After he flew in it was my intention to change my opinion of him, thinking that I had done him an injustice.

Thus I drove as far as the first elements of my battalion which were flooding back. The Russians were firing Stalin Organ rockets amongst them but the enemy was nowhere to be seen! With a loud voice I succeeded in halting the battalion, disentangling the men and placing them in a more favourable position. When the men saw me, their confidence was restored and they allowed themselves to be led. Leadership is primarily a matter of confidence! There was no trace of Captain von H. A man who had cover in a shell crater could not be made to abandon it. Enraged I shouted at him; suddenly I heard a whizzing in the air. I threw myself down lightning-fast and saw the shell explode in the crater in which the coward had hoped to find his protection . . .

Two days later I met Captain von H at the regimental command post in the gorge at Baburkin. He was without headgear and had gone to pieces. Apparently he had lost his nerve when a massive Russian barrage began, ran from the Battalion command post without cap or belt to the neighbour on the right, the artillery detachment of 113th Division. The weak and cowardly had followed his example and soon the whole battalion was streaming back. It

---

7. For understandable reasons the name is withheld (note from 44th Infantry Division editor).

suffered more losses in doing so than would have been the case if it had stayed where it was.

That evening a meeting was held attended by Captain von H., my regimental commanding officer, the commander of the artillery detachment, a Major Steffens and myself. At once I criticized Captain von H for his action. Suddenly he went outside, there was a shot and soon afterwards he returned with the remark that an aircraft had shot him in the leg. We all exchanged disbelieving glances: I took H's pistol from the holster and lo and behold there were traces in the barrel that it had been very recently fired! I accused him at once of having shot himself in the leg and wanted to shoot him on the spot. Colonel Boje relieved me of the pistol and said the matter had to be investigated. At that von H disappeared into the adjacent dressings bunker of the SP-gun detachment. From their medical officer he obtained an authorization and was flown out of the Pocket the same night, having flown into the Pocket only for the pretence of having been a veteran of Stalingrad.

On 8 January it rained leaflets from the heavens: they contained the Russian offer in exchange for capitulation. Amongst other things they promised us the immediate restoration of normal rations, treatment of the wounded, they would allow the officers to retain their side-arms and guaranteed a quick return home after the cessation of hostilities. We all had a good laugh and Sixth Army command declined. Through frontline loudspeakers German emigrés and defectors called upon us ceaselessly to come on over. Despite the evil situation the men were neither rattled nor impressed. Nobody thought then that Hitler's army would be deserted and sacrificed for the sake of some vague point of prestige.

On 10 January 1943 all hell broke loose: the enemy's major attack began. I still see in my mind's eye today a corporal with his MG group in front of me, set up in the north-west angle of our triangular position. The previous evening I had discussed the situation with him, and that we would probably have to make the Pocket smaller. The consequence would be pulling back to the western end of Baburkin. He looked at me very calmly and said: 'Herr Major, I am not moving back from this position, come what may. If we have to move farther east, then it will be all the more certainly into the hands of the Russians. I prefer to die here!' I lay in the position with my staff, rifle in hand, and kept looking to the left to my heavy-MG group. Belt after belt was fed through the chambers: finally our people took to the rifle butt and entrenching tool, and then it fell quiet.

We shot to kill every possible target: every tank commander who opened the hatch too soon, every Russian who came closer without adequate cover fell victim to our fire. All connections were torn down. One almost doubted that one still lived. In this state of mind night surprised us. After a talk with the regimental commander 134th Infantry Regiment battlegroup was transferred to positions at the western end of Baburkin. Here there was still a 2cm AA gun, also the commander of the anti-tank troop of 44th Division with some 7.62cm guns fixed on captured jeeps. A few howitzers were still able to fire – thus we could carry on.

I received a telephone call from Pitomnik. My old friend Luftwaffe Major Freudenfeld was ringing from the airfield, he wanted me to visit him soon. He had discovered my whereabouts through reading in Army Orders about my award of the Knight's Cross and wanted to see me. By chance we had met up in the unlikeliest situations in all the theatres of war. At Stalingrad, Freudenfeld was in charge of the arrivals and departures of supply aircraft. The same night with the consent of my commanding officer I drove to see him in a Volkswagen.

The journey there was creepy. To better indicate the 'roads' in the snowy waste, horses' legs with the hooves upwards had been planted in the snow. I spent a lot of time asking directions before I could find Freudenfeld's bunker at Pitomnik. The airfield looked dreadful. Parts of shot-down or damaged aircraft lay everywhere. At the centre of it two marquees had been erected for the wounded. Every so often a runway would be cleared to enable approaching aircraft to land. Often Russians would divert an aircraft off course by means of false beacon signals. Now and again an aircraft would land in No Man's Land and a fierce battle would break out for possession of the aircraft's load of supplies, equally valuable to friend and foe alike. Generally the Russians would gain the upper hand and drag the aircraft to their side with their T-34s. Freudenfeld discussed the situation with me and was astonished that I knew nothing of the facts. There was to be no relief for the soldiers at Stalingrad: the fortunes of war had changed. The loss of Pitomnik airfield was only a matter of time: it was already under observed artillery fire from north and west.

This conversation made such an impression on me that during the night I drove to my divisional commanding officer Lieutenant-General Deboi[8] in

---

8. Heinrich-Anton Deboi (b. Landshut, 6 April 1893, d. Soviet camp Voikovo, 20 January 1955). Ended First World War as Lieutenant. 1925 Reichswehr, Captain. 1934 Major, 1939 Colonel. 2 May 1942 as Major-General, CO 44th Infantry Division. Decorations: 1942 German Cross in gold; Knight's Cross.

Rossoshka valley where I talked to him and his Ia, Lieutenant-Colonel Radtke.[9] They were both thunderstruck. The Army had deliberately played down the gravity of the situation to their division and now he sat as though cast in stone as he heard from me the hopelessness of our predicament.

The ring around us was being pulled daily ever tighter. Baburkin had to be given up, and on 16 January[10] we lost Pitomnik. Thus the fate of Sixth Army was sealed. The small airfields at Gumrak and Stalingradski could not be called substitutes. The main front now ran above the aerodrome. The airmen blew up the last intact machines, and we were happy to pull out of this unfavourable spot next day. In the clear light of day one could see columns of German soldiers making for the city from every direction. They were fired on by the enemy artillery and the Russians had mastery of the air. An appalling scene in this situation: on the road lay a group of German soldiers, victims of a bomb. Many had lost limbs; the blood had frozen to ice, nobody had attended to them, nobody moved them off the roadway. All the columns had simply gone past them, concerned only with their own hopeless situation. I gave them dressings, lay them together and left a medical orderly with them to wait for a lorry to take them away. There was no lorry. The constant life-and-death struggle made us forget that for weeks we had neither washed nor shaved, that we had not had what you might call a night's sleep and that the majority had bad frostbite.

After the loss of Pitomnik we travelled through numerous ravines to Gontchara where we were to defend. In these gorges the rearward sections of the Army had dug many bunkers. In a flak bunker Luftwaffe personnel told us that every week they received seven sacks of mail for their Abteilung, including illustrated magazines; even axles for the lorries. At the same time 44th Division received a total of three sacks. That was how they rationed it out to the infantry!

About 21 January we went into positions at Gumrak. Units and stragglers continued to stream from the west into Stalingrad. I co-opted into the defence everybody whom I considered fit for the front. One night two German soldiers appeared from the Russian side with bread to lure us over. On the other hand Russians were still defecting to us! They were two Kulaks who had

---

9. Lieutenant-Colonel Radtke is listed as missing since 28 January 1943.

10. This and other details up to 31 January have been amended since the author's memory fails him as to dates, e.g. the loss of Pitomnik was 14 January, not the 16th. He dates the loss of Gumrak at 25 January, whereas the Soviets took the airfield on the 22nd.

been sent to Siberia and in 1942, when the situation on the Russian front was very serious, had been released from their punishment camp and sent to the front. They had not believed their officers when told that we were encircled: they rather thought it was the opposite! I sent them back at night, for we had no food to give them.

On 22 January the Russians made another attack with T-34s. The tanks drove along the edges of the gorge in which we had our positions and outflanked us so that we were sitting in a trap. We raced out between the tanks, which were firing from all barrels. On the way my dear company commander Captain Schmid received a serious wound in the hand from a shell splinter. Later I stopped a lorry to take Schmid to the airfield. I discovered that he got aboard a Red Cross aircraft but the Russians shot it down.

In the Gumrak gorges were many bunkers with wounded, some of whom surrendered while others decided to come with us. Also so-called stragglers, or better said, cowards, sat in hideouts with food and provisions-bombs they had stolen, awaiting the fall of Stalingrad. The Romanians were especially prominent in this respect.

For days we had had no artillery support. When Russian SMG-companies attacked us in the Gontchara gorge on 23 January, I was wounded in the upper thigh. We had to retreat before this superior force. Anybody sick or wounded who was found in the bunkers by the Russians was killed off. I knew that there was an anti-aircraft position at Gumrak airfield. They would have to be involved in the last battle if there was any chance of bringing the Russians to a standstill. I ordered the Battalion to defend the west side of Gumrak and went to the AA commander. He was flabbergasted when I described the situation to him. He had not been informed that the Russians had taken Gontchara. Briefly stated, all barrels were lowered to fire horizontally and this held up the Russians. I looked for a dressing station but found none: those where the post still existed in name only were overflowing, the wounded lying at their doors. Medication and dressings had been used up.

Luckily I found Captain Brand of our artillery detachment in a Russian shop. He had a field kitchen with steam up. He had been wounded in the arm and was hoping to fly out from Stalingradski. He actually did so even though his wound was not all that bad. With some wounded of my battlegroup I got lost while heading for Stalingrad and landed up at the 100th Division regimental command post at the Flying School. Here at last I got my wound bandaged.

The German troops in this sector looked shattered. No wonder, for since

22 November the main enemy pressure had been against the western front of the Pocket. On 25 January in a bunker near the GPU prison I found some wounded men from my battlegroup. In the cellars long arguments took place between the Generals von Seydlitz, Daniels,[11] Lenski, Deboi and others about the situation, particularly whether or not we should surrender. Paulus had decided, urged by his Chief of Staff, not to capitulate. But now the point had been reached at which an end had to be put to the unequal struggle. We had no aircraft, panzers or artillery. Behind some ruins lay German soldiers still using rifles against unarmoured targets. The Russians drove past our position on the Zariza gorge flying great red flags and playing music over loudspeakers: it was pure mockery.

On 26 January in the GPU cellar when I asked General von Seydlitz if the military commanders intended to terminate the unequal struggle with a clear order, I received the answer: 'The troops have to face the Russian attack tomorrow and then cease fire!' I did not understand this and consulted my regimental commander who was lying ill in the cellar. The pointless struggle had disturbed the balance of his mind, and I had to persuade him that in this situation suicide was not the only answer.

So irresolute was the military leadership that the final decision – as in most operations in Russia – was left to the regimental or battalion commander. On 19 January Colonel Boje drove over to the Russians under a white flag to make contact for the purpose of bringing the fighting in our sector to an end. Farther south of us several divisions had already ceased fighting. Our own neighbours were agreed, and shortly afterwards Boje came back with a Russian captain unrolling a cable to usher in the surrender. During the journey the Colonel was shot in the foot. All soldiers, most of them unfit for the front through wounds or frostbite, were thankful that finally a clear relationship had been established. That morning our battlegroup received its last serving of horsemeat soup. There was no more ammunition to be had. What else should one do in such a situation? We had practically fought to the last shell, the Battle for Stalingrad had been decided.

Paulus seemed to find some good reason not to capitulate under any

11. Alexander Edler von Daniels (b. Trier, 17 March 1891, d. Bielefeld, 6 January 1960). Ended First World War as Lieutenant. 1922 Captain, 1932 Major, 1938 Colonel: 1 April 1942 as Major-General, appointed CO 376th Infantry Division, 1 December 1942 Lieutenant-General. 12 October 1955 released from Soviet captivity. Decorations: 1941 German Cross in gold, 18 December 1942 Knight's Cross.

circumstances before 30 January. On 31 January the last signal was sent from Sixth Army to Führer-HQ. The Field-Marshal sat in a car and was driven into captivity. A number of men remained in hiding with stolen food until 7 February when discovered by Soviet troops. I returned to Germany after more than ten years in captivity. In 1949 I was sentenced to 25 years' hard labour for alleged atrocities committed by 44th Division: I was amongst the lucky ones released in 1953.

29. FRIEDRICH RANDHAGEN:

My Escape over the Don Bridges[1]

Friedrich August Randhagen (b. Rossleben, 21 June 1912, d. Querfurt, 18 June 2005). Qualified as blacksmith, then served his compulsory RAD. 1939 Staff Corporal, Workshop Company, 2nd Panzer Regiment, 16th Panzer Division. After the war trained at Eisleben mining school. From 1979 he spent his retirement at Rossleben.

In my report I would first like to describe the last day before the encirclement of Stalingrad as I experienced it. Upon reaching the Volga north of Stalingrad, Division immediately instituted measures to build winter quarters for the repair of all vehicles.

The town of Kalatch was already bulging with all Army supply services. Accordingly other areas had to be sought which might not be favourable for the centre of operations, but with the approach of winter there was not too much time available to think about it. Our regiment therefore moved down to Potemkinskaya south of Kalatch. It had no large buildings: in the houses available the men found lodging, but inspection pits and bunkers had to be constructed for the vehicles and equipment.

Because I had also been trained in explosives as an ordnance technician, I was put in the advance party. At this time the temperatures were below zero so that explosives were necessary for much of the work. We were kept updated as to the events involving the regiment. We could not get spare parts for panzers. In particular we were short of panzer motors and drive gear for tank tracks. All towing vehicles, 18-tonners, were employed to bring in broken-down but otherwise battleworthy panzers to cannibalize the guns. This shows that the Army as a whole could not be guaranteed desperately-needed spare parts.

Because the Don, a major water obstacle, could only be crossed by a few bridges – a 32-tonne bridge north of Kalatch, four lighter bridges at Kalatch

---

1. This report was published in *Unsere 16*, issue 181, 46th Year, published in July 1988.

itself and south at Zymlanskaya – Romanian pioneers had built a pontoon bridge, but this could only be used by light vehicles. Our assembly and operational areas had to be east of the Don, therefore facing the steppe, because all Russian rivers flowing west have a steep bank on the west side.

On 18 November I received orders to proceed with the rations lorry, an Opel Blitz three-tonner, and Corporal Hilpert to the provisions office at Kalatch, to the field-post office and the regimental command post at Stalingrad. The general situation was very tense and unsettled. It looked like being the last run before the trap closed. At Kalatch we were told that the heavy bridge to the north was already blocked. We would therefore have to detour to get east of the Don. The Rollbahn led past many cemeteries of the fighting divisions. The sound of heavy artillery, constantly increasing, made us suspect the worst.

It was already dark when we got to Kalatch. We could only pick up meat and sausages at the divisional veterinary company. The bakery company had already pulled out. Russian tanks had made great efforts to advance along the Don high road to Kalatch to capture the bridges. They had air support and anything that showed a light below received rocket flares and a stick of bombs. Briefly now and again we would illuminate the area fully. We noticed Russian soldiers on the Rollbahn, but without weapons. Our plan was therefore to step on the gas and force our way through without regard to losses. We each had only a pistol and so our chances were less than favourable.

When we had to make an involuntary stop we saw that the troops were Romanian. Without weapons, most of them barefoot in temperatures of -10 to -12°C, they all wanted a ride. Luckily the lorry was of closed construction and it was not possible for a stowaway to get aboard. Two sat on the forward mudguards but they did not appreciate the fast, bumpy ride and soon got off. The Romanian Army holding the bridgehead south of Stalingrad had caved in at the Russian advance, taking to its heels and leaving everything standing. With his troops advancing from the bridgehead and the north, the enemy closed the ring around Stalingrad.

We arrived with the lorry at our advance party command around 2300 hrs. It was still quiet. One still felt relatively safe so far from the front. Towards 0300 hrs, however, the alarm came: Everybody load up and prepare to leave! When everything was ready – I had had to load my Klöckner-Deutz all-wheel-drive by myself – I was given a suicide mission. I had to take another lorry, an Opel Blitz, which was already loaded up, amongst other things with 150 cotton padded jackets, 200 pairs of felt boots, 50 pairs of snow chains and ten each of oxygen and acetylene bottles. What the other lorries had aboard was not revealed for lack of time. With six vehicles under the command of a corporal we were to proceed to a meeting point from where we were to infiltrate the Pocket.

Our lorry had damaged couplings and did not make the rendezvous. We had not been given the best vehicles for the operation. The corporal, my co-driver, got into another lorry and told me to repair the damage and then catch up. Two fingers were broken on the coupling, but from where was I to get replacement parts? A passing workshop-troop of Hoth's Army took pity on me, and despite temperatures of -20°C they had my lorry driveable after five hours – but the access road into the Pocket was now closed.

When I reported back next day to my command post I had to take over my previous vehicle and join a convoy waiting to leave. We were to head south towards Zymlyanskaya to the last remaining bridge over the Don for the west. The very weak pontoon bridge put up by the Romanian Army had collapsed under the demands made of it and had settled on the river bed 40cms below the surface. Stakes marked the direction of travel. On the other side of the river we drove through mud to the Don high road. The all-wheel drive of my lorry proved reliable: I was also towing a Kübelwagen equipped with a twin AA MG: the car had to be towed because it had no fuel.

After crossing the Don our party under Lieutenant Soltmann found quarters in a small village off the Rollbahn. Here we had to wait until we received orders where to meet up with the remainder. The Russian Army was not interested in our fighting forces heading for Stalingrad nor in pursuing our dispersed units. Only with small troops of Cossack cavalry did they cause constant unrest. As 1942 drew to a close everything had to be done to protect the vehicles against the icy cold. The batteries were removed and kept in the lodgings, the cooling water drained off, the vehicles packed with rush-matting. Our CSM, Staff Sergeant Werner, an old warhorse, had a motto: 'The vehicle entrusted to you is your Homeland – keep it always in running order!'

Because the provisions had to be shared, the local peasants helped us fish with explosives in a frozen branch of the river. In the Don village churches the Russian Army had stored major stocks of rape and cereals. For New Year's Eve it was intended that each man should have a litre of home-brewed schnapps and a box of Shoka-Kola from the iron reserves, but this idea was abandoned, for we were ordered to move out at 1800 hrs when the present would be distributed. It all went quite differently from what had been planned, however.

An iron ring surrounded Stalingrad, and Hoth's relief army had received another assignment. The enemy was now pursuing German troops and threatening with his forces, particularly tanks, to cut the still open Rollbahn towards Shachty and create another encirclement. For our party, instead of orders linked to New Year celebrations, we were urged 'Save yourself, who can!' The confusion was so great that everybody attempted to leave the village and reach the Rollbahn. For my diesel lorry I was given only 20 litres of fuel and two litres of oil. I was fortunate to have another 50 litres of light weapons-oil in a canister. I poured it in – and the diesel 'refined' it!

In this situation, which I would define as chaotic, it was a case of every man for himself. The lorry was made driveable as quickly as we could, we put snow chains over the front wheels, dismounted the twin MG from the VW and packed it inside. A small fire was lit below the oil sump to warm the engine. We were still a long way from our destination, we still had to get across a bridge.

From the surrounding villages along the Rollbahn lightly wounded and seriously wounded men still able to walk were trying to thumb a lift to the west. Lacking winter clothing, having almost nothing except hospital dress in temperatures of -20°, this hapless column made its way along the side of the road – a picture of misery I shall never forget as long as I live. My co-driver and I decided that despite our load of explosives, we would take as many wounded as we could. These wounded men were to be our salvation to cross the bridge in the town.

A patrol of field-gendarmes fetched out from the convoy every man apparently fit for the front and arranged them into squads: an officer was to lead this mob, in which nobody knew anybody else, into the Unknown! I converted my co-driver into 'a wounded man' by the use of three packs of bandages to keep him out of the clutches of these people.

At the river crossing there were scenes impossible to describe. The ice of the river was still not thick enough to drive a vehicle across it. Many tried it all the same, the ice gave way at the midpoint and the vehicle sank to the bottom. The wounded inside my lorry were my free pass to use the bridge. On the other bank were ambulances waiting to take them. Because even here the river had a steep bank on the western side, with my all-wheel drive I had to tow two ambulances up the slope. Not until these were safely up and my almost frozen wounded were transferred into them, could I continue my journey to Shachty. There my co-driver rid himself of his unnecessary dressings. All the foregoing happened on New Year's Eve, 1942.

30. FRANZ RECHBERGER:

As a Runner at Stalingrad[1]

Franz Rechberger (b. Hagenberg/Upper Austria, 20 May 1922) worked on the land until his call-up into the Wehrmacht. At Stalingrad he was attached to No 7 Company, 2nd Battalion, 54th Jäger Regiment in the 100th Jäger Division. He was released from Soviet captivity on 30 September 1947 as an invalid. Later he found work in a chemical factory, and finally worked as a clerk. He retired in 1982 and lives at Wiener Neudorf.

Until I was captured on 31 January 1943 I was with 2nd Battalion as a runner under Sergeant Darsow at No 7 Company. Actually I was to have gone to a military hospital at Tchir on 11 November to have my itchy and suppurating skin disease treated. This had developed as a result of the unhygienic conditions at Stalingrad. We had not changed our underwear and shoes for weeks. My lymphatic-nodes were very swollen and hurt so much that I could hardly walk.

On 10 November I reported myself off duty at the position and went in the rations wagon back to the *Tross*. Next day my medical officer Dr Ellinger[2] told me that my ailment would be very protracted and without question I needed a stay in a military hospital. A fellow messenger, Leading Private Paul Glauer, was of another opinion and said it was advisable to remain where I was. He suggested I might like to stay with a 70-year-old Russian woman and her two grandchildren until I got better. With his front experience he had often in the past given me very good advice, and so I followed it this time. Had I known that ten days later we would be encircled by the enemy, I would definitely have gone for the military hospital!

Two months later on 15 January 1943 I returned to my comrades-in-arms

---

1. This report was printed in the journal celebrating the 40th reunion of 54th Jäger Regiment (11 to 13 August 1989).

2. Dr Karl Ellinger (b. 20 November 1917, missing at Stalingrad since January 1943) was battalion surgeon in the 54th Jäger Regiment, 100th Jäger Division.

in the company. My ailment had naturally not yet healed; it would later prove life-threatening for me in captivity. At this time 2nd Battalion lay on both sides of the numerous gullies which, as all those running from the west towards the Volga, passed north-north-west of Hill 102. On the evening of 26 January we headed south in a blinding snowstorm. Near the flying school we went north into new positions. On the evening of 28 January we were informed we would be moving farther south-east to a position well back. At that time the Pocket was being ever more tightly closed around us. The battlegroups were given the opportunity if they so desired to abandon this hopeless situation and try to break out to the west on their own initiative. Seven of us decided to attempt it the following night. Nothing came of this, however, for we were ordered to join another battlegroup. On the evening of 29 January a corporal led us to a position on a slope. We did not know if we had neighbours or how far away the Russians were. Next morning we saw that they were not far ahead, and very active. They were bringing up ammunition, and careless of cover. We concluded that they would soon be attacking.

About 1100 hrs there was light MG and mortar fire. To our right, from behind the ruin of a house, about 200 German infantrymen appeared waving a white cloth on the end of a pole and approaching the Russian lines. When we saw that we decided quickly what was best for us. We did not want to surrender, therefore we ran a zig-zag course up the slope to find cover in a trench. The Russians fired at us with MGs, but Hintermüller, Lord and I reached the trench unscathed.

For the following night, which was to be our last at liberty, we crept over to a colleague from a motorized unit who had a bunker. This was more a hole in the slope of a gully than a secure position. Nevertheless we felt relatively well hidden, and had the luxury of a stove and some wood. Now we opened our last cans of preserves which we had gathered up after a low-flying aircraft dropped them in the snow. We accompanied these with a 'special coffee' made from the last beans in the haversack, pulverized with an axe and boiled in melted snow. Then we lay down to sleep and to gather our strength for what lay ahead. Previously we had burnt our service/pay books (*Soldbücher*) and decorations.

As a result of our hardship and exertions we slept so soundly that the arrival of twenty Russian tanks at the end of the gully failed to awaken us. Great was our surprise to see them next morning stretched out in a line. The gun barrels were pointed over our heads towards the gully rim but there was no firing. Despite this ominous situation our friend from the motorized unit sauntered up the slope in order to see if his unit had any news. When he returned he told us that surrender negotiations were being held between Paulus and the Russians. His best news was that today, probably for the last time, the field kitchen was making a meal from all that remained in the larder and we should make sure we got some. I took our mess tins and went up to the field kitchen the same way as our friend had done, the tank guns pointing at my back. From the crest I saw a number of lorries, amongst them one with a steaming cauldron of stew on the loading flap. The cook had his hands full pushing aside all the containers being forced at him. When I saw how many people there were around this field kitchen, my hopes of getting anything sank to zero.

At that moment one of the tanks fired, and the shell hit the forward part of the lorry. I turned and ran towards the gully, the tanks and my comrades waiting for their meal. Before I got to the edge of the gully I looked round and noticed that while smoke was rising from the fore-end of the lorry, steam was still rising from the stew-end. And not an infantryman in sight! I made up my mind quickly, ran back to the cauldron, dipped the three mess tins into the thick stew, filling them so full that the liquid was slopping over the sides, and then dashed back to the gully. While the infantry were still slowly appearing from under cover, I had long rejoined my friends in the bunker with the stew.

After a while my friend from the mot.-unit returned with the news that Paulus had capitulated and we all had to go into captivity. As a soldier mindful of his duty my friend wanted to immobilize his vehicle. While debating with himself whether to use a round set hammer or hand grenade, I looked at my poor feet and suggested that the four of us should drive into captivity rather than walk. No sooner said than done: we got in. Thus we four friends drove at marching pace in our Kübelwagen, amidst the countless shambling companions sharing our fate, towards an uncertain future in captivity.

When we met the first Russian, an officer, he slipped his long legs nimbly into the Kübelwagen without making us stop. Hooting the horn on the orders of this officer, we made much better progress, and we overtook the long columns of prisoners streaming north-east away from the city. After a few kilometres a little outside the city where the road forked our comfortable journey came to its end. The Russian made us stop and gestured to us 54ers that we should get out. Then he told our host from the motorized unit to drive on as his chauffeur! At the same moment as he roared off hooting the horn again, we were surrounded by Russians who robbed us of watches and lighters with loud 'Urr jest!' and 'Mashinka jest!'

Now there began for us the six-day death march, rightly mentioned today so frequently. Countless of our comrades did not survive it, dying of all kinds of frostbite and maladies brought on by frost, and whoever could not keep marching was shot by the ruthless guards. In this tragic manner we lost our comrade-in-arms Lord from Ostweide/Silesia. He was so exhausted that not even our appeal to think of his wife and children waiting at home could bring him to his feet one more time.

At the end of the six days, despite frostbite in both his feet, my best comrade and friend Josef Hintermüller from Linz reached with me Camp 'Ilmen', but at the end of February or March he also died. Suddenly I was alone among so many men and felt dreadfully abandoned: there was not a living soul from earlier times with me. After four years and eight months captivity I had the great fortune to see again my Austrian homeland and loved ones.

31. JOSEF ROSNER:
The Hell of Baburkin[1]

Josef Rosner was a machine-gunner in No 2 Company, 1st Battalion 134th Grenadier Regiment in the 44th Infantry Division. After returning home he lived at Zurndorf/Burgenland, where he died a few years ago.

Always, whenever I read anything about Stalingrad, those gruesome and pitiless months I was forced to spend within the encirclement flood my memory. I endured the whole of the first campaign in Russia, that fearsome first winter with massive snowfall and temperatures below -35°C, and the fighting for Kiev and Kharkov. When the Russians broke through at Kalatch on 19 November 1942 and four T-34s captured the bridge over the Don, across which all the Sixth Army's supplies passed, we had to pull back, the Russian infantry behind us with light mortars. Eight days without sleep: we slept on the march! Regimental commander was Colonel Arthur Boje:[2] Battalion commander Major Eberhard Pohl.[3]

At Baburkin the Organization Todt had dug out a position: MG position, communicating trench and for each squad a bunker without a roof. We occupied the position and were soon sleeping the sleep of exhaustion. Suddenly Steiner ran from the listening post into the MG position shouting, 'Herr Corporal, the Russians are marching towards us!'

Immediately the first parachute-flare went up from the MG position: the

---

1. Appeared in the Journal of the Comradeship of Members of the Former 2nd Viennese Division and also 44th Infantry Division, later Reichs-Grenadier-Division *Hoch- und Deutschmeister*: issue 153, December 1998 and *Kamerad Stalingrad*, 2002/2003. The two different accounts were consolidated here.
2. Arthur Boje (b. Berlin, 3 August 1895, d. 18 April 1981). First World War, Lieutenant. Joined Wehrmacht in 1935: Battalion commander, 1940 CO 134th Infantry Regiment. In Soviet captivity until 1955. Decorations: Knight's Cross, 5 February 1942.
3. See Eberhard Pohl's own account, No. 28 'The Defensive Battle at Baburkin'.

ground was black with Russians! They opened fire with their MGs. We replied in kind, every fourth round in the belt a tracer bullet. The flare went out, the Russians advanced, but nearly all of them were mown down by our MGs. At dawn we found five Russians only 30 metres from our MG position, all with a hand grenade in their hands, having died about to hurl it into our position. Colonel Boje came past in his amphibious vehicle and praised us: 'You did that well!' There were two battalions of Russians, and we were lucky to have had the prepared trenches, for ahead of us was open country without cover, and no Russian had made it through! Over the next few days we received heavy mortar fire. Our snipers dug in behind the Russian corpses and awaited their chance.

Thus the days passed and Christmas neared. There were four men in our squad. The day before Christmas Eve, in imitation of a tree, we tied a couple of strings of coloured paper to the rifle of the fallen Bartl with steppe grass and stood it in front of our bunker. Next day as far as one could see or hear nobody fired. Suddenly our Major Pohl came through the communicating trench with his adjutant. He offered us consolation and cried with tears in his eyes, 'That you are still alive to see Christmas Eve!' We instead were rather thinking of our relations, fathers and mothers, far away in the Homeland . . .

The Russians set up loudspeakers and we heard German carols. Then came the invitation: 'Austrians! Come over to the Red Army! Hitler has lost the war! Every minute a German soldier dies in the Pocket!' A messenger arrived and said, 'That is all propaganda. In a few days we shall be relieved.' It did not come true.

So it went on: three hours at the MG position: three hours' sleep. The bunker was covered with tarpaulin, steppe grass: the greatcoats of the fallen were the carpet. The cold persisted. Since October we had not changed our underwear or boots and the lice made us itch.

Next day we came under heavy mortar fire again. The rations were being cut. Because of snow flurries the Ju 52s could not land. Most of our food now came from the half-starved horses under the snow. Horsemeat soup made from melted snow . . .

January 1943 arrived. The Russians stepped up their attacks: on 8 January their aircraft flew above the Pocket once more, dropping leaflets which read: 'Austrian comrades! Come over to the Red Army today! If you do not, on the 10th we shall fetch you out with our weapons.' I stood in the cauldron of hell which was Baburkin, keeping faithful watch at the MG position. Thousands of tiny stars looked down on the lonely MG gunner under the night sky. I thought of my dear homeland Austria, so far to the west, and I thought also of my girlfriend, working on a farm in the Leithatal/Burgenland.

On the morning of 10 January – the sun rose red – there broke out around the Pocket an artillery barrage the like of which I had never heard before during all my experience of the campaign in Russia. Thousands of shells rained down on our pitiful positions – hell on Russian soil! There were now only thirteen of us from our company and we had fired the last belts of ammunition: the MG boxes were all empty. We had received neither supplies, ammunition nor food. Forward at the MG post the T-34s came into our field of fire, infantry riding on the hulls, all carrying machine-pistols each with seventy-two rounds in the drum. Behind the tanks came a battalion of Mongolians. Two tanks were mined, the tracks ripped off. Colonel Boje, our regimental commander, deployed five self-propelled guns against the T-34s. We lay between them: I fired eight belts then the gun jammed.

A Mongolian came through the trench and threw a hand grenade at my MG: I received splinters in both hands and in the right eye. He aimed his machine-pistol at me and shouted. 'Stoi!' Had his gun jammed or was the drum empty? I still had two rounds in my pistol, shot him dead, hid myself amongst all the bodies lying around and feigned death. Soon the other Russians arrived, leapt over me and threw hand grenades into the bunker.

When night came I crawled out of the trench and, ducking low so as not to be seen in the light of a parachute flare, crept past the still burning SP-guns. The gun crew were all dead. At midday I reached a flak unit: they put dressings on my wounds and gave me my first hot meal in four days. A lieutenant appeared and enquired my unit. '134th, 1st Battalion – rendezvous at Rossoshkatal!' There I met Colonel Boje and Major Pohl. There were only eighty of us gathered there on that 11 January to occupy the village of Gontshara. All had frostbite and were wounded. The Russians had put their tanks outside the Pocket and two Russian battalions of infantry attacked us with light mortars. We fought house-to-house. The Viennese Storva had only one Russian machine-pistol against the Russian attacks. Colonel Boje arrived at one end of the village with two quadruple AA guns and fired tracer into the houses, which went up in flames. Most of the Russians inside fried.

We were forced to withdraw. Hundreds of severely wounded lay around the main dressing station. There were no more flights out, for the Ju 52s were being shot down by AA fire and Russian fighters, 'Ratas'. There was no proper food, just soup made from melted snow and the remains of frozen horses which had starved to death. On 19 January we arrived at Gumrak to be ordered: 'Battlegroup Boje retreat to the suburbs of Stalingrad to the Stalingradski airfield three kilometres from Gumrak!' Storva, Stöckl and I were scarcely able to stand, all wounded and in danger of freezing to death. We had not changed our underwear for four months and still wore our summer boots in temperatures of -35°C. Laboriously we crept into the Stalingradski airfield bunker. 'This is the end!' I thought, as did my comrades-in-arms.

But then came a different ending. At 1400 hrs on 20 January a soldier of the airfield control shouted into the bunker: 'Whoever can still walk, come with me, aircraft have landed!' From three bunkers pitiable figures staggered towards the aircraft. When we got to the He 111s the Russians began firing on them with 10.5cm guns. One He 111 burst into flames. The aircraft gunners hauled Storva and me into the machine as the thirteenth and fourteenth to be rescued: we flew off through AA fire and had to survive an attack by Russian fighters. Fortunately we came through in one piece and made a safe landing outside the Pocket.

From there we went – weighing only 40 kilos! – in cattle trucks to Cracow for delousing. We were not taken to the Reich immediately but to a military hospital at Zakopane. There the splinters were removed and my frostbitten hands and feet treated. All my toes were amputated. On 10 February 1943 I was discharged cured to the Convalescent Company at Strebersdorf.

32. OTTO SCHÄFER:

Infantryman in the Most Forward Frontline[1]

Corporal Otto Schäfer (b. Hagen-Eckesey, 27 July 1923), pre-war trade, car sprayer. In April 1942 conscripted into 76th Division and completed his basic training in Cologne. After Stalingrad he served in Italy and the Ukraine where in July 1944 as platoon leader he was wounded and discharged from the Wehrmacht that autumn. After the war he resumed his pre-war trade and obtained his master-qualification in 1962. He lives in retirement in his home town, Hagen.

After eight weeks we were notified: you are going to Russia. We were taken through Poland and Hungary, de-trained and marched behind the troops: the Russians had retreated, so that our progress was not fast. We wore field boots. After a long march we stopped and simply fell asleep where we were: suddenly a general appeared and bawled us out, the rifles have to be stood up, etc. Finally we reached the unit to which we had been drafted, a heavy-MG Company. Our General was called Rodenburg. there were a lot of Berliners amongst us: our replacement mob's barracks was at Potsdam. We marched day and night. I well remember the piercing look of a colonel who wore a monocle and bawled us out if men fell over too often.

Then we heard the first shooting. The fighting was harder because we were heading for Stalingrad. On the advance through the steppe, Russian aircraft would drop bombs. On this Rollbahn to Stalingrad we saw three Soviet lorries which had been carrying ammunition. Only the driver's cabin still existed but looked like a sieve, the Russians hung down and were still burning.

At night we made camp in a field, each man had to dig his own bed with an entrenching tool. I was too lazy and thought: next morning we'll be packing up and going. Then I noticed the flying sewing machines coming and that one

1. This report is based on an interview between the Editor and Otto Schäfer on 10 October 2003 at his home in Hagen.

220

ought to dig a bit deeper down. What I shovelled out was enough for a whole street corner!

After that we went to the Kotluban gorge. There we came under fire, but only mortars. Finally it grew quieter and we were ordered to go to a regimental command post to protect it. We arrived in the evening and had no trench but were attached to a gun company and shown into bunkers.

I was a machine-gunner in the end section. I slept through an attack. In the morning my platoon leader, Corporal Karger, a giant of a man from Berlin, came and shouted, 'Schäfer! The Russians were attacking all morning while you dossed down.' To the left and right of me my comrades lay dead while I had been dead to the world. At the time I had a bout of dysentery and in between pulling my trousers up and down I had to bring up ammunition.

I had brought four boxes of ammunition to a ridge. My Corporal was to the left of me, a Leading Private ahead. I set the boxes down. At that moment the Leading Private was shot through the head, I saw the hole appear at the rear where the round had passed right through: the Corporal had fallen dead, shot through the heart. They were both carried down: I ran back up to fetch the ammunition. Everything was done at a fast tempo. A gunner came up to me. He had an eye injury. He told me, 'We have no more men, you have to take over!' I went back up to the MG and found the gunsight shot away. I asked him, 'Where are the Russians?' He replied, 'They have all taken flight'.

I had thought they were our troops. The sun was so bright that their helmets shone. The two of us then swept the area with MG fire. From a distance, the mass of running Russians looked like black clouds: if one kept pouring fire amongst them many would fall. I was not very experienced in firing a machine gun because until then all I had done was carry ammunition, therefore the gun had jammed from overheating. A colleague fetched me an asbestos cloth: meanwhile the Russians were making another attack and so I had already pulled the barrel out – a heap of them lay round about – fitted another one and, when it heated up, exchanged it for yet another. Then my Lieutenant, Haberland by name, came by to bring me the asbestos cloth, was hit, spun around and fell dead. Therefore I have never forgotten his name.

Then we dug in at this spot. In the evening when I looked out: Ach! So many Russians lay there. After that we had a week of nothing but mortar fire. We had dug our hole 'so nicely' that a hit anywhere nearby would spray us with splinters: a heavy-MG is a prominent feature. We spent the whole time sitting ducked down thinking, careful! The next one is for us! Eight days of it. From my position I could see the airfield at Pitomnik. Then we were withdrawn and topped up with replacements and went to the rear. We were topped up three times in all while I was there because so many of our men had fallen. We were mentioned in the Wehrmacht Report, and if you got a mention there it meant you had suffered high casualties. Somebody must have noticed my name for I had to step forward in the name of the remnants of the battalion to receive a speech in praise and my decoration was recorded in the book although the medal was not available.

Next we had to build our winter quarters into the front. They were really irreproachable given the circumstances: all the trenches from one to the next were deep: we had a bunker with a stove on which bread could be toasted, pans on the wall, everything beautifully done. That was in November. There was no fighting at these winter quarters.

One day the Order of the Day announced: we are encircled, we have to shorten the front, pull back, destroy everything. We did that, in the night it snowed. We had to abandon our positions and embark on a long march, sleeping as we walked. They said that the positions where we going were all ready, but in fact they only existed sketched in on the map. After two days we saw the horizon was black with Russians. In an abandoned trench I found a sack of grain which I took along, thinking it might come in useful. Now we had to dig in damned quick because the Russians advanced at once. To the right of us, about a kilometre away, was a large wall where the mortars were situated. They were the first thing the Russians collected up. I was supposed to take an order there but I played dumb and so somebody else went. At that moment the Russians attacked and scooped up everything. I would have been scooped up with them! The Russians were closing in on us by the simple process of capturing one trench after another. We needed to excavate a communications trench to the nearest gun but it was so icy cold that we could not make any progress, but at least we had some mobility.

We dug in ever deeper: the Sergeant had a kind of bed, the others sat. Then we began to suffer casualties, men being shot dead. A shell landed just in front of our guns, one man had his head blown off, it fell into his hood. We carried him away. The snow lay deep and we were almost all in – we had had hardly anything to eat: at the beginning we got by because there were horses available for meat. Afterwards all we had was some millet seed in water, a slice of bread with jam, sausage and butter, nothing else. That was it at least from October onwards, in July there had been enough. Strangely we were not too short of tobacco. If the troops got this they were content. When the Russians attacked once, we stood there all day and smoked hundreds of cigarettes. They reduced your appetite and made you a bit warmer. Thus the Russians over-rolled the front little by little. The meal or soup in the evenings had to be fetched from the rear. The bodies of our dead colleagues marked the path. They lay there, the corpses looted by their comrades because one stole what one needed for survival.

One day there was a snowstorm and we got no food all day because the food carriers could not find us and we could not find them. I remember that if we all went together to fetch our rations we could not go on a moonlit night or we would come under fire. Once when I was not there another food carrier returned, our man had been shot in the head. I said, I had better check, there might have been something in this pail. I found pieces of bone in each ice-cold mess tin. My colleague was holding a mess tin after emptying the pail. The pail was a carrying canister from the main kitchen: the rations were then poured into mess tins and then brought to the frontline. They could be brought by hand because there were not so many of us. The comrade who fell, I remember he was a Berliner, had six children and would always divide up the rations so that he had some over. We sat around and looked at each other. Because of his death the mood was somewhat changed, and I thought, look in his haversack to see if there is any food in it. I found a tin of meat which I took and ate when I was on sentry duty. Thus I survived Stalingrad.

Later I organized some grain for our bunker. At first we had it raw to give us something to chew on, that was important. Then we took the hand grenades, unscrewed the handle and removed the detonator. This provided us with powder to roast the grain. On the debit side it meant that we no longer had any hand grenades. The method could also be used to heat water in the mess tins and we could also have a little wash: this did us good.

I spent Christmas in the company trench: parcels were distributed. From somewhere I obtained a piece of bread and went off to an empty bunker. I was happy to be able to sleep a whole night and had brought with me some combustible material to light in a corner. New Year's Eve was spent outside. The Russians were quite near us and kept saying we should go over to them, there would be food, etc. We always replied with a burst from an MG. Nobody was prepared to go into captivity unless there was no other way, and then maybe. We knew how bestially they treated people! Therefore a lot of comrades preferred to shoot themselves. Today we know what those in captivity had to suffer. Only 6,000 came back, out of 100,000! That is 94,000 dead in their camps! In our unit there were Russian Hiwis who took up the rear when we advanced. My field flask was always empty very quickly because

I have a dry liver. Then I would go to the Hiwis and beg a refill. They were treated as if they were Germans. They were only used at the rear with the *Tross.*

We also had lice: I scratched my legs so much that I could no longer bear to put my boots on. The medical orderly sent me to the doctor and said I should put salve on it. That was my great fortune, for the doctor then sent me off to the military hospital. At that time I was fairly run down, had boils on my legs and face. I went on the ambulance bus: the hospital was located in a large barn a 45-minute drive from the airfield. There were at least a thousand wounded lying there, in rows in the straw, without blankets, covered only by greatcoats. In the corners there were a couple of beds for the very serious stomach-wound cases because they could not lie in the straw. It was warm inside but there were no washing facilities and it must have been difficult to sleep. Near my spot was the operating table. It was screened off by tent canvas: operations went on day and night. I always heard the screams until the patients received anaesthetics and fell unconscious, and then I heard the sawing!

Because I had some time before the bus came to take me to the airfield I wandered round for a look. In one corner there was a great pile of bones and arms, but no corpses. I have to mention that before getting to the hospital I saw a large open area with many dead horses which nobody had taken away. When we were in the trench in which I had found the grain I met some Romanians who were cutting up parts of a horse. I gave them a couple of roubles in exchange for some of the meat which we roasted over a fire. Before the Russians came, one could usually find something in an abandoned bunker.

I was eight days in that hospital at the end of December, Christmas had gone. I remember I got lost there. I must tell about the episode with the man who had been shot in the stomach; I think that was an officer. He spoke to me in the hospital and said, 'Come here and have my rations. I cannot eat, I cannot keep anything down, everything hurts.' I was happy to do so and visited him the next day as well. However he said no, it is another man's turn. When the food was distributed in that barn, everybody sat with the lid open and one got one's share in the lid. The food was good and tasty, better than in the field. It came out of a great vat and when everybody had been served they would shout: 'Fire at will!' and the vat would be stormed and everybody would clean it up inside with their filthy hands. A female Russian civilian worked in this hospital as an assistant: she would bring a can into which one could have a pee and cleaned it out afterwards. Once I tried to count the number of lice in a sock and gave up at 150. I could even hear them wriggling

I had so many. My eczema was gradually clearing up even though I wasn't treated for it. I just lay around idle.

It was 8 January 1943 – on the 10th the offensive started – when we were told to prepare to fly out. Fifty wounded, fifty from the inner section or twenty-five. They were counted off and got ready to board the bus; a medical orderly came up to me and said, 'Get ready and dressed, you're coming with us!' I replied, 'Don't we eat first?' He came back with, 'Those that are flying out are not getting anything else to eat here!' I got ready, came out and saw a lot of canisters with pudding. Quickly I put some pudding in my mess tin: the medical orderly saw me and said, 'What's your game? If I report that, you won't be flying out. That is for distribution here!' I ran after him and begged for a small piece. I have to say that medical orderly was a good sort! I offered him my watch for a slice of bread, but he said, 'I already have so many watches!' That was not so comradely. I found it surprising that there still was a bus. We drove for 45 minutes and reached the airfield. It was just a field with some tents. I asked where we could get warm here. 'Nay, there's enough blankets, just cover yourself over!'

'And when will the aircraft be coming?' The answer: 'It depends on the weather. If it's bad, none come.' I: 'So how long might we have to stay here?' Reply: 'Could be up to eight days, or suddenly they come.' We went into the tent and covered ourselves with blankets to keep warm. There was a huge pile of blankets, but they had so many lice that we threw them aside and moved around until we warmed up. Towards morning we heard the sound of aircraft. Somebody shouted: 'Out you come!' and then we had to go to the aircraft. The runway was totally iced over. The aircraft was an He 111. Several of us got in. Ahead were two Hungarians or Romanians, still carrying their weapons, and nobody said anything. They finished up in the tail of the machine. The aircraft had a plexiglass nose: I didn't think it looked all that safe but I was assured it was. I moved up, noticed that the Hungarians were not ahead and then suddenly fell into the bomb bay, legs up, and hung there. If the crew had opened the doors I was have fallen out!

As we took off I noticed that we were being fired at, but thank God we were not hit. We heard the crack of AA shells. The flight was 350 kilometres and I could hardly believe it that we were offered a meal when we landed. The aerodrome, with airmen's quarters, was quite different to what we were used to with the infantry! Loaves were piled up, I ate two without drinking anything. Then we were put aboard a passenger train in which we stayed for the next nine days until our legs swelled up because the wagon was so full we had no space. On the way more and more soldiers got in, with neat uniforms but some with jaundice, and we were still filthy and infested with lice. Some of the men got up into the luggage netting. After that everyone had lice!

When we reached Cracow we were deloused in a transit camp. It had big rooms where we had to bathe in tubs. I found this so wonderful an experience that I did not want to get out. I was able to shed the scabs from my leg. Then when I stepped out of the tub I toppled over and fell unconscious. When I awoke I was in hospital, I think it was called Marienhospital. The food was heavenly! I had the urge to keep scratching but I no longer had lice. Some of the men had head lice: their heads were shaved until the infestation went. I retained my hair. I ate day and night, at midday at least five servings and got my weight up by 43 kilos over the next few weeks. I never could satisfy my hunger, however. My typical weight was 70 kilos.

There was a doctor at the hospital from my home town of Hagen. They used the puncture needle on me believing I had water in the abdomen, but not much was drained. The thing was, Stalingraders were flooding in for treatment and so I was sent forward to Zakopane, a lovely village in the mountains south of Cracow. Here a young doctor sent me on to a hospital near Vienna, but I was given hardly any treatment there and even had my parents visit.

33. KARL H. SCHWARZ:

The Final Days of XI Army Corps[1]

*Karl H. Schwarz (b.1914) was a Captain on the Staff of XI Corps under General Strecker.
He was captured on 2 February and remained in Soviet captivity until 24 December 1949.*

On 1 July 1942 I was transferred to the Staff of XI Army Corps as Weapons
and Equipment Officer (WuG) a month after I had been promoted to
Captain. My immediate superior was the QM, Lieutenant-Colonel (General
Staff) Karl Ulreich in the Corps of which General Strecker had taken
command on 1 June.

After home leave I was to return to my unit on 12 December, as my leave
pass stated. Next day I took the train for the front. The amazing thing was that
nobody spoke about, or enquired about, the rumours. How is it possible, I
thought, that such a significant event as the encirclement of an Army can be
kept hidden from all the population for four weeks?

This uncertainty was very soon resolved. At Dnyepropetrovsk we stopped
alongside a hospital train returning to the Reich with wounded men from all
units of the Sixth Army. Of those who could still speak and were looking
forward to the journey home, we then learned a great deal about the sad
reality. What was to become of us we discovered soon after when all officers
were sent to the transit camp at Rostov. Here, officers returning from leave and
also stragglers whose units had been disbanded or wiped out in the Stalingrad
Pocket, were registered according to their usefulness for the front.

My roommate was Captain Ott. We had reported on the second day and
requested to return to our units in the Pocket. The answer was always the
same: 'What the Sixth Army needs is infantry, pioneer and signals officers and
nothing else! What would you do in the Pocket? There are no weapons or
ammunition to be distributed. Forget your orders! If anyone is asked for from
the Pocket, he can count on being flown into there.'

---

1. This report was published in *Unsere 16*, issue 193, 49th Year, July 2001.

The days in the camp passed in an eternally unchanging rhythm: breakfast, situation conference, distribution of orders, break for chess, cinema and a nap until the next meal: only at Christmas was the monotony interrupted. The next morning I reported to the Chief QM, told him about our experience and did at least find out that whoever was to be flown into the Pocket would be kitted out first with winter clothing. The camps were full of greatcoats, fur and felt boots, and from the commanding general down to the lowest ordnance officer all, including the rearward services, were given the best: only the infantryman in the foremost frontline or the open steppe or, if he was lucky, a hole in the hard-frozen earth in which to live and fight, had nothing to keep him warm.

These circumstances and the doing-nothing-about-it slowly got on the nerves of Captain Ott and myself. When one of our sleeping companions, the commanding officer of an artillery detachment, was requested by his division and flew in, we asked him beforehand to call the Army WuG to request our presence there, since we were both anxious to reunite with our comrades. On 27 December we received orders to fly in: a day later we were taken to Novotsherkassk, where I reported to the Ia to ask if he had anything for General Strecker. An adjutant explained to me the current situation and it was soon clear to me that daily the chances of Sixth Army surviving got less and less and that – without it being said in so many words – there was no more hope for it. When the Chief of the General Staff, Major-General Schulz, heard that I would be flying in to join XI Corps he summoned me, pressed a tin of sardines in oil into my hand and said, 'Schwarz, give that to my friend Strecker and tell him, that is all I can do for him. Good luck!'

On 29 December all was ready. Because they always had to reckon with being shot down, the crew of our Ju 52 wore parachutes. When I asked where ours were, I was told that passengers did not need them! At that I tucked myself into the cockpit behind the pilot to discover what I was supposed to do if we were shot down and the crew baled out. Thank God I never had to find out. The weather was so bad that presumably the Russians did not feel like flying, and we only saw their AA fire at so great a distance that it could not reach us. The airfield at Pitomnik lay enveloped in thick fog, and a landing was not possible. The provisions were dropped over where the Pocket was reckoned to be according to calculations, and the next morning we were back at Novotsherkassk.

Two days later we repeated the operation but it was not until 3 January that Pitomnik was clear to land. I was met by Lieutenant Lex, reported myself returned from leave to General Strecker south of Hill 137 and gave him the tin of sardines from Major-General Schulz[2] with his exact words. After that I reported to my QM, Lieutenant-Colonel Ulreich, and my 'old heap' had me back again. The joy of everyone was great! I believe that they all felt a glimmer of hope at my arrival, for if somebody flew in from 'outside' the situation could not be so bad as they sensed it was. I wanted to do nothing to destroy this confidence.

Over the next few days I busied myself preparing an inventory of the stock of existing weapons and ammunition. I went to the ammunition dumps at Pitomnik and Gumrak and the subordinate divisions. The supply situation was disastrous! The daily requisitions were submitted in the knowledge that nothing could be done by the Army. We had lost half our weapons on 28 November, and ammunition would only be available from store for a short period. Even then it could only be supplied to those units which most sorely needed it, provided that there was enough fuel to transport it.

After the Russian terms of capitulation had been rejected, on 10 January the enemy began his offensive from the north-west, west and south to tighten the Pocket and extend the territory between it and the Army Groups Don and A. The losses in men and material in our divisions were enormous. On 12th the Corps had to relocate its command post to Gorodishtche. On 15th the airfield at Pitomnik came under artillery fire for the first time and was captured next day by the enemy armour spearhead. Of fourteen aircraft, eight were destroyed; only six of them were able to take off at the last moment for Gumrak, where five broke up on landing. Even before the loss of Pitomnik soldiers surviving from wiped-out units, stragglers and deserters had formed up into gangs to search for provisions-bombs dropped by our aircraft. The contents would then be taken to old positions or abandoned bunkers to be shared out. In this way the soldiers still fighting would not even receive the paltry 50 grams of bread daily which was their entitlement.

Because more and more of these groups were beginning to appear, on 14 January a pioneer lieutenant came to our HQ with his men. He had the job of collecting up the provisions-bombs, storing them and keeping watch over them until they were distributed to the troops. He required from our QM

---

2. Karl Friedrich Wilhelm Schulz (b. Polnisch-Nettkow/Silesia, 15 October 1897, d. Freudenstadt, 30 November 1976). First World War, Lieutenant. 1939, Lieutenant-Colonel, 1941 Colonel, as Major-General from 27 November 1942 until 1 March 1943 Chief of the General Staff, Army Groups Don and South one after the other. 1945 Commander-in-Chief, Army Group South. Knight's Cross 1942, Oak Leaves 1944, Swords 1945.

permission to hold field court-martials on the spot and execute forthwith the marauders who were becoming increasingly numerous and brazen. General Strecker was informed, and it was decided that all troops appointed to collect up the provisions-bombs should wear an armband by which they could be clearly identified, but they could only use their weapons for self-defence or other urgent need. Not being fully in agreement with these rules, the pioneer lieutenant returned to his very difficult task.

On 17 January General Strecker announced that on the day following, the last field post delivery out to the Reich would be made. Whoever wanted to write should do it now. Since I had to go to the ammunition dump at Gumrak the next day I was given the job of taking the final private post of the Staff to the presumably last aircraft. Surgeon-General Dr Spiegelberg[3] came with me to inspect the assembly point for the wounded at Gumrak.

On the morning of the 18th, armed with a compass and wearing borrowed skis, we set off cross-country. The snowy landscape, whose war wounds were softly overlain with fresh snow, reminded me of a peaceful mountain holiday resort. We were very thoughtful, for we knew that our days were numbered. I said that I would prefer to do away with myself than give the Russians the opportunity to slaughter me as they had done to the soldiers I had seen in an abattoir at Kharkov.

'Under no circumstances!' Dr Spiegelberg said, and he told me the story of the lieutenant and his people in a bunker overrun by the Russians. After a few days and not believing in the possibility of relief the lieutenant killed himself. Next day German troops won back the position, the men were freed but the lieutenant was refused a burial with honours for having 'deserted the colours'. This story impressed me very much, and from that moment on I decided that I would do everything possible to return home.

As we approached Gumrak, the landscape changed decisively. Upon and skirting the road lay the frozen-stiff corpses of hundreds of soldiers, lightly covered by snow except where tanks and vehicles had shattered glass-hard bones, and only heaps of grey uniforms and spatters of blood indicated that here a man had once lived and breathed.

---

3. Dr Hans Spiegelberg (b. Elbing, 9 November 1889, d. Lütjensee, 5 January 1975). Studied in Berlin, active military surgeon, First World War, then practice in Danzig. 1926 46th Medical Abteilung, Wuppertal. 1937 Oberfeldarzt (Lieutenant-Colonel, Medical Corps), 1940 Oberstabsarzt (Major, Medical Corps), from 17 January 1942 Korpsarzt (Corps Doctor) of XI Army Corps. During captivity he was promoted to Generalarzt (General, Medical Corps).

Dr Spiegelberg agreed with me on the time and place to meet for our return. I went to the commandant of the airfield, showed him the letters and mentioned the wishes of General Strecker. He accompanied me to an aircraft, one of many which had landed at Gumrak that day, and gave the large envelope to the pilot. The short runway seemed to me to be as long as a CSM's route march. Hundreds of wounded men lay, kneeled and stood before the aircraft, all observing us with hostile eyes. No doubt they thought, here were two officers who could make it even more difficult for them to reach the Reich or at least safety. A sergeant exercised iron authority: first those on stretchers were loaded, then the aircraft would be crammed full until it was hardly possible to bar the door. On such a short runway and so overloaded I thought it would be a miracle if the machine got off the ground! Yet the pilot did it, and my only thought was: May he land somewhere safely! I gave no thought to the letters which, in the event, 'State' control ensured never reached their destination.

Another picture etched itself indelibly in my memory. When I went to the ammunition dump, I noticed an abandoned lorry near the road. A soldier was crouching on the running board, between his icy hands a frozen loaf of Army bread. His eyes stared into the distance as he nibbled unsuccessfully at the last piece of treasure in his life. He would not survive the next hour and then others would come to relieve him of bread, greatcoat and cap, and then wait for death themselves.

At the ammunition dump I received lists detailing the current inventory and afterwards met Dr Spiegelberg, who had no medical supplies and had been helpless to attend to the wounded at the assembly centre. Thoughtful and silent we returned to Gorodishtche. I rang the Army and requested that the ammunition be moved to Stalingrad because I thought we would not hold Gumrak for long. 'Unfortunately we do not have any more fuel!' they replied. The lorries could no longer move, and the horses had long since been slaughtered and eaten.

Therefore everything remained where it was. On 22 January Gumrak fell, and on 23rd Stalingradski. The last air connection to the outside world had been lost. On 25 January Paulus gave his Russian prisoners to the Red Army: the same day the 'Führer' said in a radio signal: 'I forbid capitulation. The Army will hold its position to the last man and the last round!'

We had been deserted and we knew it! Perhaps that was also the reason why officers and men, without orders, following only the customs of discipline and training, accomplished feats which never appeared in any report, nor ever

231

would. It was also the time in which the divisional commander of IV Corps, mindful of his responsibility, surrendered to the Russians with the remnants of his men in order to save them from a senseless and unnecessary death.[4] And it was also the time of desperate attempts to break through the perimeter into the endless white Russian steppe, the time of the most fantastic rumours and promises. Thus many men believed, even in our HQ, that radio sets would be parachuted down with which groups of up to thirty men could call up aircraft to come for them. But no radio sets were ever dropped and we never saw another aircraft except for a single one which dropped two tonnes of provisions.

All and sundry discussed breaking out. Most were convinced it was impossible to break through the encirclement in the prevailing cold without food and ammunition. Yet there were some who thought it worth a try. With the approval of General Strecker, on 29 January the O2 from our Staff, Lieutenant Pöthke[5] with the adjutant of our artillery commander, Lieutenant Lex, set off at dusk to reconnoitre the route along the Volga. After four hours they returned and reported that on the west bank every bunker and hole in the ground was bristling with Russians and that there were sentries within listening distance watching the Volga, probably put there in the expectation of such attempts to break out. At that, hope perished even amongst our optimists until somebody had the idea of getting a captured Russian vehicle ready, and loading it with petrol drums and cans. The officers who wanted to try it would lie concealed beneath tarpaulins while a Hiwi and assistant up front drove. Out of fear for the consequences if they were caught, the Hiwis had begged to be allowed to remain with us when the Russian prisoners of war were handed over, but they were prepared to drive the lorry through the Russian lines. A lorry was made ready with great enthusiasm, loaded and tarpaulins provided, but before the limited list of escapees had been drawn up, a chance mortar round put paid to this last dream with a massive explosion. Fate or coincidence?

On the evening of 25 January all the officers of the 71st Infantry Division's artillery regiment assembled at the command post of the regimental commander. After one last 'Hoch!' for Germany all the officers shot themselves

---

4. The Commanding General of IV Army Corps was General Pfeffer: only Lieutenant-General Schlömer with his XIV Panzer Corps surrendered prematurely, on 29 January.
5. Lieutenant Hans Reinhold Pöthke (b. Plappeville, 29 November 1909, d. in Jelabuga camp, 11 July 1946).

at the word of command. In his quarters, seeing how hopeless was the situation, General Stempel also shot himself.[6]

On 27 January XI Corps had assembled in the cellars of Factory 2 of the tractor works in the north of Stalingrad. On the 28th, following an attack on height 102 in the north-west of Stalingrad, the Pocket had been split after the intentions of XI Corps had been clearly identified the day before. Thus XI Corps was in the northern Pocket, and the remains of many divisions in the centre and the Army Staff with other remnants in the southern Pocket.

On the evening of 28 January the splitting-up of the Pocket was reported to Army Group with the intention of setting up a new 'defensive front' along the northern perimeter and in the western approaches. Involuntarily the image of a dead chicken came to my mind: it had lost its head, but its wings were still flapping and its legs twitched as if it could and would still escape its fate. Thus it was with our remnants. Reflex movements announced the onset of their death.

General Strecker had a clear vision with respect to the duties he owed his soldiers and those above him: 'We do not have the right to do what we wish! Obedience is the duty of every soldier! I do not know a time when "being a soldier" ceases to apply to generals. Only Paulus can give the order to abandon the struggle. I am against unnecessary sacrifice, but obedience and discipline are the pre-requisites for every human community!' How many actually did fight to the last round we shall never know but the one who had insisted on complying with the (Führer's) order (not to capitulate) did not obey it himself. Paulus and General Schmidt surrendered themselves to the Russians on 31 January.

On the afternoon of 30 January I was alerted. A bomb which failed to explode had come to rest in the room near where General Strecker had his quarters. In this room we stored what remained of the infantry ammunition, hand grenades and 3.7cm AA shells. The fireworks display had this bomb gone off is best left to the imagination. But it lay there peacefully between the ammunition boxes after making a round hole in the roof. I defused the bomb and reported to General Strecker, who had withdrawn to the other end of the cellar, that everything was safe again. As I did so I noticed that the radio was

---

6. Richard Stempel (b. Chemnitz, 18 June 1891 d. Stalingrad, 26 January 1943, suicide). 1937 Colonel: from 1 April 1942 as Major-General commanded 371th Infantry Division. From 1 December 1942 Lieutenant-General. He shot himself because he believed mistakenly that his son had fallen. Decorations: German Cross in gold.

turned on and everybody was listening to it. This was the room in which the officers of the QM Staff and the artillery commander's staff had their quarters and in which I also had a plank bed. When he heard the voice of Göring, General Strecker left the room in silence.

On 1 February we were alone with General Strecker in the northern Pocket – we, that is to say, the Corps HQ, the remnants of 16th and 24th Panzer Divisions, the remnants of 76th, 113th and 389th Infantry Divisions, and anyone else who had gathered around the tractor works. Towards evening General Strecker assembled us and announced: 'General Paulus and everybody still alive in the southern Pocket have surrendered to the Russians. Our situation is hopeless. Therefore, as senior commander in the Pocket I give you the freedom to act from now on as your conscience dictates. Any further defending is pointless.'

On the morning of 2 February the Russians set out to eliminate the final bastion around the tractor works. But we were out of ammunition and the Russians knew that we would eventually fall into their hands without a fight. Thus a reconnaissance aircraft of the Army Group reported in the early afternoon of that day, 'In Stalingrad fighting has ceased.'

All survivors of the Corps HQ remained in the cellar. Since it was only a matter of hours until we would be captured by the Russians, we destroyed our weapons: we broke our pistols and rifles into their component parts and threw them to all points of the compass. The same happened with the radio equipment except for one set which we kept back for the case of remaining in contact with the outside world. On the evening of that day each man prepared for imminent captivity in his own way. I had an old sleeping bag which I cut up and made into a warm cape with a hood by use of needle and thread. In the days following, cold would be our worst enemy, and so everybody did whatever he could to ensure that he would be able to withstand a long and cold march. The last tins of provisions were shared out equally and we enjoyed the hot tea which somebody made on the home-made petrol-can oven. Somebody had also turned on the radio, and between the conversations we heard music from the Reich, overlapped by 'News for the Wehrmacht'. In this broadcast those in the homeland sent messages to their relatives and friends whom they hoped would still be alive on the various fronts. We all listened silently, but suddenly all heads were raised: 'Lieutenant Pöthke is informed by his wife that he has become the father of a healthy son!' At the news everybody jumped up. We got Pöthke off his plank bed, somebody brought him a cognac from a secret supply and we drank to the health of father, son and wife. We did not 'clink', for the bottle was passed from mouth to mouth, but the joy and enthusiasm were none the less, and some of the men were dewy-eyed with pleasure. The great event was reported at once to General Strecker, who came to our room and congratulated Pöthke with serious words touched with emotion. Unhappily, Pöthke never had the fortune to know his son: in July 1946 he died after an operation in the Jelabuga officers' camp.

Shortly afterwards – everybody else was still talking – General Strecker took me aside and said, 'Schwarz, have a look outside to see what's up!' I went up the steps from the cellar and stood for a while at the entrance. The great square in front of the works lay in darkness. I could see no movement, just now and again somewhere behind the black ruins on the far side of the square a flare would go up and illuminate an area of the snow-covered surface. About fifty metres in front of the cellar entrance our last 3.7cm anti-tank gun had been positioned there the day before. Protected by rubble and burnt-out vehicles I reached the gun and its two-man crew. They told me that since dusk all had been quiet. Only now and again in the distance did we hear a rifle fired. The gun was down to the last couple of rounds of ammunition. I told them that General Strecker considered all further resistance pointless, that they should disable the anti-tank guns by removing the important components and then report in our cellar. When I got back downstairs I made a full report to the General, who called an orderly officer and told him, 'Put guards at the entrance without weapons. If Russians appear, bring them to me at once!'

After a brief, restless sleep 3 February 1943 dawned.[7] Russian soldiers were brought before General Strecker and the interpreter told them that the Commanding General of the northern Pocket would only negotiate terms with a general of the Russian forces. The soldiers left and after a short while re-appeared with a Russian staff officer who requested General Strecker and Colonel (General Staff) Grosscurth[8] to follow him to the Russian HQ. They returned around midday. General Strecker called the Staff together and informed us that he had received the agreement of the Russian General for the

---

7. The north Pocket surrendered on the morning of 2 February so that the remaining dates in the account have to be put back by one day.
8. Helmuth Groscurth (b. Lüdenscheid, 16 December 1898 d. in Soviet captivity, 7 April 1943). 1916 volunteered, later served with Reichswehr. 1939–40 as Lieutenant-Colonel, head of Abteilung. Heerswesen (Army affairs) at OKH. 1940–1 1a (No.1 Staff officer) 295th Infantry Division; 1943 as Colonel, Chief of XI Army Corps General Staff. He was active in the conspiracy against Hitler.

whole Staff to use their own vehicles to travel into captivity, but unfortunately no Russian vehicles were available for the purpose.

I was told to make as many lorries as possible driveable and I set about the job with the armourers, ordnance staff and mechanics. There were many wrecked lorries on the large open place in front of our cellar: whenever we found one with a motor in running order we changed the battery over, tanked it up from other vehicles and replaced the damaged tyres. It was clear, however, that this would be the only one we could muster. I drove the lorry to the cellar entrance and reported the fact to the General. He thanked me, and I returned to my party to continue the search.

A short time later I saw officers climbing aboard the lorry. As I approached, Lieutenant von Platen appeared on the lorry with a list in his hand and said, 'This lorry is full, Schwarz, you are not on the list and we are leaving!' This was a dreadful blow! I had flown into the Pocket to join my colleagues, I had conjured them up a lorry, a runner, and now there was no place for me aboard it. I was not ashamed of the tears which rose into my eyes. Later, with distance and the knowledge that nearly all of them who left with this lorry would not survive 1943, I naturally asked myself if Fate had not played a hand in the game once more.

Yet there was something else that day which restored my faith in human nature. While we were searching the wrecked lorries for anything usable, a Russian soldier took the wristwatch from my armourer. Nearby was a Russian major with blond hair, blue eyes and an immaculate uniform, not like any of the Russians we had ever seen before. I made a gesture in the direction of the armourer, but the officer had seen it. He addressed the soldier who made no reply. The major repeated his order in a sharp tone at which the soldier turned and spat at the officer's feet. The Major gave him another order: the soldier made an unmistakeable gesture. At that the Major drew his pistol, shot the man dead, removed the wristwatch from his pocket and returned it to the armourer. We did not think such a thing was possible! Everyone who had seen it looked on in disbelief. At that time Russian soldiers were answerable only to their own immediate superior; a situation which was amended not much later. I saluted the Major who, as I learned later from our interpreter, was a Siberian and responsible for our transportation into captivity.

We had not been able to render any other lorries driveable but with new-found confidence as the senior officer I returned to the cellar in order to inform the remainder of the men they should make preparations for the march and hold themselves in readiness. Gradually 1400 hrs approached and we had still received no orders. I went with the interpreter and asked the Major what we should do. He informed me we would set off as soon as the guards arrived. I asked him to order the guards to prevent Russian soldiers plundering the prisoners along the way, which he promised to do. After I went back into the cellar we waited until 1500 hrs and then the difficult march into captivity began. As expected, hundreds of soldiers waited in the gulches along the way for the opportunity to strip us of our belongings, but were deterred by the readiness of our guards to shoot. Therefore our 130 men were probably the only ones who, thanks to the Siberian Major, arrived to the wonderment of those who awaited us to learn that we had managed to hold on to our meagre possessions. In gratitude I gave the leader of the guards a pocket lamp with green, yellow and red lights and had difficulty in resisting being embraced and kissed, so grateful was he! I told my people to mingle in amongst the other prisoners to prevent their being robbed of boots and other possessions when the march continued. At the collection point a note was made of our names and branch of service; then we waited for the next day, when our long haul through the deep snows of the steppe would begin. The Sixth Army and with it my XI Army Corps was dead.

34. HELMUT SPIETH:

Back over the Don[1]

Helmut Spieth (b. Esslingen, 7 May 1920) qualified in commerce, 1937–9; conscripted into 35th Infantry Division November 1939. In the advance on Stalingrad he was attached to 4th Signals Regiment, 4th Panzer Army. After the war he worked in commerce and lives in retirement today at Baltmannsweiler.

It was November 1942, south of Stalingrad. We were in the steppe on the edge of a gully. My comrades Egon Solke[2] from the Sauerland and 'Wastl' – Sebastian Grassl from Königssee – and I built a small bunker as an improvement on our tent for the coming winter. We obtained the wood from the ruins of Stalingrad. We were in dried-up inhospitable territory, no bushes, trees or water.

Attached to the close-range reconnaissance signals company – a special surveillance unit – of 4th Signals Regiment, 4th Panzer Army, our job was to listen in to, and take bearings of, enemy radio traffic in the local neighbourhood. Elements of 4th Panzer Army on the way to the Caucasus had been detached from the Kalmuck steppe to reinforce Sixth Army towards Stalingrad.

It so happened that on 18 November Wastl and I had to return to our company, about 40 kilometres west of our position. To do so we crossed the Rostov–Stalingrad highway and railway line between Abganerovo and Tinguta to Sety, a small farmstead with a couple of houses in the steppe on the dried-up river bed of the Donskaya-Zariza. After we had left our bunker that day for Sety, the Russian preparations for their great counter-offensive were not visible. Our supplies of winter clothing were late, due to arrive on 17 November.

---

1. This report appeared in the magazine *Kameraden*, KA 3/2011; reproduced here with the approval of the author.
2. Wehrmacht auxiliary Egon Solke (b. Limbergen, 28 November 1920, missing at Stalingrad 3 February 1943). Leading Private Sebastian Grassl (b. Ramsau, 2 February 1907 died in Soviet captivity in Astrakhan on 2 October 1945 according to the German War Graves Commission).

On the night of 20 November there was an alert. Prepared positions had to be re-occupied. With two colleagues and an MG I moved into an infantry foxhole east of Sety. At first all was quiet until suddenly we saw four armoured scout cars appear on the horizon to the south-west. Assuming that they could only be German coming from that direction, we were relieved. After we recognized our error by the red stars painted on the vehicles, a messenger appeared with orders for us to pull back.

It was already too late: the Russians had discovered us and cut off our line of retreat. Our only choice was to head north. Luckily the dried-out river bed had a steep bank about two metres high . On the other side the terrain rose gently. The armoured cars drove up to the river bank and opened fire with everything they had. With the last of our energy we dragged ourselves up the slope, finding cover from the Russians' MG bursts. I am still not sure how we emerged unscathed from the hail of fire! Had the Russians had too much vodka at breakfast and couldn't shoot straight any more?

Behind the elevation we were out of sight and decided we must re-establish contact with our company. In the featureless steppe it was difficult to orient oneself. An armoured personnel carrier appeared, this time with a black cross on the side. The crew was on reconnaissance and pointed out the direction in which we should head. From that one may infer that we had no knowledge of the situation and no idea of the respective positions of friend and foe.

Late that afternoon we reached our unit at Businivka without further incident. There was little time to rest, for in the evening we had to stand guard with a quadruple AA gun at the edge of the village. The night was cold and short: Russian tanks were advancing. We had no anti-tank guns and so had to move out. Apparently the Russian advance was hesitant and so we could head for Kalatch in the assumption of being able to reach the west bank of the Don over the bridge there. At Kalatch we came across a large provisions warehouse and were intending to stock up but decided against it upon noticing some Russian tanks standing a few hundred metres away from the entrance along the highway. Therefore, nothing for it but to head into the steppe! The territory was full of fleeing German soldiers. They were jumping aboard vehicles, on the running boards and radiators – sheer chaos!

When we reached the highway, the Russians were hot on our heels. They did not fire, but merely rammed the fleeing lorries into the roadside ditches. Our vehicle, making thick smoke, was evidently not worth the trouble. The tanks did not pursue us, there was no shooting – an incomprehensible situation. We were just outside Kalatch and the Russians could have captured the town without much opposition. Either they had orders not to proceed or were short of fuel and ammunition.

The Russian spearhead from north of the bend in the Don was already in the Kalatch area, but we did not know that when we reached the town. Just beyond the first houses we had to ford a dried-up river bed; after that our journey ended when the motor gave out. I had the opportunity of passing radio equipment in the lorry to an artillery unit and then, without being aware of the current situation, went into the nearest house to sleep.

The noise of vehicles next morning brought us back to reality very quickly. The tumult was due to the bridge over the Don, a few hundred metres farther on beyond the town limits, having been crossed by the Russians. In the early morning ten German panzers, actually Russian tanks which had fallen into the hands of 71st Division, should have been repainted, but there was no paint for the black German cross. Everybody knew them, even the forces defending the bridge. Suddenly firing began on the Don heights and MG salvoes destroyed the silence. Then it dawned that these were not the captured tanks arriving, but the Russians! After a brief, violent struggle the bridge and a bridgehead fell into Russian hands. Now everything German streamed through the town southwards. I found a place on a lorry fully loaded with fuel, a rewarding target for a tank shell! We came through unseen, however. The remainder of the Company had met up. The cold, with an icy wind from the east, made itself noticed. In the open lorry there was a serious danger of freezing to death so that we kept watch on each other to ensure that neither fell asleep.

We had escaped from the clutches of 13th Mechanized Corps. We celebrated Christmas in Krasny Kut, a couple of houses on the frozen Don. That day we received the last message from our comrades in encircled Stalingrad. The source of the stream of men heading there was exhausted: hardly any are known to have survived to the end. They all remain 'Missing at Stalingrad'.

In the first days of the New Year we crossed the frozen Don between Rostov and Bataisk, went from there to Taganrog and later Dnyepropetrovsk, where 4th Panzer Army units were resting. In the weeks previous we had received precious little information about the dramatic events which had played out on both sides of the Don and Volga.

My comrade Egon Solke, who had stayed behind in the bunker, is listed as missing since 3 February. 'Wastl' Grassl was admitted to the military hospital at Millerovo with jaundice. He survived the war.

35. HANS STAUDINGER:
With the Luftwaffe Ground Staff[1]

Hans Staudinger (b. Bad Wimsbach, Wels/Upper Austria, 16 February 1920, d. Gunskirchen, 2003). February 1940 compulsory RAD service; 15 October 1940 conscripted into Luftwaffe, Fels am Wagram. He served in the Russian campaign until February 1943 with a short-range reconnaissance squadron of Hs 126s.

No 2 Group *Immelmann*/6th Squadron was raised at Wels. Squadron commanding officer was Colonel Rudel.[2] In June 1942 we went by train to Kursk-Shishigry towards Voronesh on the Don, then via Kupyansk–Millerovo–Tazinskaya–Morosovskaya–Oblinska–Chirskaya where we crossed the Don bridge at Kalatch to Karpovka. From here our Ju 87 Stukas bombarded Stalingrad without a break. On 19 November the enemy broke through on two sectors of the front, and on 22nd we were encircled in the Stalingrad Pocket.

The flying and technical personnel were flown out to Tazinskaya; we of the ground staff had to parade, and *Battalion Immelmann* was formed with other Luftwaffe servicemen. As a butcher I should have gone to the kitchens but I preferred to remain with my comrades. Then we occupied the frontline. The Russians had dug in along the Kalatch-Stalingrad railway line while we lay in the open with MG 42s in foxholes. We had very little to eat, some horsemeat and soup with bread.

---

1. This report appeared in the December 1998 edition of *Stalingradbund Österreich*, Nr. 39, 14th Year.

2. Hans-Ulrich Rudel (b. Konradswaldau/Silesia, 2 July 1916, d. Rosenheim, 18 December 1982). Stuka pilot and only recipient of the highest degree of the Knight's Cross award, i.e. with Oak Leaves, Swords and Diamonds. 1936 entered Luftwaffe, 1941 Lieutenant with Stuka Wing 2 *Immelmann* of which he became commander in the rank of Colonel in 1944. His total of 2,530 operational flights was unequalled. He was forbidden to fly by Hitler on several occasions following the amputation of both legs, but he took no notice. 1945–6 US PoW. Later military adviser, notably to the Argentine Government.

At the end of November I had a look around from our earth bunker and counted seventy Stalin Organs, which opened fire over our sector at 0800 hrs. During the night in temperatures -30–40° we had to scout close to the Russian positions.

At Christmas I received from my sister a kilo-packet with frozen apples which we ate immediately. On 8 January we were still in the same position and were exposed constantly to music and invitations to: 'Come on over, you will get a loaf of bread every day, and don't forget your mess tins! If you do not surrender, however, then we shall wipe you out!'

On 10 January the Russians launched their major offensive. Our kitchens, where I ought to have been, received a direct hit: all six men there were killed. We wanted to bury them, but then we were told, 'Leave everything where it is, the Russians are coming!' We fled over the frozen river Karpovka. My comrade Bardasch and I had three blankets each to protect us against the cold. I was lying on a slope with my carbine at the ready when suddenly a Russian was lying not ten metres away and pointing a machine-pistol at me. Neither of us fired: I wanted to go home to my mother. The Russians bombarded us without pause with mortars. A mortar exploded nearby: my comrade Bardasch was seriously wounded in the stomach, and I had splinters in my left leg. I gave Bardasch one of my blankets. As they carried him away I said to him, 'Say hallo to my parents when you get home.' He was flown out, although after 10 January no stretcher cases were taken.[3]

On 14 January I got to Pitomnik. What I saw there was gruesome. I was told, 'Disappear to Gumrak!' There I was given a sleeping place in a closed goods wagon. On 19 January I hobbled to the airfield, where provisions-bombs had been dropped for us, from which I removed two Army loaves. A field-gendarme saw me and shouted. The thick fog was my fortune – I ran quickly to a tanker which belonged to our squadron. The driver, from Cologne, hid me; I gave him a loaf of bread for his help.

Meanwhile a Ju 52 had landed. Hundreds of infantrymen stood around it: naturally they all wanted to be flown out. A lieutenant stood in the hatch holding two pistols and shouted down: 'Men, be reasonable, another twenty-five He 111s are flying in, you will all get away from here!' A high-ranking officer got into this Ju 52 with two trunks. The machine took off with him alone! After the war I discovered that this had been General Hube, who had

---

3. If such an order existed it was not observed, for many reports mention stretcher cases being flown out.

lost his left arm in the First World War and was being flown out on Hitler's personal order. After that the weather took a turn for the worse and not a single aircraft landed there subsequently.

At 0900 hrs on 22 January at Gumrak railway station I met Sepp Riess from Mattighofen with whom I had completed basic training at Fels am Wagram. He had a serious wound to the feet and could not walk. As a radio operator he knew that Gumrak airfield was to be given up that day. When we reached it, the airfield was deserted. As so often already, my luck was in again: an He 111 landed and rolled towards us. Cases of hard sausage were unloaded. Thirty to fifty men appeared suddenly from foxholes, wanting to be flown out. The Luftwaffe Lieutenant ordered that first the wounded should approach: I was to go aboard as the sixth man. The aircraft took off with fifteen men and four crew and landed safely, after a 500-kilometre flight, at Stalino-Makeyevka. In Germany I lay in hospital three months before receiving leave. Later it was reported that there had been no survivors from Battalion *Immelmann* at Stalingrad.

My brother Hermann[4] had also been in the encirclement at Stalingrad, with 100th Jäger Division, and was also flown out wounded. Unhappily he fell on the Vistula front in October 1944 at the age of seventeen and a half years.

After his recovery Staudinger rejoined his unit and served at Kharkov and Byelgorod. Later he was taken prisoner by US forces in the Sudetenland. After the war he returned to his trade of butcher and innkeeper at Gunskirchen.

4. Hermann Staudinger (b. Bad Wimsbach, 4 April 1923), was a butcher and innkeeper in his home town and died there on 14 February 2006.

36. ADOLF VOSS:

My Wound Saved My Life[1]

Dr (Jur.) Adolf Voss (b. 4 December 1911, Hagen, d. 30 November 2005 Hagen). Lived for some time in Paris and Lausanne. Qualified as lawyer in 1937. Because of 'political unreliability' was refused civil service position. He spoke English, Italian, Spanish and Russian, and in the rank of Lieutenant(S) – a civilian serving in the Wehrmacht with an equivalent military rank – was sent to Bulgaria and also served with 79th Infantry Division during the French campaign. Transferred to 16th Panzer Division, where he became a personal friend of its commanding officer, General Hube. To perfect his Russian, at the beginning of 1941 he was sent to the Eastern European Institute at Breslau.

The invasion of the Soviet Union began within a few days. The Russians had taken it out on the German prisoners: they were strewn on the battlefield with sexual organs cut off, with a hatchet in the back – all quite gruesome. Colonel Müller, our 1a at 16th Panzer Division HQ, told me, 'Voss, so many Germans have been murdered, we have to take revenge. Pick out 300 Russians from amongst the prisoners – no Ukrainians – who are to be killed in reprisal for what was done to our prisoners. This must be advised to the men!'

I replied: 'Herr Colonel, I accept the assignment!' I made a list of the names of the selected prisoners, family status, children, etc., returned to him and said, 'Herr Colonel, will you please sign here!' He declined. He was a rigorous type with red stripes down the side of his pants, but on the Staff of 16th Division there were still good men of whom I could mention some names. On the entire advance of the division from Breslau to Stalingrad I saw no Wehrmacht crimes of the type which are alleged nowadays: in this single case I acted to prevent it. I was well liked in the division because I always let everyone know what I knew.

At Kharkov I once interrogated a Russian General. General Hube always wanted to know what I had found out from the prisoners. He also wanted to

---

1. This account is based on an interview with Dr Voss at his home in Hagen on 29 March 2003.

convert me into a 'proper' officer. I was interested in the armoured reconnaissance company and as a Lieutenant drove with one such unit from Stalino
to Stalingrad for the first time in my career. I did a small amount of
interpreting at Stalingrad, but finally there was nothing more for me to do
there for we had some Russian Hiwis who helped me with the translating. I
had a very good relationship with two of them.

My commanding officer with the reconnaissance unit of 16th Panzer
Division was named Dörnemann. The Russians lay opposite us on the
northern front. The divisional HQ with Hube and his officers was located in
a gully whereas I had tanks pass lightly overhead of my trench. I was assigned
to a unit with the job of expanding and defending the northern front. All I
saw of Stalingrad was a couple of giant clouds of smoke. Occasionally I left the
frontline for the Volga, from where I often brought back grapes and other
fruit.

On leave in Münster I contacted Dr Portmann, the secretary of Bishop
Galen. I had met him first on campus where I prevented his being nabbed by
the Nazis. I took Galen's sermons with me to the front and distributed them
there: even General Hube and his officers were interested in them. In a
conversation about the bishop, Captain von Alvensleben stated: 'Graf von
Galen is a gentleman from the parting in his hair to the soles of his shoes.' By
means of this conversation at HQ the problems in the Homeland came under
discussion. I had the impression that in General Hube's HQ there really were
no National Socialists. Later Hube flew from Stalingrad to see Hitler at
Obersalzberg to tell him the truth about Stalingrad. After leaving Hitler,
Bormann[2] came up behind him and said he should visit again. Hube replied
that he had said everything there was to say. On the flight out from Obersalzberg he came to grief. He flew his own aircraft; whether it was an accident
or if he took his own life remains unknown.

One day at the end of November 1942 the commanding officer, with
whom I had a good relationship, came to the northern front. He had a leather
measuring tape with him and wanted to know how many metres it was from
our trench to the next. We had a talk and he asked who would try to jump it.
I volunteered. It was actually absurd to want to measure the distance, and
even more to actually try to make the leap, for the Russians were so close over
there that we could see their steel helmets. On the way back I was shot in the

---

2. Reichsminister Martin Bormann (b. Wegeleben/Halbestadt, 17 June 1900, d. (disputed)
Berlin, 2 May 1945) was Head of the NSDAP Party Chancellery.

neck. This would save my life. Through this experience I learned that nonsense often can be found in sense, even amongst the military, but also sense in nonsense, namely, in this concrete example, that my life would be saved through it.

Dörnemann arranged for me to be transported out by ambulance. From the forward lines I was brought to the 16th Panzer Division main dressing station where the wound was provisionally treated. After that I went to a field hospital where the wound was handled in an amateur fashion. I then crawled on my belly across a huge field of stubble to a Ju 52 and found a corner in the machine. Somehow I squeezed in; there were already some wounded men inside. I was happy when we landed at Stalino. From there I had an eight-day journey direct to Ulm, where my wound was operated on. When I came out of the anaesthetic I asked 'Where is the bullet?' They answered, 'No, we couldn't take it out!' So I still have it in my neck at the time of writing. Unfortunately the nerve was affected and I have a plexus paralysis.

In April 1944 Dr Voss was transferred to the Führer-HQ at Rastenburg then to the Army General Staff in Berlin on account of his knowledge of Russian, Department Foreign Armies East. He was discharged from the Wehrmacht as a result of his wound at the end of 1944. He passed his final State examinations in 1952 and worked later as a State attorney and notary public at Hagen, where he lived until his death in 2006.

37. HELMUT WALZ:

Close Combat in the Tractor Factory[1]

Helmut Walz (b. 22 August 1922) trained in commerce and was conscripted into the Wehrmacht in 1941. After the war he founded a business with 350 employees selling ironware and sanitary installations. He lives in Pfinztal-Berghausen.

In the summer of 1942 I was a 20-year-old infantryman in No 7 Company, 577th Infantry Regiment, 305th Infantry Division when our unit was thrown into the fighting at Kharkov. It was a major battle to escape encirclement. That was our baptism of fire. After that we headed south-east, to where exactly, nobody knew. Naturally we badgered our NCOs at every opportunity but learnt nothing. Hennes, our Lieutenant,[2] came from Sulzbach, Lieutenant-General Oppenländer[3] was our divisional commanding officer. 'Force the enemy to retreat and keep going forward' was our motto. I belonged to a mounted advanced detachment.

Thus, often hard pressed by the Russians, we arrived at Stalingrad in September 1942. Many civilians still lived in the city. We obtained quarters in a white-painted children's home, the children still being in occupation. There was no problem with either the children or their carers. They

---

1. This report was published in the journal *Kamaraden*, KA 1 and 2, 2011, pp 35–6. It is based on an interview with Helmut Walz by Frau Agnes Moosmann of Tübingen in her house in 2005.
2. Lieutenant Hermann Hennes (b. Würzburg, 5 April 1921, fell at Kurmen 17 October 1942 according to the German War Graves Commission).
3. Kurt Oppenländer (b. Ulm, 11 February 1892, d. Garmisch-Partenkirchen 17 March 1947). First World War Lieutenant, then accepted into Reichswehr. 1938 Colonel, 1941 Major-General. April 1942 commanding officer 305th Infantry Division, which he relinquished due to serious illness 1 November 1942: according to another version he was relieved of command. 1943 Lieutenant-General, 1944 transferred into the Führer-reserve. Decorations: 1942 German Cross in gold and Knight's Cross.

understood why we were there and we tolerated each other. The city and its great industrial plants were subjected to repeated violent bombing raids by our Stukas: their bombing was pinpoint accurate. They also knew where this big children's home was, for neither the house nor the children ever came under attack.

When we left it we went into the tractor factory, occupied by German soldiers. The fighting there had become very bitter and ruthless. Inside the barricades there had once been a meeting point for the 'hoi-polloi' and NCOs where we would drink with a certain regularity whenever it was possible in the evenings. This rendezvous was now seldom visited. The casualties were enormous. Many of my comrades had fallen or were wounded, always in the evil close-quarters fighting; but on 17 October it was hell! I observed a lieutenant at an MG indicate a new target. Then he stumbled and fell. The loud sounds of battle, shouting and general panic prevented the MG crew from understanding what had happened: all lost their heads and ran over him, trod on his face, trampled him underfoot. The desperate struggle continued without a break. I was a member of an MG team and we had fought our way into the tractor factory. My comrade Schappel was at my side carrying the MG. When I saw a couple of shell impacts and ricochets nearby I threw myself to the ground and shouted, 'Take cover, Schappel!' but he kept going and fell into a large bomb crater. There he lay, wounded, nose and mouth full of dirt. I cleaned him up and searched for his wound. When I opened his jacket and saw the size of it I doubted that he would survive. Blood and air bubbles were issuing forth from a gaping hole. A round had entered near the backbone, passed through his left shoulder-blade and lung and exited at the right side of the upper torso. It looked as though his innards were only being held in place by his uniform. I gave him dressings as best I could: actually I wrapped him up completely in bandages, some outside his uniform.

'The war is over, isn't it, Helmut?' Schappel groaned.

'Yes, Schappel, the war is over. I promise I shall get you out of this: just rest here quietly. I shall look for a doctor, you are seriously wounded. Can you hear the air?'

He answered: 'Yes.'

I improved his dressings and made him more comfortable. Then the noise of battle got louder and I heard foreign voices from a bunker about five metres in front of me. Russians! I crept behind a fragment of standing wall and called out to them to surrender. Nothing happened. I primed a hand grenade and threw it into the bunker entrance, a hole in the earth. There was a dull explosion and then a Soviet soldier climbed out, blood trickling from his nose, ears and mouth. No doctor would have doubted this to be the sign of serious internal injury. Therefore I thought it was safe for me, that there was no danger, and left cover. At that the wounded man drew a pistol and aimed it at me.

We were only a few metres apart. 'I did not want to kill you!' I shouted, but realized at once that all that mattered now was who was faster. At the same moment as I attempted to draw my service weapon I suddenly saw stars; rigid and confused as to what was happening, I tried to shout for help but could not speak. At my mouth I felt a lot of blood and some broken teeth. The Soviet bullet had smashed my chin, and the upper and lower jaw. The soldier had shot me in the face. When one of my colleagues saw this, he went into such a rage that he threw his whole weight on the Soviet soldier, knocked him to the ground and trampled him underfoot until he stopped moving.

Lieutenant Hennes gave me a temporary dressing and laid me in the bomb crater. As he was climbing out, he saw an armed Russian advancing. Suddenly Hennes' steel helmet flew off: a sniper had shot him in the head from another direction. My lieutenant looked down at me, ran his hand over his face, staggered back and somersaulted into the crater. Dead! I watched horrified as brain matter flowed out of his shattered skull. It was a clear liquid, no blood.

All this happened near a railway embankment. There were very many tracks through Stalingrad, and goods wagons had often been left in sidings. I now crept through these. Behind them was a trench, and near it on the roadway lorries of 14th Panzer Division drove past. I was seen and one stopped. 'Comrade, we'll take you to the dressing station!', they promised and brought me there in their vehicle. After a cursory glance a medical orderly said, 'We can't do anything for you here – go at once to the main dressing station(HVP)!'

The comrades from 14th Panzer Division drove me to the HVP even though they were at the end of their strength. The doctor who examined me – a Stuttgarter – said: 'He must be operated upon at once – it is already swelling up.' This meant that the wound would have been very difficult to treat later on. Therefore my face was cobbled together temporarily at eleven that evening. I was not able to tell them to fetch my friend Schappel quickly, but I believe that death would already have claimed him at this time.

Thus for me the war was over, but the price I paid was high! At the end of October I was flown out to Stalino, where I was stripped of my filthy and bloody uniform and washed and scrubbed thoroughly. The gaps in our ranks

249

were so enormous that I think I must have been one of the last survivors of my detachment. In any case, after I was wounded my company was disbanded.

I underwent many operations to restore my upper and lower jaws, enabling me later to eat, chew and speak. Then I was awarded the black Wound Badge and given a job here and there in administration. Finally I was to get a special gas mask so as to be fit for the front again. The special issue seemed to cause great difficulties, for repeatedly I received instructions to go to this or that town to some gas-mask supplier or other. In the end nobody knew where such a gas mask could be made or what they should do with me, and so I used my instructions for short visits home.

One day I had the feeling that a sergeant was going to write me up 'fit for the front' without a special gas mask. Quickly I removed my badly-fitting false teeth and jaws. He was so horrified at what he saw that there was never again a question of a 'fit for the front' docket. This wound did not heal for many years, but then through the skill of facial surgeons it was repaired so well that today there are only a few striking scars to be seen.

38. HELMUT WEGMANN:

My Angel was a Female Russian Doctor[1]

Helmut Wegmann was conscripted into the Wehrmacht on 3 December 1940, first to 105th Ersatz Infantry Battalion at Heidelberg and then to Russia on 3 October 1941 as paymaster to 198th Infantry Division. On 15 April 1942 he joined No 3 Company, 79th Panzer Grenadier Regiment and took part in the fighting at Kharkov.

On 27 August 1942 I wrote to my family: 'Am already over the Don and just short of the Volga near Stalingrad.' In a letter dated 30 August: '. . . and I am sitting in a trench five kilometres outside Stalingrad. We can see the Volga. The terrain here is simply featureless: a huge steppe of sand. It cannot be any worse in Africa. That there is heavy fighting here is understandable. One does not surrender such a city without a fight. The worst thing is the aircraft. You are never safe from one moment to the next. Neither day or night. It is particularly bad at night. Then they turn up in rough groups and drop their bombs.' Those were my first impressions and experiences in the first two weeks.

The 16th Panzer Division had the job of building a northern front, facing inwards to Stalingrad and outwards to the north. In the first few days we received an Order of the Day from Adolf Hitler in which we were informed that Stalin had sent out a large number of divisions from Saratov. Thus we had to reckon with a major attack.

The constant bombing – fragmentation bombs – caused tremendous damage to our vehicles. Splinters damaged the radiators so that the vehicles could not be driven. We were forced to place them in the Balkas, gulches incised into the steppe, so that the bonnet was protected inside sandy recesses. The fighting troops dug foxholes to give themselves some protection. I never kept count of the number of foxholes I excavated! The fighting was so furious that we might lose and then regain our position several times a day. The

---

1. This report was published in the divisional journal *Unsere 16*, issues 195 and 196, 50th Year, January and April 2002.

casualty rate was so high that on various occasions I had a colleague fall at my side. In the evening we received our 'human supplies'. A totally inexperienced lieutenant brought them up. He was attached to my section. Next day in my foxhole he received a fatal splinter wound in the chest. We suffered our heaviest losses when we had to abandon our positions in the face of overwhelming Russian forces. My comrades fell like rabbits at a hunt. We noticed now the pressure coming from the direction of Saratov. My proud company, No 3, 79th Panzer Grenadier Regiment, was reduced after three weeks fighting from 150 men down to 20. As a trained private soldier, I was one of the 'highest' ranks. Our company was disbanded and transferred to the battalion reserve.

If what we had experienced until now was appalling, now hell began in the truest sense! We were called upon day and night to free our comrades encircled in small groups by the Russians. This was – it must be said – cruel in-fighting always involving more casualties. Already in September we were having problems of supply. Ammunition and food were scarce. Supplies arrived at irregular periods. We could neither wash nor shave. The worst was when colleagues were wounded or fell. How often when we retreated, and then after a short time made good what we had lost, we could not bury the dead or obtain medical treatment for the wounded!

In this worst-ever phase of my life I made a pledge: I decided that in peacetime, if I could escape this hell and see the Homeland and my family again, I would work for the good of the community.

It was 25 September 1942. A large number of my comrades had been encircled. In order to hold the whole line, this encircled section had to be regained. A Captain gave my squad orders. We got into our armoured personnel carrier (APC), our aim being to drive the Russian occupiers in close combat. If we reached a certain enemy-held position we were to jump down hurling hand grenades and recapture it.

It was towards 1700 hrs when we set out. The setting sun was behind us because we were heading for the Volga in the east. The attack was to be made in a wedge formation. The guns on the Volga opened fire at once because we could be seen easily against the horizon. Within a few minutes three of our APCs had received direct hits. The vehicles and men were lost. The Captain stopped the attack immediately and we returned to our departure point. We spent the night in the open with the APCs. Towards dawn when the rising sun lit the battlefield from the east the attack recommenced.

Because the sun was rising in the east and there was a light mist it was not so easy for the Russian guns to make us out. We reached our objective without coming under fire. I gave the instruction to hang the carbines around the neck and prime hand grenades. For the imminent close combat we put rifle ammunition in our pockets. About twenty metres before the Russian trench I ordered: 'Throw hand grenades and after they explode jump down!' The APCs would then withdraw. Now the Russian guns on the other side of the Volga opened fire. When I jumped out a shell exploded nearby and a splinter hit my trouser pocket, igniting a box of rifle rounds stowed there. I felt a heavy blow at the rear of my left thigh, collapsed and was enveloped in smoke. I shouted: 'I am burning!' because I thought I had been hit by tracer fire. Not until the smoke had cleared did I see that my toes, the whole leg, was facing the wrong way. Why that should be was at first not clear to me. The driver of another APC had been shot in the head through the viewing slit; he had died at once. His vehicle was removed from the scene of the action and used to convey the wounded to the dressing station. As I was the first man to have been wounded I was laid alongside the dead driver. Thus within half an hour I was inside a field hospital. Where it was or what it was called I have never discovered.

I was attended to first in a tent. The left trouser leg was cut away. Now I saw for the first time what had happened. The explosion of the rifle ammunition had broken the upper thigh bone and twisted the leg. Eight rifle cartridges were removed from the wound. Now I knew exactly what the problem was. They would operate late that evening. After treatment I wrote a letter to the girlfriend who would later be my wife.

I underwent major surgery that same day, 26 September 1942. The people in the operating tent – just as in the film *Der Arzt von Stalingrad* – told me that it had lasted four hours. The twisted leg had been put straight, the outside of the upper thigh opened up and fitted with a drainage tube. This was necessary because the explosion had forced powder, dirt and other material into the upper thigh, that meant a lot of suppuration. It was many months before this suppuration terminated. They also attempted to remove fragments of the cartridges, but even today there are at least 100 tiny splinters still lodged in the upper thigh. During the operation half of my smashed upper thigh, which had been forced upwards into the bowel by the twisting of the leg, could not be removed by reason of my weak state. That was only achieved in the autumn of 1943 in the Julius-Spital at Würzburg after complicated surgery.

After the operation I was brought to a hospital marquee for forty to fifty patients. I was told it was one of the marquees used by sportsmen at the 1936

Berlin Olympic Games. The person in charge in this marquee was a Russian female doctor from Kharkov. I learned that she had placed herself at the disposal of the Wehrmacht to secure a livelihood. I was 22 years of age and dirty, but she noticed that I had not touched my breakfast on the morning of 27 September. I did not have the strength to lift anything, nor do anything which required any effort. On her rounds in the marquee she noticed my condition at once. She sat herself on the metal framework of the bed and fed me like a child. That happened at every mealtime.

After about two weeks she told me that she was being transferred as a female assistant and interpreter to the senior Surgeon-General at the Stalingrad front. Her substitute would ensure that the foregoing condition of good care would be maintained. Despite her new assignment she kept her job at this field hospital. She would take her leave before each journey, of two or three days' duration, and enquire how I was after her return. To comply with my request for something different to eat, for example something sour, she organized it in her own way.

After about five weeks she explained to me that with my fever – always above 39° – I could not have my leg put in plaster for transport out. That was naturally an incentive to get my temperature down to 37.5° every time it was taken: then my 'angel' was satisfied. Thus on 8 November I could write home: 'Finally I have managed it! This morning I got my plaster cast for the journey, so that in one or two days I can be flown out to Stalino and then forwarded on. I will soon be back in Germany!'

Before I was taken to the airfield, I took my leave of the female doctor on a stretcher, thanking her for her help and care. At the airfield there was no aircraft in sight. After about an hour an Italian machine came over but instead of landing the crew parachuted out some containers and the aircraft then disappeared. Nobody knew if there would be others flying in. The ambulance driver had no option but to return to the field hospital. Now there was no bed for me: I was put on the floor. My 'angel' was also disappointed. Later she came to see me and said that next morning a convoy with panzer protection was going to Tchir. There would be some ambulances in the convoy. If I wanted to chance it I could go along. A bird in the hand is worth two in the bush, I decided.

We left next morning. The ambulance driver told us he had to maintain his speed within the convoy without regard to ourselves. The journey passed over undulating country. My fellow patients and I alleviated our suffering, when the pain got too bad, by screaming. Halfway between Stalingrad and Tchir was a hill which changed hands between the opposing belligerents several times daily: we had to pass through it. We could peep out of the windows of the ambulance. It was devastating: masses of burnt-out German panzers and Russian tanks lay strewn about the terrain: worse still were the many victims lying in the open. Today the spot is marked by a Russian monument.

Finally we got to Tchir, the last railway station on the Don before Stalingrad. Here the German supplies were stored in halls while it was still possible. We went towards Dnyepropetrovsk aboard the next empty goods train. Every wagon had five supine, and about twenty standing, wounded. On the way the train was subjected to an act of sabotage: a bomb exploded under the track and derailed the locomotive. The stretcher cases particularly suffered by being thrown about. My plaster cast held, but other patients were not so fortunate. Later I was told that I had been given a very resistant alabaster cast. That had been very lucky for me. Did I have my 'angel' to thank for that too?

The journey continued to Lemberg. It was Sunday evening. One can imagine the circumstances in the goods train as regards food or sanitary necessities on such a run! On the Monday morning we taken to a clinic for a decision to be taken about our further treatment. After the doctors saw and cleaned my wound, they decided: immediately to Germany.

On 28 November 1942 Helmut Wegmann was admitted to the Julius-Spital at Würzburg. After several operations which saved his leg from amputation, he was discharged from the Wehrmacht on 27 July 1944. He fulfilled the pledge he made at Stalingrad by voluntary church and social activity.

39. KARL WOLF:

The Most Difficult Days of My Life[1]

Karl Wolf from Perchtoldsdorf/Austria served as an NCO with the signals section of 44th Infantry Division.

Much has been written about Stalingrad, and as a signaller I had to pass on many reports of experiences. On 16 November 1942 a motorcycle messenger came to me reporting his return from the workshop detachment. He mentioned the great unrest amongst the Romanian, Hungarian and Italian divisions fighting on our side against the Russians. They were at the great bend in the Don: the pastureland was similar to that of the Danube. It was also said that Russian troops had crossed the frozen swampy region in temperatures below -35°C.

This was reported to my command post who dismissed it as rumour. Between 17 and 18 November they would be surprised to see the true position. With greatly superior forces the Russians had forced their way into this weakly occupied area, therefore at our backs in the direction of Manolion, Warsenaya, Dopruskaya, Popov, Surovikino and Tchir. We had taken special care in the preceding weeks to convert our trenches into winter quarters because we had been ordered to hold the area. Every free minute had been used to expand the trenches sufficiently for eight men. But now our orders required us to abandon them in haste! Since we could not bring all vehicles and equipment with us, we destroyed what had to be left behind. Our orders said we were to fall back towards Stalingrad. The temperature was below -35°C, night began at 1400 hrs,[2] starry skies but very dark: the moon was never seen. The roads along which we marched to our ordered position were lined by ammunition trucks, columns of vehicles – all out of fuel – and other rearward services and guns of all calibres which could proceed no further.

1. This report appeared in the journal of *Stalingradbund Österreich*, Nr. 5-7, 3rd Year, 1985.
2. Central European Time: It was actually 1600 hrs at Stalingrad when darkness began to fall.

We saw gigantic quantities of provisions stacked up for the troops operating in the region, so that the food crisis of the first Russian winter of 1941 should not be repeated. We saw huge amounts of Christmas packages from the Homeland which had been brought up shortly before by goods trains. We looked at these in anguish, knowing that these packages, sent with love and financial sacrifice, would be consigned to the furnace. Acts of destruction of this nature occurred in the supply dumps to the stacks of ammunition and massed vehicles. Nothing could be taken along, and it was for this reason that from the outset the Pocket experienced extraordinary difficulties in the question of provisions and supplies. Much had been destroyed in the individual units beforehand. Most soldiers had only a small pack and a haversack in the frontline.

Signal connections between the individual units were very complicated and intricate. The entire telephone network of many divisions had been wrecked and the radio-telegraphy apparatus was only usable to a limited extent. It is worth mentioning here that nearly all aircraft fell undamaged into Russian hands before the encirclement, with all their equipment and fuel. Our victories of previous years had led us to believe initially that there was no possibility that we should not be able to break out from it.

Our main frontline was entirely barren. Every man had to use bayonet or entrenching tool to dig his own foxhole in the frozen earth as best he could. With a superhuman will to survive and the desire to be able to call the humblest protective hole his own for a short time, under a hail of rifle rounds and MG bursts, at first only accompanied by the sparse fire of field-guns, he would excavate a trench which after hours of backbreaking toil was no greater than 1.7 metres long, 50 centimetres wide and 10 to 15 centimetres deep.

On the early morning of 23 November, especially on the western front in the Baburkin-Karpovka-Bol and Mal Rossoshka stretch, we heard the deafening roar of aircraft motors. All eyes looked upwards and with what joy we saw at low altitude the familiar Ju 52s, He 111s and Ju 88s, protected by fighter aircraft. It was strangely quiet, for from nowhere did the Russians fire. We ourselves believed these were the first units which had come to relieve us, or at least bring in the supplies, war materials and food we lacked. As if drawn up by a magnet the soldiers rose and waved to the aircraft. Was this not a glimmer of hope for the future? Yet scarcely had this squadron reached our position than did their bomb bays open, and down came the devastating, very much feared Molotov cocktails known by front troops. Next came bombs of all calibres, dropped by the He 111s and Ju 88s. We realized at once that these were German aircraft captured by the Russians. This scenario was repeated on several occasions.

We suffered terrible casualties. The cries of the wounded who had lost limbs, or were otherwise seriously wounded, were very distressing even for us who had already had much experience of warfare. As always one tried to help one's comrades with whom one had fought shoulder to shoulder and gone through the same joys and sufferings. But what use was that here! There was no bunker in which to operate, and dressing materials had long been used up. There was no food, now and again a man would give away his so-called iron ration. The wounded were attended to as well as possible, we made attempts to ascertain where a dressing station might have been set up, here and there we found a doctor with only very few medicaments if any. Often a doctor would attempt to amputate hands and feet, attached to a body only by fragments of flesh, but without any possibility of taking prescribed precautionary measures against infection, or using anaesthetics.

A provisional dressing station was set up in a gully at Baburkin because that was the enemy's main focus of assault. Amputations were carried out there, but one had no idea where to begin with the patients. There was nowhere to put them and, lacking the means to keep them warm, after a few hours they froze to death. All that remained was to add them to the accumulating piles of corpses.

Once the numbers of dead had reached staggering proportions, it was decided to fill a gully with the dead and fallen. In the circumstances it was not always possible to identify every man. It would generally not be his own best comrades who brought the corpse to the mass necropolis at Stalingrad, but the next best. Ten thousand men lay dead there, unburied, for no grave could be dug in the bone-hard earth. This would be left to a later time. The air attacks using German aircraft persisted for some time. An assortment of heavy and light artillery and Stalin Organs would join in as they flew over.

Russian tanks found our pitiful foxholes fair game and came over in great numbers. The Russian tank drivers had got wise to the fact that our worn-out, exhausted and hungry troops could not be dislodged from their holes by mortar or MG fire. Therefore they drove over these trenches and then turned round on them, so that the men lying inside them were crushed by the heavy tracks.

In the days following one frequently saw several Ju 52s arriving at a considerable height to land at Pitomnik or Gumrak airfield bringing food and war material; but this was only a fraction of what was needed. From day to day their numbers grew less: if it was foggy they would not come at all. We noted in horror how often these machines with their precious and necessary loads were shot down. The same fate was meted out to aircraft taking off from the Pocket with wounded aboard. I was myself an eyewitness when fourteen Ju 52s with wounded aboard, and soldiers clinging to the tailplane for dear life, were shot down with no survivors. This was often repeated. On another occasion it was a Condor aircraft[3] which had loaded more than seventy wounded and was brought down at low altitude. Here again there were no survivors.

The first days of December 1942 were black ones for our division. One company after another was wiped out by the enemy. The fighting grew daily more bitter: there was no time to rest. After fourteen days we received some bread and sausage. Each man got a slice of bread weighing 50 grams and a quarter-spoon sized piece of sausage.

On Christmas Eve 1942 the front soldiers, who had had to endure much deprivation and sorrow, experienced their most difficult hours. Not only that they had already spent four weeks, starving, freezing cold and without letters from home, and had continued to do their sworn duty faithfully despite there being no prospect of success: but at dusk the Russian loudspeakers, which had been installed deliberately close to the German lines, called upon them to surrender – the battle was pointless and had already been lost. They guaranteed us free passage into captivity and promised us warm rooms and food. All this babble was 99% wasted!

Then came the worst of all: they played us over the loudspeakers 'Stille Nacht', 'O Tannenbaum' and other carols and marches from the Homeland. There can scarcely have been a single soldier who did not dearly wish to see his loved ones at home once more, and of course at such times one tends to resort to tears. We were not only there to protect our own skins, we had also to do our duty for our wives, children and parents. We knew that right now their thoughts would be with us. That night there was no fighting. On both sides an absolute ceasefire reigned. The same happened on New Year's Eve. At midnight both sides fired salutes. Writing home from the Pocket was pointless, we knew that no post would go because the priority of every aircraft leaving was to take the wounded.

On 1 January 1943 we received an enormous artillery barrage. On the days following we were the recipients of all varieties of Russian exhortation to come on over. Their aircraft dropped leaflets giving fairly accurate details of our

---

3. He means here a Focke-Wulf 200 four-engined long-range aircraft.

dead, shot-down aircraft and our reserves of supplies. The calls to surrender were endless. With growing impatience the Russians let us know that on 10 January they would begin the annihilation of everybody they found in the Stalingrad Pocket.

Now the promised major attack by the Russian armies actually began. It started with an artillery bombardment of the German defensive front using just about every kind of gun imaginable. Then came incessant bombing, massed tanks rolled across our lines, especially the trenches, to crush the men in them and finally hordes of Russian infantry attacked. This resulted in the Pocket being compressed by stages, softening up those within it. As luck would have it our field kitchen was hit by a bomb. Recently it had ceased to cook anything in any case, but occasionally it had been possible to boil up dirty, blood-soaked snow so that rarely we all had a lukewarm beaker of melted snow to drink.

From one hour to the next our ranks dwindled. Anybody who could still walk or crawl was in the forward trenches, from a general to the most junior soldier. Only rarely did one find there somebody from one's own unit. Everything was criss-crossed: the signals connections were only possible through the major posts and points. There was no point in shouting, commanding, procuring and arranging any more: all that mattered was 'Look after yourself, then perhaps God might help you.' Wherever you looked there were abandoned and wrecked bunkers and vehicles or similar in flames, which had served soldiers as quarters.

That 10 January after close combat I had to visit the dental bunker because I had had two teeth damaged and the nerve was exposed. 'Sit yourself there!' A foot-operated drill was used, the nerve was removed without anaesthetic. It felt like he had taken out my whole brain! It was all over quickly, however, and the hole closed temporarily. Then the dentist said to me: 'I don't know, but haven't I seen you as a civilian?' I could not speak. I looked at him more closely and when the treatment finished I said, 'You don't come from Perchtoldsdorf, do you?' Scarcely were the words out than he replied, 'Yes, I am that Ratzenberger[4] near the church!' Then there was an explosion near the bunker, a bomb had fallen, we could not talk. I often remember my dental treatment in the gully at Baburkin. Ratzenberger never made it back home . . .

The Russians persisted with their demands that we should surrender, not

---

4. An NCO Franz Gustav Ratzenberger (b. Vienna, 21 December 1911) died in Beketovka Camp on 11 April 1943, according to the German War Graves Commission.

forgetting to bring with us our weapons, equipment and vehicles undamaged. Then we would all get together and General Paulus would rendezvous at a particular spot to negotiate the handing over of the surviving soldiers. Only a few ever gave a thought to surrendering: we had seen and experienced enough – scarcely describable – when we had lost a sector of the front and then regained it. We would find our people tortured and mutilated in the most bestial and sadistic way, hands and feet cut off, eyes, mouth and lower torso re-arranged so as to be unrecognizable, a bayonet in the head or chest; exhausted, starving and wounded men crawling, half naked with legs, hands or sexual organs missing.

We had to see all this: nobody could help the still living comrade, crying out, long since out of his mind, for there were no medicaments. Comrades who in their last vile agony cried out for mother, wife or children and wanted to tell them something before they died. Praying, cursing and gesturing in pain. Nobody could help when the temperature was -45°C. There were no cases of enemy tanks running over the crawlers. All these men were heading towards Gumrak and through the gulches into the city centre of Stalingrad, but few made it. There was nowhere food or warm clothing to be had. Although many Ju 52s, Ju 88s and He 111s flew in, not many reached their goal. Most dropped their provisions-bombs over the Russian advanced positions. Now and again some of them fell into our hands, but we no longer had the strength to open them and had to leave them where they lay. The Russian AA defences had grown very strong: their aircraft attacked from low level everything that moved. Even the Russian prisoners who moved amongst us, the Romanians and Croats experienced the same fate. Yet all this could not break our will to fight to the last breath, although we knew what we were up against. We were very well informed of the fighting will and endurance of the men beyond the Pocket, who had tried to hold up the Russians, and that to their rear the front had been pulled back behind the Donets at a smart pace so that there was for us no hope any more.

Arriving at Gumrak airfield, at daybreak we were confronted again with the most hideous sights: men hanging on to the tailplane of aircraft, thinking that they could escape the Pocket in such a manner; scarcely off the ground they would fall to the ground like blocks of stone. Russian fighters were at work: the consequences of shooting down aircraft loaded with wounded do not bear description. Also here in the days to come it was hell on earth, the horrific images remain with me with dreadful clarity to this very day as if I had experienced them only a few hours ago.

From 0600 hrs on 18 January the Russians unleashed a dreadful artillery bombardment with everything they had against the southern and western front sectors. Bombs and grenades dropped around us without pause, and it was more than one's life was worth to raise the head for a look. We had heavy losses; again nobody could help the wounded and those shouting out for assistance, again came the massed attacks with tank support. Despite that, the enemy was beaten off with heavy and bloody losses, losing many tanks destroyed in the process.

At 1600 hrs there was another bombardment. It was very dark; one could see hardly anything. There were terrible scenes in the dressing stations. Comrades, Russians and refugees died in their hundreds of wounds and frostbite. Bombs rained down. Around Gumrak the station building and hundreds of railway wagons were wrecked, dead and mangled soldiers lay all around them, the same in the camps for the wounded and prisoners. Dead comrades and Russians were piled up into protective walls. There was nobody any more who could provide help and treatment or medicaments. The earth was churned up, railway tracks bent and ghostly: between them the wrecks of aircraft, guns, lorries, tanks, railway wagons. In the camps the wounded, scarcely able to move, lay in bunks. From the upper bunks excrement, urine, pus and blood dripped down on those below who scarcely knew where they were or whether it looked good or bad for them. No narcotic, no dressing was available. The stink was bestial – feet and hands froze off to expose bone. Then one saw soldiers chewing on some such fragment of flesh.

The most ghastly situations occurred when in their helplessness soldiers gave themselves the coup de grâce. Many thousands begged for it, but there was hardly a seriously wounded soldier whose wish was fulfilled.[5] They died alone, utterly alone, but calling out to the heavenly hosts: 'What is it that I have done, that I must suffer so and cannot see my loved ones again?' I am not ashamed to admit it: for many I made the sign of the Cross, because my faith had taught me to do so. There was no break, pause or sleep.

On 23 January 1943 we were so tightly wedged in with the Russians that no soldier paid heed any more to another. Columns of our own troops and

5. Under German military law it was punishable by court-martial to give the coup de grâce to another whether he had requested it or not. Other authors mention one or two cases where it might have been done to relieve a man of the most intolerable pain, or if he could not be moved and was likely to be tortured to death by the Russians if found alive, but otherwise it appears to have been rare. [Tr].

262

Russian wounded pushed forward in the same direction, lying on tent canvas or blankets, comrades one had known for years whose hope now was to escape the massacre or find help. The icy cold and snow storms made it difficult to organize men reduced by hunger to skeletons. Hands stuck to metal parts and froze. The rifle served primarily as a crutch to assist walking, and as a support whether the man was upright, kneeling or creeping along. On the ground one could make out the silhouettes of comrades, but also Russians, Romanians and Croats, crushed flat.

Few there were not suffering from one or more of dysentery, malaria, typhus, jaundice, pneumonia and pleurisy. One can imagine how the men looked, constantly exposed to bitter cold, without help or care, no change of socks, underwear or shirt for weeks and months. Everything was soaked with blood, pus, urine or excrement. Lice, wherever they were found, caused great discomfort. Erysipelas and scabies were rife.

Naturally that led to soldiers collapsing in exhaustion, becoming unable to move, and falling asleep, to die where they lay. Many of these poor creatures, who now had given all for their Homeland, Fatherland and loved ones, often held a picture in their hands of wife, children, bride, parents or a religious figure. What would have been going through their minds in these their last days, hours or minutes? I can imagine it, for I was numbered amongst them. All those of the fighting troops who got to see the Homeland again, can only speak of a miracle or an act of Providence without unleashing an angry word against the enemy, who was in the same situation. There were also many in the Pocket who never went hungry, had enough clothing and could care for themselves.

After the murderous fighting had slackened off many were aware that falling asleep meant certain death. Who still had his senses tried to move himself, to find something warm by way of clothing, footwear or headwear from the fallen. It was also no different for Russian women, men and children in the Pocket.

Because I still had a radio set, we could receive reports and were therefore able to keep up to date to some extent with what was happening in the outside world. Here the fighting was almost entirely at its end; thus one could watch a German aircraft drop provisions-bombs and even land. The dying went on, the mass necropolis gathered up its victims, old and young, at a fast tempo. The whipping snow storms in low temperatures gave cover to one's comrades, friends and enemies, war material, foxholes and bunkers alike.

Many of our colleagues wore bits of uniform of Hungarian, Romanian,

Italian, even Russian issue. The fighting was at its end, the Russians were not worried about taking enemy soldiers captive, only dealing with those who got in the way of their advance. These latter they would thrust aside, those crawling or lying on the ground would be trampled upon or driven over. Occasionally one heard rifle, pistol, MG, mortar or artillery fire, but who fired it and at whom could not be established. Certainly much of it was suicide. Many cried in pain and despair, many had lost the balance of their minds and could not be calmed, many pulled terrible faces because they were out of their senses. By now it was clear to everyone that relief or escape was no longer possible.

How I got back to Austria I can only relate from what two signals corps comrades from my Homeland told me, who had been spared the horror and death of Stalingrad because I had sent them on home leave two days before the encirclement. They both told me that they had been sent to an airstrip to where wounded men had been brought out from the Pocket. Here there were hundreds of dead comrades lying around, but also some who occasionally moved. Both noticed the yellow collar patches and piping on my shoulder straps: I was one of the few signals corps men amongst the wounded. They did not recognize me as I lay there stiff in the icy snow but – trained in first aid – knew I was not dead because they could still move my limbs. Therefore they could justify bringing me out of the reception camp. I was wrapped in a blanket and taken to a train for Brest-Litovsk. They went through my pockets and exclaimed, upon seeing the entries in my service/pay book, 'This is our Old Man!'

Later they accompanied me to Vienna. I had forty-one wounds in my body and my state of health was so bad that the duty surgeon told my wife she should prepare for the worst: because of the injuries to my head and back I would only be a burden to her. The wounds healed quickly, as did the erysipelas and diphtheria. I weighed on reception 38 kilos but this soon increased, so that in August 1943 I could leave the hospital on two walking sticks.

What I have portrayed here can only be understood by somebody who experienced it himself, or something similar. Fortunately all this suffering and dying could not be recorded for posterity. Thank God those we loved in the Homeland were spared these dreadful horrors.